P9-EKI-211

THE GODDESS

LIVING WISDOM

THE GODDESS

SHAHRUKH HUSAIN

SERIES CONSULTANT: **PIERS VITEBSKY**

Little, Brown and Company
BOSTON NEW YORK TORONTO LONDON

Contents

First American Edition

Conceived, Edited, and Designed by Duncan Baird Publishers, London, England

Associate author: Clifford Bishop

Editor: Clifford Bishop
Assistant editor: Ingrid Court-Jones
Designer: Sue Bush
Picture research: Anne-Marie Ehrlich
Cartographic design: Russell Bell
Commissioned artwork: Hannah Fermin

ISBN 0-316-38005-9

Library of Congress Catalog Card Number: 96-78853

10 9 8 7 6 5 4 3 2 1

Published simultaneously in Canada by Little, Brown & Company (Canada) Limited

Typeset in Times NR MT

Color reproduction by Colourscan, Singapore
Printed in Singapore by Imago Publishing Limited

Introduction

In his book *The Golden Ass*, the Greek philosopher Apuleius (b. AD125) described the goddess Isis reciting all the different names under which she was worshipped by the peoples of the earth (see p.33). Despite their numerous attributes, titles and powers, all these female deities emanated from the same source, the ultimate reality that can be described as the Goddess, wherever or however she appears.

The Goddess manifests in many different forms, some of which shatter the stereotypes that are commonly associated with womanhood. Sovereignty, war and hunting are all within her remit. She is autonomous, sexual and strong. The sum of all her parts is a total divinity which the human mind is incapable of fully defining.

To assert the dominance of the Goddess in the same way that patriarchal monotheisms assert the dominance of God, some feminist writers drop the definite article and simply designate her "Goddess". Her essential quality is all-inclusiveness: she contains all opposites within herself, including male and female, creation and destruction. And she recognizes that life and death are of

ABOVE *A wooden figurine of Kwan-Yin, goddess of mercy, from Sung dynasty, China,* c.*13th century* AD.
BELOW LEFT *Modern papier maché and plaster figures used in the Durga Puja festival, honouring the goddess Durga, in Varanasi, India.*

equal weight, held in balance to preserve the order of the universe. The multiplicity of the Goddess is expressed in the Nag Hammadi scriptures, a collection of largely Gnostic texts which were written in the 2nd or 3rd centuries AD, and discovered in Egypt in 1945. One of the scriptures is written throughout in a female voice, which may be that of Isis, or the Gnostic Sophia (or Wisdom). The voice refers to itself as "Thunder: Perfect Mind":

For I am the first and the last.
I am the honoured one and the scorned one.
I am the whore and the holy one.
I am the wife and the virgin.
I am the mother and the daughter.
I am the members of my mother.
I am the barren one and many are her sons.
I am she whose wedding is great, and I have not taken a husband.
I am the midwife and she who does not bear.
I am the solace of my labour pains.
I am the bride and the bridegroom, and it is my husband who begot me.
I am the mother of my father and the sister of my husband, and he is my offspring ...
Give heed to me.
I am the one who is disgraced and the great one.

CENTRE *A Mesopotamian frieze depicting the Tree of Life, guarded by winged females, c.9th century BC.*
BELOW Venus and Love, *painted by Lucas Cranach the Elder in 1509.*
BELOW *A print of Lakshmi, Indian goddess of luck.*

The Goddess Rediscovered

The prevailing theories of human prehistory have been regularly rewritten throughout the 20th century. The abundance of archeological finds dating from the Paleolithic and Neolithic periods, coupled with the absence of any documentation, has fuelled much fantasy and speculation. Among the objects that have been most tellingly reinterpreted since their discovery are the Venuses, or female figurines and symbols. Many of these, when first found, were described in similar terms to the ivory figurine unearthed in 1937 at Dolni Vestonice, in eastern Europe: as "diluvial [from the flood] plastic pornography".

Since the Second World War, there has been a powerful, persuasive and growing international trend to describe these figures as Goddesses – emblems of fertility, but even more importantly of the interconnectedness of life and death. They have been seen as proof of the existence of ancient matriarchies, and as timeless symbols drawn from a mythic well that is – and always has been – shared by all humankind.

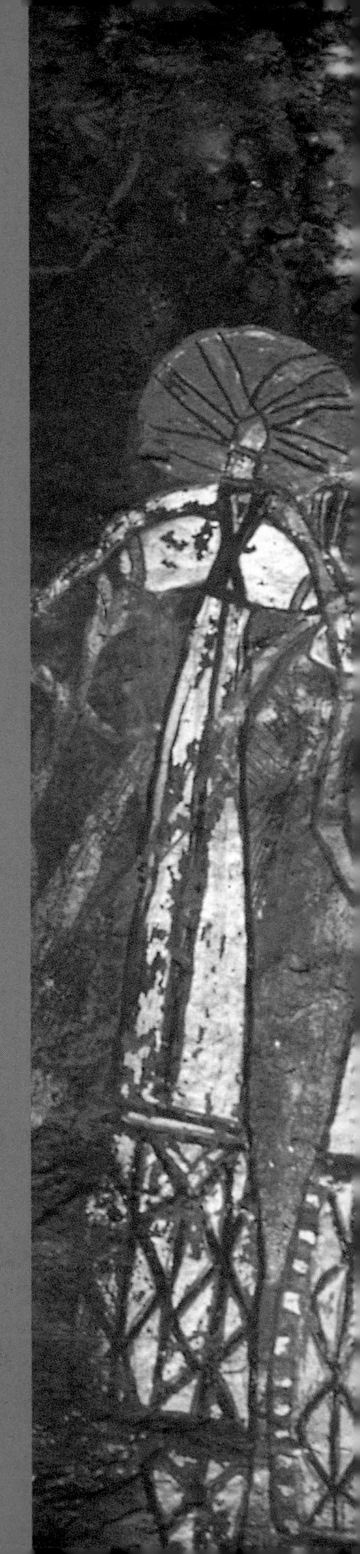

A woman in the process of giving birth, painted by Aboriginals in Arnhem Land, Australia. The figure is usually described as the "Old Woman", or All-Mother, who arrived in northern Australia in the form of a serpent, and gave birth to the Ancestors of the people. Aboriginal images such as this have been the subject of a continuous, although fluid, oral tradition for thousands of years, so that, unlike their European counterparts, their meaning has not been completely lost.

Recent discoveries

The term "prehistory" came into general use only in 1865, after the publication of a book called *Prehistoric Times*, by the British scholar John Lubbock. The book advocated the ideas of the French customs inspector, Jacques Boucher de Perthes, who in 1841 had been the first person to link human chipped-stone artefacts with the fossil bones of extinct animals. According to Boucher de Perthes this meant that the story of humanity extended back far beyond accepted biblical accounts. The newly discovered antiquity of the human race fuelled a vast international programme of exploration and excavation in search of prehistoric remnants.

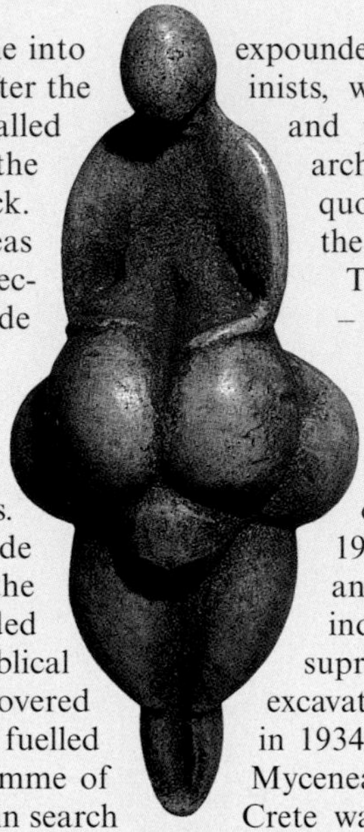

Some of the most striking finds were Paleolithic engravings, figurines and paintings, depicting women, especially in their role as mothers. Their vulvas, breasts, buttocks and pregnant bellies were always prominent, in contrast to ill-defined heads and limbs. The figurines in particular attracted popular attention, and soon earned themselves the title of "Venuses". They were generally described as archetypal images of femininity and its functions, but from their first discovery there were occasional suggestions that they might be evidence for the ancient, widespread belief in a universal Mother Goddess.

The Venus of Lespugue, a typical Paleolithic female figurine (with exaggerated secondary sexual characteristics and a featureless head) c.*20,000BC.*

This idea did not gain widespread support until the latter half of the 20th-century, when it was enthusiastically expounded by academics, artists, feminists, witches, ecological activists and polemicists. Much of the archeological evidence they quote only came to light during the 20th century.

The Indus Valley civilization – which disappeared early in the 2nd millennium BC and left behind a large number of female figures, which seem to have been votive offerings – was identified in 1921. The royal graves at Ur, in ancient Sumer, whose relics indicated the worship of a supreme fertility goddess, were excavated by Sir Leonard Woolley in 1934. The existence of the pre-Mycenean Minoan civilization of Crete was suggested only in 1896. Excavations on the island began in 1900 and, to date, no images of adult male gods have been found on any of the Neolithic sites: males are always portrayed as infants or children, diminutive next to the figure of a Mother Goddess. In 1974, on the Cycladic island of Phylakopi, a religious sanctuary was discovered that had been abandoned since 1120BC, when male votive figures were only beginning to appear alongside earlier, predominantly female imagery, indicating the waning of the Goddess-worshipping Minoan culture and the spread of the male-dominated Mycaenians. Perhaps the most impressive of all Neolithic finds, the goddess-filled buildings of Çatal Hüyük in modern-day Turkey, were not explored until the mid-1960s (see p.14).

Minerva Visiting the Muses on Mount Helicon*, by Hans Jordaens (1595–1643). Minerva aided and inspired the quests of many heroes, and the muses were patrons of arts and artists. Ever since classical Greece, muses have been used as a divine imprimatur for the idea that women merely inspire men, who are the actual creators. This stereotype has coloured most theories of human evolution and prehistoric culture, in which it is males who are described as cutting flints, painting caves or inventing new tools.*

THE FEMALE AS ARTIST AND CREATOR

Many of those commentators who accept that Paleolithic Venuses are fertility figures, or even representations of the Goddess, nevertheless assume unquestioningly that they were made by men. The large number of Venus figures, and the comparatively tiny number of similar works depicting men, is taken as an indication of the male fascination with women as the source of life.

However, in 1996, Le Roy McDermott, the Professor of Art at Missouri State University, USA, suggested that the characteristic distortions in these figures – such as swollen bellies, large breasts and buttocks, short legs and tiny feet – were consistent with pregnant women sculpting their own self-portraits. In a series of photographs, he demonstrated that the foreshortened view that a pregnant woman would have while looking down her own outstretched body was comparable to the appearance of Venuses, such as those of Lespugue (see opposite) or Willendorf, when examined from the same angle.

McDermott also used the photographs to explain more subtle distortions in the Venus images, such as the navels, which tend to be large, elliptical and too close to the pubic triangle. The heads of the figures are featureless because, in a world without mirrors, the artists could not see their own faces. If this theory is correct, the vast majority of Paleolithic sculptures were made by women, lending weight to feminist arguments that women, and not men, were the original craftspeople, artists and transmitters of culture from generation to generation. The possibility that the Venuses are self-portraits does not mean that they cannot have had some ritual or religious function.

The Paleolithic and Neolithic ages

The Paleolithic era has so far yielded approximately 1,000 complete or partial images of the female form, including sculptures, reliefs and engravings. The earliest of these were created between 27,000BC and 26,000BC, within an area of 1,200 sq. miles (3,000 sq. km) that spans the major part of Europe.

There is considerable disagreement about the original intention behind these images. It is possible that they were meant to be representations of actual women; that they illustrate ancient canons of beauty; or that they are examples of ancient pornography or erotica. They may even have been used to illustrate the birth process to first-time mothers. However, the most widespread opinion identifies them as priestesses to the Goddess, or as the Goddess herself, incarnated as an ancestress. For example, Marija Gimbutas, a 20th-century archeologist who has revolutionized modern understanding of the Stone and Bronze Ages, suggests that the figurines were "symbolic or mythic figures, used to re-enact seasonal and other myths".

This view is echoed by other commentators, such as A. Marshack, author of *The Roots of Civilization* (1972), for whom the figurines evoke "storied images" connected with the seasonal cycle and renewal of life. Both experts link the figurines to an earth goddess or her officiators, through their role in her ceremonies. This view is especially plausible because of the likelihood that Paleolithic societies, in common with all known pre-scientific peoples (and many cultures that are technologically advanced), practised a form of fertility magic.

Vulvas scratched into a rock face at Abri Cellier, in the Dordogne, France, during the Upper Paleolithic period. On the whole, what would now be described as erotic sexuality plays very little part in the Paleolithic representations of genitalia. Clay triangles and circular pendants embellished with a seed or an eye were common ways of representing the vulva. These were probably worn as amulets, and alluded to the productive functions of both women and the earth, the seed providing a common metaphor for human and vegetable life.

Fertility was almost certainly the foremost function of any Paleolithic Goddess. This is indicated by the emphasis in Venus figurines on pregnant bellies, pendulous breasts and wide, full buttocks. Often the hand of a figurine draws attention to its pudendum or its breasts, leading some researchers automatically to assume a symbolic emphasis on the primary sources of creation and nourishment. However, the beliefs of past, unrecorded cultures must be analyzed with special caution, because a symbol whose meaning appears obvious to one culture or age may prove to signify something very different to another. It used to be assumed, for example, that Egyptian pyramid images of women holding their breasts related to sexuality or the nourishment of infants. But, following early

19th-century work on the Rosetta stone (a tablet discovered in 1799, containing Greek text along with its hieroglyphic translation), these images proved to be gestures of mourning.

The similarity of some Paleolithic figures to those of the Neolithic period (beginning *c.*10,000BC), suggests the possibility of a coherent religion that continued from one age to the next. Marija Gimbutas designates the region containing this tradition "Old Europe". It included the area around the Aegean Sea, the Balkans and eastern central Europe, the central Mediterranean and western Europe. The Goddess-worshipping tradition that at one time permeated this area survived, in Crete, into the latter half of the 2nd millennium BC.

MARIJA GIMBUTAS AND THE INTERPRETATION OF SYMBOLS

Marija Gimbutas is indivisibly linked with the study of the prehistoric Goddess. In the course of her thirty years of field research, Gimbutas noted an overwhelming resemblance between Stone Age figures of the Goddess and different animals and birds, particularly water-birds. These resemblances can be seen in figures more than 26,000 years old, and traced through Neolithic images into the paintings and pottery of Bronze Age Crete. Surveying a vast number of pots, figures and engravings, Gimbutas identified bird-like posteriors, or egg-shaped thighs, breasts and hips, as indicating a hybrid of woman and water-bird – the bird-goddess, familiar from mythologies around the world.

Gimbutas also compared various symbols, inscribed on the back and legs of goddess-images, to different features of liquid and its life-sustaining properties: a doubled V means running water; the painted, downward lines on goddess jugs and icons represent rain. Similar symbols on breasts denote milk. On the backs of the thighs they signify amniotic fluids. In this way, Gimbutas linked the Goddess with the primary element – water – and established the basis for her theory of a Paleolithic creatrix, forming herself and the world out of the primordial fluid. Gimbutas further noted that the owl-like eyes of the Goddess, adorning tombstones, shrines, temples and altars, connect her with death and the afterlife, extending her function from mere creator to the Universal Great Mother, whose "powers pervade all nature".

A storage jar from Knossos, Crete, c.*1450BC. Marija Gimbutas interpreted the double-axe as a goddess motif. She argued that it had evolved from the butterfly, a common symbol of the soul.*

There is considerable variation in the sizes, styles and types of female image found among the enormous number of clay and marble figures excavated from the period between 7000 and 3500BC. They range from the monumental goddesses found in the rock-temples of Malta to tiny figurines, and include the Goddess asleep, in the process of giving birth and in a worshipping or blessing stance.

A baked clay statue of a Mother Goddess, seated on a leopard-throne, from Çatal Hüyük, Turkey, c.5750BC. The archeologist, James Mellaart, suggests that this was the century when statues of a male god (in the form of a bull) disappeared from the local religion, indicating the triumph of agriculture over the ancient practice of hunting.

The archeologist James Mellaart, who directed the excavation of the Neolithic site at Çatal Hüyük, in Turkey, in the 1960s, described the rooms in the various buildings as shrines that would have been reserved for Goddess worship. Critics suggest that they could equally well have been assembly rooms for gatherings of hunters. On the other hand, the buildings uncovered by the partial excavation of the area are mostly temples, and only the Goddess appears on walls and reliefs, making Mellaart's proposition the more likely. For Mellaart, the development of an agricultural economy suggests a growth in the power and importance of women, because traditionally they were the tenders of the soil.

The theory that the people of Neolithic Çatal Hüyük possessed a formulated religion and cosmogony is also corroborated, to some extent, by the excavations. Paintings on the walls of temples depict vultures near headless bodies, raising the possibility of a belief system in which the Goddess reabsorbed the dead, probably for the purpose of regeneration. The heads of bulls were found juxtaposed with corpses in burial chambers, suggesting an extension of this theme (the shape of the bull's head has been compared to the human uterus, and its horns to the fallopian tubes, so placing a dead body near to a bull's head would be a way of preparing it for rebirth). The bull has also been interpreted as the male god, or consort (and son) of the Goddess. In one shrine, a goddess appears to have given birth to three bulls' heads, and the sacral bull subsequently found in Celtic and numerous other cultures may have survived from the Neolithic period.

A powerful case can be made for the reconstruction of prehistoric religious and social attitudes, based on the analysis of archeological findings – including the structure of settlements and individual buildings. However, it is difficult to assess the accuracy of the resulting theories in the absence of vital, supplementary information, which is no longer available. The 20th century has made great advances in the study of past and present cultures, but the danger still exists of refracting ancient beliefs through a distorting contemporary lens.

THE GODDESS AND THE LION

The familiar and widespread association of the Mother Goddess with lions has probably existed since Paleolithic times. The earliest evidence of the link between lions and motherhood was found in the Chapel of the Lioness in the cave sanctuary of Les Trois Frères, in the Dordogne in France, where a lioness and her cub are engraved on an altar. On the wall is a lifelike image of another lioness, engraved in the middle-Paleolithic period (between 18,000 and 14,000BC).

The feline aspect of the Goddess appears again in the Paleolithic temple of Pech-Merle, in France, in the shape of an unusual red figure known as the Lion Queen. Perhaps the most spectacular lion-image of all is that of an Anatolian Mother Goddess high up in Yasilakaya, which was once the Hittite capital. The centre-piece of an imposing scenario of figures, she is more than 6ft (2m) in height and sits mounted on a lion as a god advances toward her. The tableau also includes a small boy on another lion. The scene probably represents a form of divine marriage (see pp.100–103), which resulted in the magical fertilization of the realm. Because the lion, with its tawny golden mane, is sometimes mythologically analogous with the sun, the image of an earth goddess riding a lion might suggest the combination of natural elements to bring about this fertilization.

Another image relevant in this context is that of a vastly-proportioned goddess, seated on a birthing throne, with each arm resting on a panther or other big cat, and the head of a baby appearing between her legs. Babylonian and Egyptian statues of goddesses with lions' heads (dating from *c.*3000BC) suggest an even closer link between the Goddess and the lion and hint at myths and rituals of metamorphosis, possibly related to the cycles of the sun. The Egyptian goddess Hathor had lion heads that looked forward and backward, symbolizing time.

In this 19th-century Indian painting, the goddess Durga, riding a lion, destroys the demon Mahisha for threatening to dispossess the gods. During wars between regional Indian princes, the altars and images of Durga were anointed with the blood of captured warriors to quench the thirst of the goddess.

Creating a Golden Age of woman

The Dream, *painted by Henri Rousseau in 1910, just before he died. The painter's own explanation of this work was that the woman on the Victorian sofa had fallen asleep and dreamed she had been transported to an ancient natural utopia.*

The idea of the "Divine Feminine" has attracted much attention because it can be used to re-evaluate the position of women in contemporary societies. Many feminists of the Western world have welcomed the suggestion that there might once have been a society based around a Goddess religion. This society, according to modern Goddess movements, was not concerned with conquest or domination, but concentrated its energies on a gynocentric (female-centred) system of organization, with the accent on peaceful interaction and artistic development.

These claims appear to be endorsed by the discovery of the civilization of Çatal Hüyük (see p.14), described by its discoverer, James Mellaart, as a "supernova among the rather dim galaxy of contemporary peasant cultures". Çatal Hüyük flourished between 7000BC and 5000BC, in what is now Turkey. It boasted a range of arts and crafts, including sculpture and painting, weaving and pottery. Its buildings and shrines – many apparently dedicated to a supreme goddess – were built on several levels and follow a sophisticated architectural blueprint. There are no defensive structures, such as hill-forts, and the 150 or so paintings discovered in the area do not depict any scenes of violence. The surviving mythologies of the region reinforce the impression of a peaceful, agrarian lifestyle.

Followers of Goddess movements claim the Neolithic as a Golden Age: populated by matriarchies based on the worship of a single, universal Goddess, which lasted for several millennia until it was gradually eroded from the 4th millennium BC onward by a series of major invasions by the so-called Indo-Europeans. The Goddess continued to command worship in many cultures, but in a less powerful and unified form. After the advent of Christianity, the Goddess is believed to have survived throughout Europe in Wicca-style religions (see pp.152–3), despite persecution during the witch-hunts of the Reformation. For modern Goddess-worshippers, the social disorder apparent today results from the usurping of the Goddess's throne. The Golden Age is used as a necessary paradigm of the future: an attempt to avert cataclysm by the recreation of a strife-free and ecologically-conscious world.

The ideal of a Goddess, it is hoped, will unite women and inspire them to create a less materialistic society where people can co-exist peacefully. In North America, where modern Goddess movements are strongest, Native American myths are used to illustrate the gynocentric ethos – in which woman is the bringer of life and nourishment, society and the earth are seen as a unified whole, and the general good is more important than the individual will.

However, even if the Golden Age actually existed, critics of the ideologies that are derived from it point out that a matriarchy preserves a state of gender domination. The gender-balance is reversed, but there is little guarantee that a Goddess-orientated civilization would lead to greater peace. Moreover, even in countries such as India, where traditions of Goddess-worship have been unbroken for millennia, women are rarely accorded the status that would seem to be commensurate with the adulation of the "Divine Feminine".

THE FIRST MOTHER

According to the Penebscott Native Americans, First Woman greeted the Great Spirit and First Man with the words, "Children, I have come to abide with you and bring you love." When she had peopled the world with many offspring, a famine came. Seeing her children unhappy, she insisted that her husband should cut her up into pieces and drag her body around a field, before burying her bones in the middle. Seven months later, as she had promised, the field was filled with corn which provided her children with food. The corn, she said, was her flesh, and they must return a portion of it to the earth to perpetuate it. The yield of her bones, buried in the centre of the field, is tobacco, the Native American symbol of peace.

To the Goddess movements, this myth illustrates the pre-eminence of the female divinity. Her incarnations as corn and tobacco demonstrate the principle of regeneration inherent in mysteries of the Goddess worldwide (see pp.70–71), as well as the social value of selflessness.

The act of First Woman resonates through the myths of Mother Goddesses of many mythologies, and the ritual in which a goddess is dragged around a field recurs among the German Celts and the worshippers of Cybele.

The Great Mother archetype

The importance of the Goddess as a symbol of motherhood can be explored and illuminated through the theories of the psychologist and psychiatrist Carl Gustav Jung (1875–1961). According to the Jungian view, the Mother Goddess as the supernatural source of the world is a concept innate in the human mind prior to birth, partly because the primary, universal human experience is of gestation. This pre-natal idea is reinforced after the birth, when the mother nourishes her child with food, love and warmth, and the child depends entirely on her for comfort and safety.

At this stage, the child experiences its mother as "numinous" (suffused with a feeling of divinity). Her most casual action is of overpowering significance, and an infant quickly begins to split her into the "good mother", who is giving and protective, and the "bad mother", who is threatening and punitive. As the child gets older, the mother gradually becomes established as a whole, and therefore ambivalent, individual, combining beneficent and harmful qualities.

This infantile process is reflected in mythical accounts of the beginning of the world, which is often depicted as consciousness emerging from chaos. Another way of describing primal chaos is as the totality of all potential forces, exemplified by the widespread symbol of the Ouroboros, a serpent that chews its own tail, and in doing so forms an unbroken circle. Within the circle are many apparently contradictory pairs: male and female (implicit in the circular mouth-womb which receives the phallic tail), conscious and unconscious, productive and destructive. At first, these are not distinguishable from each other.

Out of this chaotic totality evolve numerous distinct entities that tend to be classified by the human mind as good and bad (and male and female). Although the mythologizing mind, like that of the very young child, conceives of good mothers – such as Sophia, or wisdom, and the Virgin Mary – and bad mothers – such as the Gorgon, with her serpentine hair and a glance that petrifies, or the bloodthirsty Sekhmet and Anath – it also evolves other, even more compelling and powerful mother figures: the ambivalent goddesses who combine both negative and positive aspects, such as Hera, Aphrodite,

A scene from the Walt Disney film, Snow White and the Seven Dwarves, *which abounds in goddess symbols: the evil crone, the goodhearted virgin and the apple, half sweet and half poisoned.*

JUNG AND THE ARCHETYPES

Jung believed that his "theory of archetypes" was of fundamental importance to the study of the psychology of religion. According to this theory, the mind of the individual is not only divided into the conscious and the unconscious, but the unconscious is further split into the collective and the personal. The collective unconscious, which is shared by everyone, consists of innate memories and historical experience inherited from our ancestors. The personal unconscious is the ever-changing product of individual experience, beginning in the womb.

The inherited memory, or collective unconscious, expresses itself in a series of symbols or "instinctive patterns" called archetypes, which become conscious through dreams, images and words, as well as expectations associated with particular people. A child has pre-existent ideas of a mother, a father or a teacher that may be unrealistic at first but are modified in the normal course of development. The first, strongest and most lasting of all the archetypes is the Great Mother, represented as the omnipotent Goddess.

The Large Standing Figure: Knife Edge *(right), sculpted by Henry Moore in 1976, and the 6th-millennium BC Turkish fertility figure (left) are part of an unbroken tradition, stretching back to the Paleolithic, of visualizing the mother archetype as a monumental, and often frightening, form.*

Kali and Hine. This tendency of the Goddess to represent the complementary opposites of above and below, creation and destruction, security and danger, is commonly symbolized, in the unconscious and in myth, by rounded images of wholeness that recall the Ouroboros. The face of the moon, which, over the course of a month, combines darkness and light, is a worldwide goddess symbol. The apple is also commonly associated with the Great Mother: it is, by tradition if not scriptural authority, the apple that Eve (whose name derives from "Mother of All") took from the Tree of Knowledge; the apple is also one of the attributes of Venus, and of the graces.

The Jungian scholar Erich Neumann made a seminal and extensive study of diverse mother symbols in *The Great Mother: An Analysis of the Archetype* (1963). He concluded that all the earliest religious works of art were "figures of the solitary Great Goddess – the Paleolithic image of Mother, before there was any Father either on earth or in heaven".

Conflict and Survival

Although prehistoric artefacts may suggest the existence of a primitive, Goddess-worshipping religion – and possibly even of matriarchies that practised it – there is no way of knowing what these objects really meant to the people who made them. To investigate the beliefs of ancient cultures, a different kind of archeology is necessary: an archeology of myth.

The recorded tales of the most ancient cultures reveal vestiges of belief systems that are older still. Many of the tales describe some primal struggle between male and female powers, but it is arguable whether these conflict-myths refer, in coded form, to power-struggles that actually took place, whether they were invented by men to explain (or justify) the (male-controlled) status quo, or whether they spring from archetypal, psychological differences between the sexes. Whichever interpretation is correct, male attempts to control religion were only partially successful: although frequently slandered and outlawed, Goddess-worship has survived into the modern world, often by the most circuitous and surprising routes.

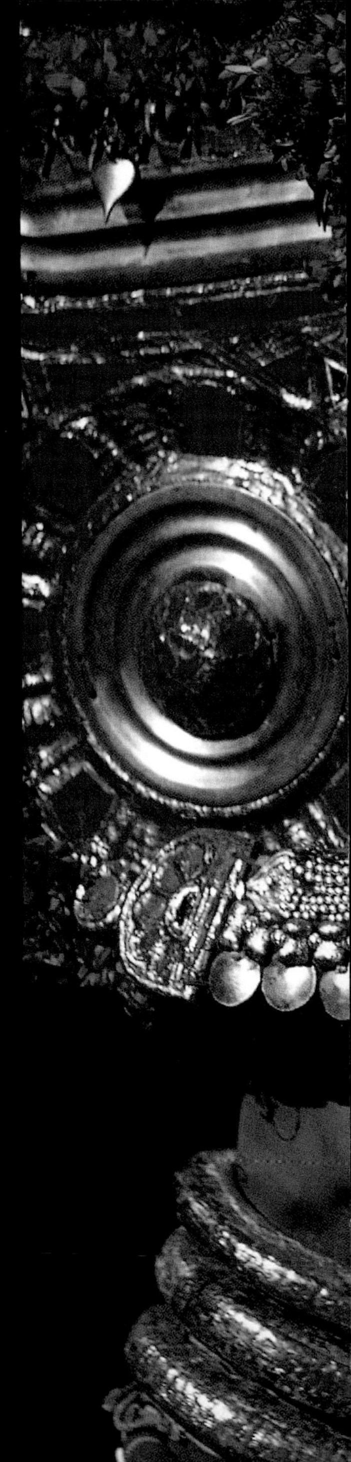

The sacred dances of Kerala, in India, share an unbroken tradition that stretches back over centuries, possibly to the Natya Shastra, *a Hindu sacred text that lays down the laws for dance, written in the first few centuries* AD. *Only men are allowed to take part in the dances – many of them not only play the part of a goddess, but become possessed by her. This man is dressed as, and possessed by, an avatar of the warrior-goddess, Durga.*

The shifting balance

The story of Tiamat and Marduk, shown here in an Assyrian relief, c.900BC, has been described as the first example of "priestly politics", in which the gods of an old, conquered culture become the demons of the new (see p.47).

The destruction of a serpent by a hero (shown here in an illustration from a 14th-century Icelandic text) spread from the Near East to become an almost universal symbolic act, signifying the triumph of light (and masculinity) over darkness (and the female).

The myths of Europe, Asia, Oceania, Africa and the Americas repeatedly describe the appropriation by males of powers that had originally belonged to women. For example, sacred objects that are now exclusively used by men, such as the flutes of the Amazonian Xinguano people or the bull-roarers (sticks that are said to reproduce the voices of ancestors and demons) of the Aboriginal Australians, are described as having once been in the custody of women, until they were stolen through force or trickery. Such myths can be interpreted in different ways. They may be archetypal expressions of an innate struggle or complementarity between the sexes. This view is supported by the way in which many societies divide the world into paired male and female elements – such as the sun and moon, gods and goddesses or the men's or women's parts of a house or village.

Alternatively, it is possible that the stories describe, however allegorically, actual historical events. This view is hard to prove conclusively, because it relies on the interpretation of myth, the decipherment of ancient texts that are partial or obscure, and the excavation of archeological sites belonging to cultures that may have left no written records. Nevertheless, the available evidence is consistent with the view of the modern Goddess Movement: that there was once a Goddess-worshipping Golden Age (see pp.16–17), which was superseded by patriarchal cultures that imposed their own, male deities.

The myths of a region frequently reflect its political upheavals. The city-states of ancient Sumer regularly fought each other, and lay on a flat, alluvial plain, which was particularly vulnerable to invasion. The structure of the Sumerian pantheon – and the relative importance of the different deities – changed constantly, and closely reflected the power struggles that took place. By 1700BC, the region had been taken over by Babylon, a city whose tutelary deity was the male god Marduk, and a tale of Marduk's victory over the goddess Tiamat (see p.47) was recited every spring equinox.

SEXUAL ENVY, CONQUEST AND THE RAPE OF THE OLD CULTURES

A common mythological theme that invites interpretation as a veiled description of a power struggle is that of the rape of a goddess by a god. Throughout history, conquerors have raped the women of the cultures that they have defeated. They have also described their gods as raping the goddesses of their victims. In the rhetoric of conquest, rape signifies mastery, and the violation of a people's divine mother brings about the subversion, and therefore weakening, of an existing national or cultural identity. Similarly, the invaders' god is sometimes described as raping the daughters of local kings. For example, Zeus impregnated Danaë, a princess of Argos; Leda, a princess of Sparta and Antiope, a princess of Thebes, in addition to many other royal daughters. Zeus went unchecked except by his jealous wife Hera, who often chose to wreak her revenge on the rape victim instead of on her husband. Zeus, meanwhile, became the father of nations in every part of the Greek world. In this way a foreign god was described as placing his genetic imprint on existing dynasties, thereby establishing his followers' rights to rule.

Myths of sexual conquest seem to acknowledge a fear, or even envy, that men experience before the birth-giving power of women. Alongside innumerable other tales, which describe different ways in which men overcame women, they also attempt to explain the kinds of social and political power that lie predominantly in the hands of men. Taken as a whole, these myths appear to be suggesting either that political dominance did indeed originally belong to women, or that such dominance is only a symbolic male substitute (and perhaps an inadequate one) for the female generative power.

In the women's rituals of the Pitjantjatjara of central Australia – whose details are always kept secret from the men – the rape of an ancestral female is the prelude to an act of vengeance, in which the man responsible is mutilated. The role of the man in these ceremonies is always played by an infertile woman. The Australian ancestress Kalwadi is an example of a sacred female whose generative powers have been appropriated by men. Kalwadi is an important figure in male initiations. She is described as swallowing boys and regurgitating them as men, but also once gained a reputation as a cannibal, with a weakness for eating the occasional child. Men searched for her and killed her, but when she was slit open, the children were not in her stomach. Instead, they were found in her womb, waiting to be reborn. Despite her innocence, her power was partially taken over by the men, who now preside over initiations in which boys are bloodied and placed in a hole in the ground, called the "womb of Kalwadi".

The Rape of Europa, *from a 1st-century AD Pompeiian fresco. Europa was a pre-Hellenic goddess, and the legend of Zeus turning himself into a bull to carry her off may be a Hellenic rationalization of ancient images showing a priestess of Europa riding a sacrificial bull.*

India

The Indian subcontinent is probably the only part of the world in which the importance of the Goddess has perceptibly increased throughout recorded history. The earliest Hindu sacred texts, the Vedas, were written between 1500BC and 1000BC. They were not primarily intended as repositories of myth, but mainly to record hymns for ritual use, as well as philosophical glosses on those hymns. However, the narratives that can be gleaned from the Vedas describe a relatively limited pantheon of some thirty-three deities. The most important of these is Indra, the warrior king and wielder of thunderbolts, closely followed by Agni, the god of fire.

Although there are goddesses in the Vedas, they are minor characters. Indra's wife, Saci, is hardly ever referred to, and is usually called Indrani (the feminine form of her husband's name) on those occasions when she does appear. The Sarasvati of the Vedas is a river goddess, and bears little resemblance to the Sarasvati found in modern Hinduism, who is a popular goddess of learning and the arts. When females appear in Vedic myth, they are incidental characters: either victims (such as Diti, whose womb was entered by Indra so that he could cut up a foetus that might grow to threaten him); relatives of the main protagonists; or agents of the gods (such as the messenger Sarama, sometimes described as a bitch, who was sent by Indra to recover cattle that had been stolen by demons).

This is not to say that the Goddess was unimportant in ancient India. There are many goddess representations surviving from the pre-Vedic Indus Valley civilization, but these seem to be mainly fertility figures who, if they survived into the Aryan civilization that produced the Vedas, probably did so as *apsarases* (river goddesses) and similar, minor divinities. However, in later Hinduism, the idea of Mahadevi ("the Great Goddess") was to flourish. The first ever mention of the Goddess as a supreme being occurs in the 5th century AD, in the *puranic* ("ancient") text called the *Devi-Mahatmya* ("Glorification of the Goddess"), which contains hymns of praise that are still in popular use. By this time, the number of Hindu gods was conservatively reckoned at more than 300 million, but they were all held to be aspects of the *trimurti*, or "triple form" of the one ultimate reality that underlay the universe, comprising Vishnu, Shiva (both minor figures in the Vedas) and the newcomer, Brahma.

A 10th-century AD Pala dynasty representation of the divine female power, from Nalanda, Bihar.

The *trimurti* was still all male, but by the 8th century, the ultimate reality was being described as comprising "six paths", of which Vishnu and Shiva were two. Brahma had already vanished, and there is only one major temple to him in modern India. The other "paths" were Surya (the Vedic sun), Karttikeya,

Ganesh and Devi, "the Goddess". Of these, only Vishnu, Shiva and Devi are still thought of as pan-Indian supreme deities, and the three most important forms of modern Hinduism are usually described as Vaishnava (Vishnu-worshipping), Shaiva (Shiva-worshipping) and Shakta (from *Shakti*, meaning female power, see pp.156–7).

Like the other Indian deities, Devi has many forms, which range from the loving wife, Parvati, to the bringer of death, Kali. Some of these, occasionally thinly disguised, have also entered various branches of Buddhism, as *bodhisattvas*, or saviours. In this form they were transported throughout Asia by Buddhist missionaries, evolving in turn as they went into countless local deities.

The festival of Gangaur, in Rajasthan. Young women carry vessels or dolls on their heads, which symbolically turn them into vessels of the goddess Gauri (another name for Parvati). This is one of thousands of local festivals throughout India in which the Goddess is celebrated openly, rather than in a disguised form, as is more common worldwide (see pp.40–41).

COMPETITION AND SEDUCTION

The tension between male and female – and between the status of women in myth and their status in Indian society – is indicated by the number of stories in which the Goddess struggles with male divinities or demons. Tellingly, these contests are not always straightforward fights: for example, in one set of stories, in which Kali challenges the power of Shiva, they agree to a dancing competition, which Shiva wins because Kali is too modest to copy his high kicks. The goddess is tamed by her defeat. She adopts an Indian woman's traditional virtues of restraint and subordination, and agrees to worship Shiva. However, in popular representations of Kali, she is far from subdued and is often shown dancing on the corpse of Shiva.

Even when the struggle undertaken by the Goddess is overtly violent, there may be erotic undertones. In one myth the River Ganga threatens to fall on Shiva and crush him so that he mingles with her waters. In some versions of the myth that describes the struggle of the goddess Durga against the buffalo demon, Mahisha (see p.15), there is an obvious ambiguity between the roles of husband and enemy. The demon proposes marriage to Durga, and when she responds with terrible threats, he interprets them as innuendo – metaphors for the "battle of love".

Australia and Oceania

The cosmological myth of father sky and mother earth can be found throughout most of the inhabited islands of Polynesia, but the relative significance accorded to the male and female participants in the creation of the universe varies greatly from place to place.

In Hawaii, Papa the earth mother is also known as Haumea, and in this form she is the patron of childbirth and agriculture. She is also venerated as the mother of the feared, much-worshipped volcano goddess, Pele. In the past, Hawaiians used to venerate rock formations resembling paired male and female genitals as if they were ancestral gods, and the complementarity of male and female is central to traditional Hawaiian religious thought. By contrast, the Maori of New Zealand traditionally regard men as being *tapu,* or sacred, while women are thought to be *noa,* or profane. Although Rangi the sky and Papa the earth are the primal parents, they take little part in the process of creation, which is mainly undertaken by their son, Tane (who is known as Kane in Hawaii), who forces them apart so that their children have room to move, and so that light can enter the world. Tane fastens the sun, moon and stars on his father, then, in searching for a wife, he copulates with many strange beings, producing the plants and animals, before fashioning himself a wife from the soil. The role of women in the Maori creation stories is ambivalent at best, and sometimes wholly negative. The daughter of Tane and Hine-ahu-one ("Woman-heaped-up-from-soil") is called Hine-nui-te-po ("Great-woman-the-night"). She is generally credited with introducing death into the world (see pp.86–7). In another Maori myth, the trickster hero Maui tries to conquer mortality by climbing up into Hine-nui-te-po through her vagina, thus reversing the process whereby every human is born from a woman's womb, and disappears at death into the grave (which is Hine-nui-te-po's mouth). However, he fails, and is killed in the attempt.

An 18th-century Maori wall slab, probably showing Maui climbing up into the vagina of Hine-nui-te-po. He was killed by the vagina's snapping, flint edges, which generated sparks and lightning.

Although Maui is a male hero, his name, meaning "left", associates him with the *noa* side of the body. He is a troublemaker, and even those of his tricks that are beneficial to the rest of humanity are achieved by breaking the laws of the *tapu.* They are also usually achieved through the highly potent relics or effects of (sometimes unspecified) female ancestor figures. For example, fire, which Maui brings to humankind, was originally kept under the fingernails of the ancestress Mahuika. When Maui goes fishing, and draws the North Island of New Zealand up out of the sea, the hook that he uses is

AUSTRALIAN TOTEMS

A kangaroo totem in the X-ray style, from Western Arnhem Land in Australia.

Among the Australian Aborigines, the deeds of the totemic ancestors, who inhabited a mythological "dreamtime" and travelled across Australia creating rocks, plants, animals and people, are re-enacted in ceremonies, so that the people themselves become their ancestors. According to Aboriginal mythology, the acts of creation must continually be performed, or else the world will languish.

The ceremonies are divided into "men's business" and "women's business", and normally the women's ceremonies concern the reproduction of physical life, and health, while the men's ceremonies concern the reproduction of the spirit.

In most Aborigine myths, the totemic ancestors left spirits in certain places, and a woman conceives when one of these spirits enters her. The particular spot where this occurs determines some of the child's totems. Sometimes these are revealed to the father in a dream, but sometimes it is the mother's right to announce the totem place. Nevertheless, through these myths, men claim the power of reproduction, because it is their ceremonies that maintain the supply of spirit children to be born into the world.

made from the jawbone of another ancestress (hooks of human bone were taboo), and is filled with magical power.

In the vast majority of Polynesian myths, although it is men who set forth on adventures, they are able to succeed only with the help of sorcerous women, who can break the normal rules. In day-to-day Maori life, also, the obligations of *tapu* represented a sometimes crippling restriction on a man's behaviour. For example, in Maori society, women enjoyed much greater sexual freedom because they were not bound to *tapu* conduct (on the other hand, they had to carry all loads, because men could not take burdens on their backs).

During the construction of Maori meeting-houses, women must stay away, or they would profane the building. However, once built, a meeting-house is dangerously full of sacred potency, and some of the *tapu* must be removed by having a high-ranking woman enter it (this is the modern version of the ceremony: formerly the woman would walk on the roof). A woman who removes excess *tapu* is a *ruahine*, and the first ever *ruahine* is said to have been the ancient ancestress, Hine-te-iwaiwa. She was an archetypal mother-figure, and one of the few Polynesian mythical women to undergo her own quest, albeit only to find herself a husband.

The Americas

When the Spanish conquered Central and South America in the 16th century, they encountered two great empires: the Aztecs of Mexico and the Incas of the Andes. They interpreted the myths of these cultures in their own terms, claiming that the peoples whom they had conquered already worshipped primitive, unformed versions of the Trinity and the saints. In this way, unwittingly, they provided the means for the survival of indigenous deities, who are still widely revered under the names of the saints they most resemble.

Unexpectedly, goddesses have benefitted more from this process than gods. The prime example is probably the Virgin of Guadeloupe, who first appeared as a brown-skinned woman in 1541 and demanded, in the native tongue (Nahuatl), to have a church built on the site of a shrine that had once belonged to the indigenous goddess, Tonantzin. There was only ever lip-service paid to the pretence that this church was for the worship of Mary. Nevertheless, the church dedicated to the Virgin of Guadeloupe is crucial to Mexican Catholicism, and one of the main centres of pilgrimage in the country. There are many other examples of American goddesses being worshipped as saints or virgins, but there have been no comparable post-conquest manifestations of male gods.

This corn- or maize-mother is one of the very few female representations ever found in a traditional kiva *– a ceremonial house where business is conducted mostly by men.*

SPINNING TALES

Men are the storytellers of the Pueblo Native North Americans, and those researchers who have investigated the Pueblo's oral traditions generally describe a male-centred mythology. The widespread trickster figure, for example, is invariably portrayed as masculine, although one aspect of its trickery is in fact a magical ability to change gender.

Similarly, studies of ritual, shamanistic bisexuality among Native Americans has always concentrated on the male transvestite, commonly called the berdache (from the Arabic *badaj*, or boy-slave). The role of "ceremonial lesbians" was only analyzed in depth in the early 1980s, and has still received comparatively little attention. The complex rituals surrounding midwifery have also not been adequately researched, despite their obvious connection to most Native American creation stories, which concentrate on the birth of beings into an already existing world, rather than the making of worlds and people out of chaos.

Women's myths are rarely found in stories, but in handiwork, such as pottery and weaving. The process of making a Navajo rug recreates an entire cosmology linking the weaver to the yarn, the sheep that produced the wool, the movement of the sun, and so on. In this way, it relates the living female artisan to the creator, Spider Woman, who wove the web of cosmic order.

However, at the time of the conquest, the Aztecs had some 300 deities, very few of which were women. There is evidence that the female principle had been systematically devalued over the preceding centuries. Quetzalcoatl, "the feathered serpent", which appears in myth as male, was originally probably androgynous, as indicated by "his" name, combining the masculine quetzal bird with "coatl", which meant both "twin" (indicating a dual nature) and "snake" (a creature that the Aztecs associated with the female psyche).

The most widely revered goddess figure in the Andes – who predates the Incas – also demonstrates some androgyneity. The fertile earth, Pachamama, is still offered libations and sacrifices throughout Peru. Although *mama* denotes fertility, it is not specifically that of a mother. The word also has male connotations, for example when pure veins of metal are referred to as the *mamas* of the mines. The benign aspects of Pachamama are often conflated with the Virgin Mary, and she is frequently referred to as Santa Tierra ("Saint Earth"), but it is acknowledged that her destructive side requires at least as much worship. She is sometimes cannibalistic, an aspect shared with other pre-Colombian female spirits, the *condenados*, who have survived into the modern day and are thought to suck a man's energy from him during sex. This trait of the Goddess is also common in Amazonian South America (see p.110).

Native American goddesses were not the only ones to resurface in the form of saints. This woman, a priestess of the Candomblé cult of Brazil, is dressed as Oxum, who was originally an African goddess of water. Brought to the Americas by slaves, Oxum was christianized as Our Lady of La Caridad.

Africa

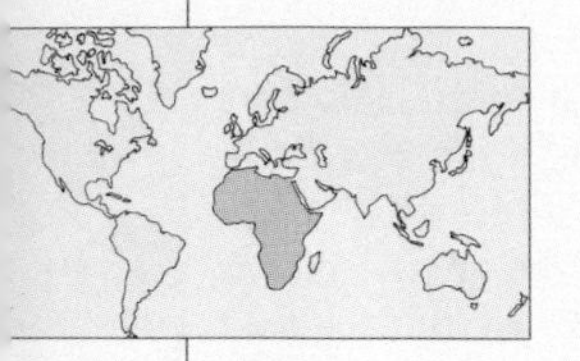

The countries of modern Africa are relics of the ways in which colonial powers divided up the continent. They often group together peoples who, historically, have shared nothing but animosity, while their borders frequently cut traditional homelands in two. Neighbouring African peoples may have completely different traditional beliefs, and often the only religious concepts that are found uniformly throughout a country belong to Christianity or Islam, and were imposed or urged upon the local populations by invaders. However, some ideas, albeit with extensive local variations, occur among a large number of widely separated African groups.

A bisexual serpent, often worshipped as a goddess and associated with a rainbow, features in the creation myths of Benin as the self-fertilizing Mawu Lisa, in southern Africa as the great python Chinaweji and in southern Algeria as the gigantic Minia, from whose body the whole world was made. Another creation motif traditionally associated with goddess figures, which is found from the Dogon of Mali to the Lungu of Zambia, is the primal egg, whose vibrations set the world in motion. In

THE SPREAD OF THE BLACK GODDESS

Rock paintings in the Tassili region of Saharan Africa, thought to be between 7,000 and 10,000 years old, show female figures bearing marks, such as crescents, that are commonly associated with the goddesses of Egypt and the Near East. The people who created these images may in fact have been influenced by the early Egyptians, but black African historians have suggested instead that they represent the original black goddess figure, from whom all others derive.

Although humankind originated in northeastern Africa, the dominant themes that recur throughout the world's myths and rituals may not have developed until humans had already moved to other regions. Such themes may then have been reintroduced to Africa by subsequent waves of migration or conquest. However, 20th-century black historians, such as John G. Jackson, have argued that coastal African peoples were accomplished mariners and explorers, who carried a matriarchal, goddess-based culture to Asia, Europe, the Americas and Oceania. According to some of these historians, the Black Madonnas found throughout Europe (see p.122) – usually interpreted as representing the psychological "dark side" of the Goddess – are simply vestiges of a time when the Goddess really was black. More recently, slaves taken from western Africa successfully introduced their deities – especially the water goddess Oya – throughout the Americas, in religions such as Candomblé, Umbanda and Batuque.

A spiritualist and servant of Oya, on the banks of the River Niger, in Nigeria.

These religions all feature possession by the gods, and, as in Nigerian possession cults, there are many more women than men in the priesthoods.

the Dogon creation story, the world was populated after the great god Amma had intercourse with the earth, whose vagina was an anthill, and whose clitoris was a termite mound. However, the first time the god approached the earth to have intercourse, the termite mound rose up to block him. Because he cut it down, the first intercourse was flawed, and produced the evil jackal, which is a symbol of all the problems of god and humanity.

Another widespread African belief is that trees are sacred, and usually female, beings. For the Ibo of Nigeria, as well as for other western African peoples, the cotton tree contains the earth goddess. Among the Ndembu of Zambia, the Mudyi tree is a multiple symbol, suggesting breast-milk, women's wisdom, death and the continuity of Ndembu society.

Among a number of African peoples, patterns of kinship are calculated through the female line. This, along with some dubious accounts by the Greek historian Diodorus Siculus, writing *c.*100BC, about Egyptian and African husbands having "to obey the woman in all things", has led some historians to propose that all Africa was once populated by matriarchal societies. The last vestiges of greatly revered, serpent-worshipping priestess-sisterhoods could be found in parts of western Africa well into the 20th century, along with stories of their earlier power and influence. The multifarious African legends about the origins of kingship also tend to support such theories. Most African royal families trace their ancestry back to culture heroes, or even gods. However, in the majority of cases, even if the first king is a god himself, and has his own store of magical powers, he derives his right to rule only from his marriage to a divine bride. For example, the Mbangalala of Angola tell of the hero, Chibinda Llunga, founder of the Lunda dynasty. Chibinda Llunga became a king when the Lunda queen, Lueji, who was descended from the primordial serpent, fell in love with him and told the Lunda elders that he would rule in her place. Lueji subsequently became sterile, and had to give Chibinda Lunga a new wife to bear him children, possibly so that, although the legitimacy of the Lunda kings derived from a divine woman, their power could be held to pass through the male line.

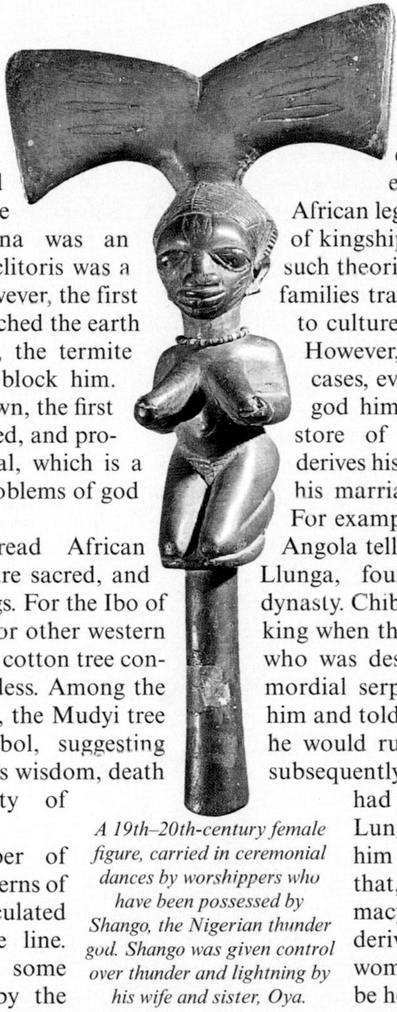

A 19th–20th-century female figure, carried in ceremonial dances by worshippers who have been possessed by Shango, the Nigerian thunder god. Shango was given control over thunder and lightning by his wife and sister, Oya.

Other forms of power that are now the province of men are traditionally thought to have originated among women. For example, among the Bapende of Zaire, a woman is said to have discovered the secret magic of the masks used in initiation rites, but for hundreds of years only Bapende men have been allowed to wear them.

The triumph of Isis

Each ancient Egyptian city had its own cosmology, which explains why the goddess Isis could simultaneously be described as the mother of the universe and as one of the four children of the earth god, Geb, and the sky goddess, Nut. However, all the cities of Egypt depended on the annual flooding of the Nile to provide them with fertile soil, irrigation and crops, and all were agreed that the Nile, as primordial water, was the ultimate source of life.

In Bronze Age Egypt, the Upper Nile seems to have been represented by a vulture goddess named Nekhbet, and the Lower Nile and delta by a serpent goddess, Wedjat. Isis was originally the protective deity of a small delta town, named Perehbet. She became assimilated to Wedjat and, when the kingdoms of Upper and Lower Egypt were united, also took over the identity of Nekhbet.

The hieroglyph of Isis's name was a throne, and she was often depicted wearing a throne on her head. As early as the First Dynasty, pharaohs referred to themselves as the sons of Isis: the lap of the goddess was regarded as the royal throne, while her breast poured forth the nectar that conferred the divine right to rule. Similar attitudes to kingship can still be found in parts of Africa (see pp.30–31).

Isis was not represented exclusively as an aristocrat. In at least one of her legends, she was described as a serving woman who obtained divine power only after she had tricked the sun god Ra into revealing his secret name and, perhaps because of her suffering while trying to find the dead body of her husband, Osiris (see pp.84–6), she was often portrayed as a particularly sympathetic deity, with many vulnerable, human qualities. She eventually subsumed all the other Egyptian goddesses.

Alexander the Great conquered Egypt in 332BC. When he died nine years later, his Macedonian General, Ptolemy, declared himself ruler, and attempted to cement his position in Egypt by establishing the cult of Sarapis, which merged Egyptian and Macedonian elements. Isis became the mother-lover of Sarapis in the new composite religion, which helped establish her cult throughout the Hellenistic world. Isis-worship spread to Rome in 80BC, and although her cult was banned in 58BC, after a scandal when one of its priests seduced a Roman matron, it was reinstated fifteen years later in response to public demand. Isis was worshipped openly at least until the 6th century AD, when her sanctuary at Philae was turned into a Christian church. Many of her attributes continued to be revered throughout the Christian world, having been absorbed into the person of the Virgin Mary.

A bronze statue, c.600–400BC, of Isis, wearing a headdress of the sun between cow-horns, suckling the child-king Horus and acting as his throne.

Isis as the winged guardian of the dead, on the sarcophagus of Rameses III, c.*1194–1163*BC. *The other end of the sarcophagus bears an image of the winged Nephthys. Isis and Nephthys were the "two sisters who speak with one voice", and in several hymns merge into a single figure.*

UNIVERSAL ISIS

As late as the 2nd century AD, the Greek historian Plutarch described Isis as "the female principle of Nature ... called countless names, since ... she turns herself into this thing or that and is receptive of all manner of shapes and forms." The Greek philosopher, barrister and initiate into the mysteries of Isis, Apuleius (born *c.*AD125, around the time of Plutarch's death), wrote a book called *The Golden Ass*, describing the initiation of a fictionalized autobiographical character named Lucius. Isis appears to Lucius, and tells him: "The primeval Phrygians call me Pessinuntica, Mother of the Gods; the Athenians ... call me Cecropian Artemis; for the islanders of Cyprus I am Paphian Aphrodite; for the archers of Crete I am Dictynna; for the trilingual Sicilians, Stygian Proserpine; and for the Eleusinians their ancient Mother of the Corn. Some know me as Juno, some as Bellona of the Battles; others as Hecate ... but both races of Ethiopians ... and the Egyptians, who excel in ancient learning ... call me by my true name, namely, Queen Isis."

Celtic Britain

The "male" and "female" Neolithic Men-an-Tol stones, at Penwith in Cornwall. Legends that may date back to the Celts equate climbing through the hole in the female stone with a form of spiritual rebirth.

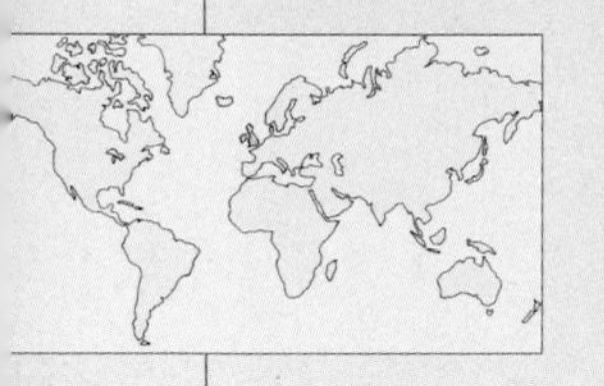

Only a tiny minority of Celtic goddesses had a widespread following. Most were merely local deities, restricted to streams, groves, hills, valleys or other geographical features. In addition, each Celtic people had its own patron goddess, and there were some eighteen distinct Celtic peoples in mainland Britain alone.

Epona, the horse goddess, seems to have had what was very nearly a pan-Celtic following, but even she was accorded different roles in different regions. Some worshipped her predominantly as a warrior, others as a guardian of the dead, and others as a healer. She appears frequently with a cornucopia, or horn of plenty, and although this was probably a Roman addition to her iconography, it is likely that she was widely identified as an earth-mother long before the Romans invaded Gaul and Britain. It was customary in Ireland for the king to "marry" the earth, to guarantee his right to rule, and as late as the 12th century there is an account of one king marrying a white mare – the symbol of Epona – at his coronation.

Epona was sometimes worshipped as "the three Eponae", and Celtic goddesses regularly appear as trinities. The Irish Morrigan was composed of Ana, the virgin; Badb, or "Boiling", the mother, who was a bubbling cauldron perpetually bringing forth life; and Macha, "Mother Death". Often, as in the case of the Irish land deity Cailleach Bheur, the goddess appeared alternately as a hag or a beautiful maiden.

Roman descriptions of the Celts emphasize the ferocity of the women and the prevalence of warrior goddesses. This is perhaps because the death-dealing crone aspect was often chosen to stand for the whole trinity, so that Morrigan, for example, despite her multiple personae, is characteristically depicted as or with a raven, haunting the battlefields.

The cauldron of regeneration, exemplified by Badb, was found throughout Celtic myth. In Wales this cauldron, a symbolic womb which could revive the dead overnight, belonged to Branwen, one of the "Three Matriarchs of the Island". Branwen's cauldron was later Christianized as the Holy Grail (just as her brother, Bran, was Christianized as Bron, who brought the Grail to Britain). Although other Celtic mythological figures have survived in Arthurian tales and medieval texts such as the Welsh *Mabinogion*, they have done so only in fragmentary forms (for example, as the sorceress Morgan Le Fay), shaped by the ideologies of the early Christian missionaries and monks.

A 1st-century BC statue of Epona, who is usually portrayed in Celtic art riding a horse or standing between a number of horses. In Germany, she was popularly depicted feeding young foals. Epona became a favourite of the Roman cavalry, and was the only Celtic goddess to be granted her own festival within the city of Rome.

THE ASSIMILATED GODDESS

Julius Caesar, writing about his conquests, asserted that the Celts had only one goddess, whom he called Minerva. Under Roman rule, the innumerable local Celtic goddesses became assimilated to the Roman figures who most resembled them. Brigit was the triple goddess of the Brigantes, who occupied parts of the British Isles, France and Spain. Her ruling aspect became associated with Juno, Queen of Heaven, while her sister-selves, who were responsible for healing and the metalworking crafts, became known as Minerva.

Early Christian hagiographers, finding her cult too popular to eradicate, canonized her in different regions as St Bridget, or St Bride. She was reinvented as a nun who had founded a convent in Kildare. However, she retained her pagan qualities. Her feast day, February 1, was the first day of Celtic spring, Imbolg, and she was regularly associated with fertility magic. Because of her earlier status as Queen of Heaven, St Bridget also became identified with the Virgin Mary.

A Celtic-Roman bronze head, from the 1st century AD, depicting Brigit as Minerva.

Rome and Christianity

The head of the mother goddess, Cybele, from 2nd-century BC Rome. The first emblem of Cybele that was brought to Rome was not an icon, but a plain black stone.

The most ancient goddess of Rome was Vesta, who was commemorated as a disembodied flame, kept perpetually burning by six sacred virgins. This was considered to be the mystical beating heart of the city, and later the empire. Other local goddess figures also, in different ways, became identified with the fabric of the state. Venus, like the Greek Aphrodite, is chiefly remembered as a goddess of love, but she also had the full complement of functions associated with any great goddess, including those of mother and bringer of death. In particular, she was said to be the mother of Aeneas, founder of Rome, and as such was the patron deity of the city. Ceres, the Roman version of the earth mother Demeter, was also called Ceres Legifera, "the lawgiver". It was said that her priestesses were the founders of the Roman legal system.

Rome was tolerant – and even acquisitive – of foreign deities. Cybele was brought to Rome from Mount Ida, in Phrygia, in 204BC, after the Cumaean Sybil predicted that her presence was the only way to defeat the conquering armies led by Hannibal. King Attalusat of Phrygia initially refused permission for her cultic image to leave his domain, and consented only when Cybele herself appeared and said that it was her wish to go. Hannibal was routed, and retreated from Italian soil in 203BC. The first Roman Emperor, Augustus, considered Cybele to be the supreme deity of the empire, and thought that his wife, Livia, was her earthly incarnation. Cybele was called the Magna Mater ("Great Mother") and "Mother of all the Gods". She was reviled by the early Christians, although one of her priests, Montanus, founded a Christian sect in the 2nd century based on the identification of Jesus with Cybele's son, Attis. The Montanists were declared heretics in the 4th century.

Other mystery cults, belonging to foreign goddesses such as Isis, Hecate and Demeter, flourished alongside those of Cybele. The term *Magna Dea* came to be applied fairly indiscriminately to all the great goddesses throughout the Roman Empire, and it has been claimed that Rome was on the verge of evolving a universal feminine monotheism until the advent of male-centred religions such as Mithraism and Christianity.

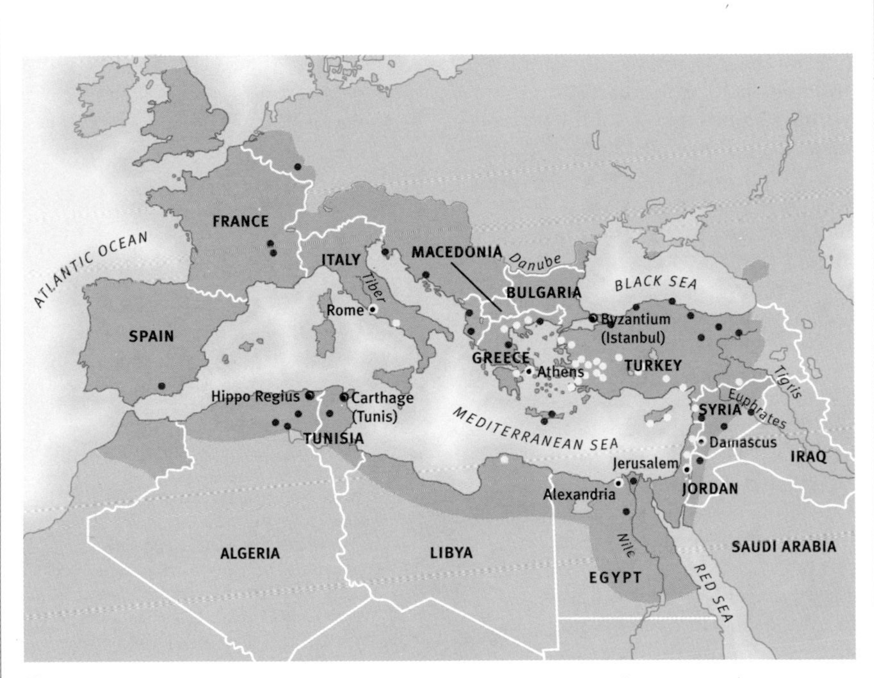

Roman Empire at the time of the first Christian Emperor, Constantine (d. AD 337), superimposed on a partial map of modern Europe, Africa and the Near East

City with a significant Christian community by the end of the 1st century AD

● City with a significant Christian community by the time of Constantine

•● Cities significant in the history of early Christianity and the decline of paganism

CHRISTIANITY IN THE ROMAN EMPIRE

Roman goddess cults were a rich source for a nascent Christian faith anxious to establish its own calendar of popular feasts and festivals. Christianity appropriated some of the most popular Roman holidays, reinterpreting them in an (often unsuccessful) attempt to purge them of their pagan associations. For example, Candlemas is the festival of the Purification of the Virgin because it falls forty days after Christmas, and the Judaeo-Christian tradition taught that a woman was unclean for forty days after the birth of a son. Yet Candlemas was originally the day honouring Juno Februata as the virgin mother of Mars, during which people marched through Rome burning candles. The celebration of Christmas borrowed most of its traditions from Roman Saturnalias and other pagan rites, such as the cutting of a sacred pine tree for the temple of Cybele. Lent derives from a period of abstention traditionally practised by women before the feast of Ceres.

The emperor Constantine (*c.*AD288–337) adopted Christianity as the official faith of the Roman Empire, partly because he wanted a suitably bureaucratic, well-organized religion to help hold his crumbling empire together. However, Constantine tolerated and encouraged the older faiths, and the Church's imperially sanctioned persecution of paganism did not begin until after his death.

The Goddess and the prophets

When the Hebrews invaded the promised land of Canaan, some time before 1200BC, they found a thriving, fertile region, occupied by Semitic peoples whose myths and religious practices were similar to those of Sumeria and Babylon. In the biblical book of Joshua, the invasion is described as a holy war against the false gods of the Canaanites. Chief among these were the "Mother of the Gods", Asherah, her daughter Astarte (Ashtoreth in Hebrew) and her son Baal. The father god, El, escaped the persecution of the Israelites, largely because he was assimilated to their own god, Yahweh-Elohim. The invading Hebrews were unable to keep elements of the local faiths from influencing their own religion. In particular, they could not suppress the idea that gods and goddesses existed as lovers or married couples. However, the bride of Yahweh, instead of being a traditional goddess figure, was held to be Israel itself, and when the people of Israel reverted to pagan worship they were described by their priests as whoring after foreign gods.

Astarte–Ishtar, represented in alabaster in the 3rd century BC (above), and in ivory in the 9th century BC (left). The Bible condemns the existence of "graven images", and in the book of Exodus declares: "Thou shalt not bow down thyself to them or serve them." However, graven images of Astarte–Ishtar found their way into Jewish ritual, in the form of the cherubim. In the book of Genesis these were angels placed by Yahweh at the east gate of Eden. In the time of Moses, images of cherubim were used to guard the Ark of the Covenant, and when Solomon built his temple he carved all the walls with cherubim, along with oxen and lions, which were ancient goddess-symbols.

Although the Hebrew prophets waged a bitter struggle against the Canaanite goddesses, they were at first only intermittently successful. King Solomon, according to the biblical book of 1 Kings, "went not fully after the Lord as did David", and "sacrificed and burned incense in high places". He probably imported Asherah-worship into Jerusalem, *c.*1000BC, along with one of his 700 wives. A wooden image of Asherah occupied the Temple of Solomon for some three centuries before it was removed (and then only temporarily) by King Hezekiah.

Any disaster that befell the Hebrews was habitually blamed on their weakness for flirting with the old deities. The unorthodoxy of Solomon's faith supposedly caused the kingdom of Israel to be divided in two after his reign, with Israel in the north and Judah in the south constantly fighting each other until 721BC, when the northern tribes were ejected from their land by the Assyrians. This deportation was also blamed on the widespread worship of "images and groves in every high hill". Subsequent kings of Judah vacillated in their attitudes to goddesses. Whenever one of the kings followed the prophets' injunctions to destroy the old altars and groves, it seems that his successor invariably replaced them. At the same time, traditional goddess worship was enormously popular among the ordinary inhabitants of the region, especially the poor.

A reproduction of a pact made in 1634 between a priest, Father Grandier, and the devil. Among the co-signatories is the demonized goddess, Ashtoreth.

When the people of Judah were themselves exiled into Egypt early in the 6th century BC, the prophet Jeremiah, typically, blamed their idolatry. However, the strength of goddess worship is indicated in the book of Jeremiah by the reaction of "all the men which knew that their wives had burned incense unto other gods, and all the women that stood by", who retaliated that, on the contrary, their troubles were caused because they had turned away from the Queen of Heaven (Astarte): it was only since they stopped pouring out offerings of drink and burning incense to her that they had been "consumed by the sword and by the famine".

Astarte was usually referred to in the Bible as Ashtoreth, a title which was a combination of her name with *boshet*, the Hebrew word for "shame". When the later, Christian, theologians resumed the attack on Astarte, or Ashtoreth, they literally demonized her, turning her into one of Satan's officers, so that the practice of offering her food, drink or unguents became, in the eyes of the Church, an act of devil-worship.

ASHERAH AND HER DAUGHTERS

Asherah was the oldest of the Canaanite goddesses, and was mentioned in a Sumerian inscription as early as 1750BC, where she was referred to as the wife of Anu (the Sumerian name for El, the father god of the Canaanite pantheon). In the Hebrew Scriptures, her name is translated as "grove", and she was typically represented as the Tree of Life, although among her many other titles she was also the "Lady Who Traverses the Sea", and the "Mother of the Gods", of whom she bore more than 70.

Astarte is only referred to nine times in the Bible (compared to Asherah's forty entries), but by the 5th or 6th century BC she was almost certainly more widely worshipped. However, there is considerable disagreement about whether Astarte was the daughter of Asherah, or merely another of Asherah's aspects, or another name for Asherah's daughter Anath, the wife-sister of Baal (Anath is not mentioned directly at all in the Hebrew Scriptures). Astarte was referred to as the "Queen of Heaven". The original meaning of her name was "womb", suggesting that she was a fertility goddess, and she was also, as patron of the coastal city of Sidon, the "Virgin of the Sea".

Festivals of the Goddess

One of the first festivals for which there is written evidence celebrated the marriage of the Sumerian king to a priestess who embodied the Goddess. *Inanna, Dumuzi and the Prosperity of the Palace*, a text probably dating back to the 2nd millennium BC, seems to be a script for this marriage, turning it into a piece of ritual theatre, with speaking roles for the goddess Inanna, her mother Ninlil, and a chorus. There are no speeches for the king, in his role as Dumuzi, the son and lover of the goddess, who is clearly a passive, subordinate character. Dumuzi was sacrificed each winter by the goddess, only to be resurrected in the spring, and there is evidence that, in another Sumerian festival, the king or a surrogate was killed to enact this myth. An annual Festival of Weeping Women to mourn Dumuzi was held in the town of Harran until the 10th century AD, and some form of springtime celebration of the dying and resurrected son, presided over by his mother, is probably the most persistent tradition of (often disguised) goddess-worship in Europe and the Near East. It survives in the modern Western world in many forms, not least as Easter.

Most festivals of the Goddess also honoured her son. They were celebrated by both men and women, and involved an element of often orgiastic sex, with the goal of magically stimulating the earth into greater fertility. For example, the ancient Roman festival of Flora ("Flourishing One"), the goddess of spring, is generally considered to be the prototype of traditional May Day celebrations. In these, until at least the 16th century in rural Europe, the young women of a village would be "defiled" en masse by the young men, or a specially chosen virgin (the May Queen)

A woman at the Durga Puja festival in Varanasi.

WIVES AND WARRIORS

India has more traditional festivals for the Goddess than anywhere else, and most follow the familiar pattern of celebrating her marriage, so that sympathetic magic will improve the fertility of the earth, or the marital happiness of her devotees. For example, the Teej festival, in Rajasthan, celebrates Parvati's journey to her husband Shiva, at the same time as welcoming the monsoon. During the Rajasthani festival of Gangaur, women pray for the well-being of their men, and it is believed that any young woman who is unhappy when she takes part in the celebrations will get an ill-tempered husband.

Some festivals celebrate different goddesses in different regions. Dussehra is marked in Karnataka by a procession of elephants, one of which carries a statue of Parvati, while in parts of eastern India it is celebrated as Durga Puja, and honours the Goddess in her aspect as the warrior, Durga. Diwali, or the Feast of Lamps, honours Lakshmi, goddess of prosperity and good fortune, in most of India, but in West Bengal is dedicated to Kali the death-bringer.

An Andalusian Christmas procession. In many Roman Catholic areas, pagan fertility festivals still exist, disguised as processions of the Virgin Mary.

would couple with a man dressed in green, representing her son.

One of the few well-recorded ancient fertility festivals that was celebrated exclusively by women was the Greek Thesmophoria, which took place in October. It was dedicated to the earth goddess Demeter, and re-enacted the descent of her daughter Persephone into the underworld. Persephone was represented by pigs, which, along with pear branches and dough cakes shaped like vulvas, were thrown into a pit of serpents. On the third day of the festival, the rotted remains from the previous year's festival were dragged to the surface, as the reborn Persephone, and mixed with seed corn, to make it fertile.

The Goddess and the Cosmos

Most cosmologies visualize the beginning of all things as chaos or a dark, boundless, formless space, sometimes described as primordial waters. From this rises the first consciousness, which has a desire to create order from the void. This is the Goddess. She forms the cosmos through her will and from her essence and peoples it with gods and humans. Around the world, origin myths show how she manifests in a range of elements from heavenly bodies to individual plants. She thus appears simultaneously as the many who exist only to serve a single purpose and the One who is unchanging. The earth is her body, a living organism in which all matter – organic and inorganic – participates.

Although the cosmos itself is everlasting, the life-forms within it enact a constant cycle of birth and death, one attendant upon the other, in order to ensure the continuity of the whole. Life, death and other inseparable pairs of opposites – such as chaos and order, darkness and light, dryness and moisture – are all subsumed within the creatrix.

An 18th-century Sri Lankan panel showing a dancing apsaras. *The* apsaras *of Asia are water nymphs, often personifying rivers. They are usually represented as the sexual slaves of a male god, but this almost certainly disguises their earlier, powerful, elemental nature, as primordial water beings.*

The three worlds

Among mythologies and religions worldwide, the most common division of the universe is into sky (heaven), earth (mortal world) and underworld (the realm of the dead, which sometimes extends beneath the sea). Ancient peoples were familiar with their world, and could observe the sky, its planets and its atmospheric phenomena, but all knowledge of the underworld was denied to them. Fear of the unknown prompted them to conjure up images of an alien realm full of darkness and dread, and to see death primarily in terms of pain, loss and punishment.

The oldest surviving myths, from Sumeria and Egypt, contain numerous accounts of goddesses – such as Ereshkigal (see p.78) and Neith – who created or ruled over all the three worlds, until the actions of a male deity either banished them to the underworld, or restricted their powers so that they became associated chiefly with the afterlife. Many other goddesses are described as visiting the underworld, usually in their youth. This is typically presented as a journey of self-discovery. For example, the Hawaiian goddess Hi'iaka went to the underworld to liberate her lover Lohiau, after he was killed by her sister Pele the volcano goddess. When Hi'iaka arrived at the centre of the underworld, she saw the waters of chaos held back by a gate. If she released them she would destroy Pele's volcanic fires for ever. But the goddess learned the importance of maintaining the balance and continuity of the world and resisted the temptation for revenge.

By contrast, the male gods and heroes of world mythology are frequently humbled by the processes of death and

THE CONTINUUM

The human mind tends to fragment and categorize what it knows. By contrast, the concept of the Goddess encompasses the entire state of being as a continuum. Within her body, which is the cosmos, the Goddess combines all the different stages of being. From this viewpoint, death is not the end, or even an ending, just as birth is not a beginning, but simply a phase in the continuum.

LEFT *A Shinto Torii arch from Tako Chiba, Japan. As an emblem of the vulva, or yoni (see pp.96–7), the Torii arch represents the continuum between life and death.*

A cross-cultural survey of mythologies reveals that many ancient cultures thought the Goddess withheld the secret of immortality from men. While women, made in her likeness, could reproduce themselves, men apparently had no existence beyond their bodies. The thought spurred them continually to seek to outdo death and gain immortality.

But those who reached the underworld and completed a period of initiation learned that the Goddess is both womb and tomb: there is no end, simply a change of being. The Goddess does not recognize life, death and rebirth as discontinuous fragments of existence but as part of a whole.

rebirth. The Japanese god Izanagi and the Greek bard Orpheus both negotiated the return of their dead wives, but failed to fulfil the conditions set by the underworld, and came away without their spouses. The ancient Sumerian *Epic of Gilgamesh* describes the hero-king Gilgamesh's journey to the underworld in a way that is directly comparable to the descent of the goddess Inanna (see pp.76–9). However, while the goddess descended at will, Gilgamesh needed the enigmatic wine goddess Siduri to direct him. Also, Inanna embraced death and made it part of her being, whereas Gilgamesh sought eternal life, but was disqualified from achieving it by his own hubris.

ABOVE *A 6th-century Viking pendant of a Valkyrie. As voyagers between the three worlds, goddess-figures were often the transporters or guides of human souls.*

The Goddess of the primordial waters

Isis and the primordial water goddess Neith, from a 12th-century BC tomb in Luxor, Egypt.

The notion of a dark, watery and formless universe pervades many mythologies. Whereas modern scientific thought would describe the earth – as well as the stars and planets – as flying through space, these older cosmologies spoke of a world floating in limitless primordial water. Sometimes the world is willed into existence by the water (who is a goddess) herself, and sometimes by a demiurge or creative entity who has been eternally co-existent within her. The concept of a creative spirit being born from water is echoed in the widespread practice of baptism to represent "rebirth" into a new faith or way of life. In Christianity, the baptismal font has been described as the womb of Mary.

The precise details of creation vary from culture to culture. In Japan, the goddess Izanami and her consort, Izanagi, formed the land from primordial waters before giving birth to their children, the heavenly constellations and the elements. In Arizona, two Hopi ocean goddesses produced land by meditating over a rainbow, while in Nigeria, Yemonja, goddess of salt and sweet water, gave birth to the sun after lying with her brother, the soil.

One powerful creator who combines disparate mythological elements is Neith (also known as Net, or Nuanet) from the predynastic era of Egypt. Defined as the "water above and the water below", she is mistress of the ocean and embodies both celestial and terrestrial water. The world and all its creatures are suspended within her. Neith was once hailed as the mighty veiled goddess of Sais, who was quoted by Plutarch as saying: "I am all that has been and is and shall be, and my robe

A festival of the water goddess Yemanja, in Salvador, Brazil. The worship of the Nigerian goddess, Yemonja, spread to Central and South America, where she came to be known as either Yemanja or Iamanje. She is typically celebrated in the Americas during the summer solstice, reflecting her role as mother of the sun.

THE DRAGON

The goddesses of a religion may be absorbed into new theologies as demons, monsters, dragons and serpents, which are usually described as dwelling in the darkness and depth of the primordial waters. Probably the first goddess to suffer this fate was Tiamat of ancient Sumer. By the time that Akkadian had taken over from Sumerian as the main spoken language of Sumer, in the 2nd millennium BC, the goddess Tiamat had been transformed from a devoted mother into an evil breeder of dragons (see below). This new depiction helped to justify humanity's allegiance to Marduk, who as her enemy became defender of right. Similarly, each night, the sun god Ra fought Apophis, the dragon of chaos, who was harboured by the goddess Nuanet in her watery abyss.

The Indo-Europeans made a virtue of the slaughter of dragons, pitting gods of light and sky against these reptilian monsters. In the 3,000-year-old Indian sacred text, the *Rigveda*, Indra mutilated the mighty dragon Vritra, at the same time assaulting Vritra's mother Danu with a deadly weapon so that her "vital energy ... ebbed away". In Greek myth, Apollo killed Python, the oracle of Delphi. The struggle of the consistent, light, male deity, representing goodness, against the changeable, dark, female divinity continued into the monotheistic religions.

St George and the Dragon, *by Uccello (1397–1475). The quest of St George can be seen in Jungian terms (see pp.18–19) as an attempt to unite the male and female sides of the human character.*

no mortal has yet uncovered." Yet she is often excluded from modern accounts of Egyptian cosmology.

As myths evolve and are rewritten – possibly for political reasons (see pp.22–3) – primordial water deities who contain the world, or make it from their own being, are often displaced by males who manufacture a universe external to themselves. In the Akkadian *Enuma Elish*, a political parable that was written *c.* 1750BC, the goddess Tiamat, who was salt water, and her consort Apsu, who was sweet, produced gods who remained within Tiamat. They fought for supremacy until Apsu decided to kill them. However, Tiamat's children learned of his plan and Ea, "Earthly Wisdom", killed and replaced Apsu. In order to avenge her husband, Tiamat "mothered a new brood" of "snarling dragons" to fight Ea, but Ea's son Marduk shot her in the stomach and split her womb, so that he could use her dismembered body to remake the world that she had already created.

The river Goddess

A 20th-century panel from a Balinese temple, showing a river sprite.

River goddesses were worshipped throughout the ancient world because of their obvious life-giving qualities. Often aniconic (not represented in any form other than the river itself), they have occasionally manifested themselves as humans in order to couple, as is the case with Ganga in the Indian epic *Mahabharata*; Boann, in the Irish mythological cycle; and Oya in Yoruba myth. Rivers are frequently referred to – for example, in Celtic and Indian myth – simply as "the Mother". They conform particularly well to the ideal of the Goddess, in that they simultaneously give life and take it: the floods that fertilize the surrounding countryside can also cause massive destruction. For this reason, wherever there are vestiges of goddess worship, it is common to see garlands and other gifts set afloat on rivers as tokens of supplication.

Rivers combine attributes of wisdom, judgement and mystery with those of life and death. The Styx, daughter of Oceanus and the sea goddess Tethys, and the river that in Greek mythology divided Hades from the world of the living, purged sinners by inflicting painful death-throes upon them as they passed through on their way to the afterlife.

THE WIVES OF SHANGO

Shango, a great hunter and thunder god among the Yoruba people of West Africa, was married to three eponymous river goddesses – Oya, Oshun and Oba. One day he saw Oya transform herself from a water buffalo into a woman, and watched where she hid her skin. She agreed to marry him on condition that he would not reveal her secret. As usually happens in myths about a hero who marries a shape-changing woman, Shango broke his promise – in this case after his other wives got him drunk. He placated Oya with her favourite food and narrowly escaped being killed.

Oba was alienated from Shango as a result of the machinations of his middle wife, Oshun, who suggested that, to please him, Oba should cut off her ear and add it to his food. In fact, Shango was enraged by his wife's self-mutilation, and the two women had to escape his wrath by turning into rivers. The waters are choppy where these rivers meet.

Oshun is specifically a goddess of women, whom she befriends and blesses with babies. She is also a vain, capricious goddess of love and beauty, who delights in colourful beads and bright metals.

In addition to being revered in West Africa, Oya, Oshun and Oba have received the status of saints in numerous South American religions that combine possession cults and Catholicism (see p.30). Oya – shown here being personified by a Brazilian initiate – is known as Yansan in Brazil, but has also been sanctified as Barbara, with Wednesday as her holy day. Barbara has also been assimilated to Oya's husband, the thunder god Shango, because of her role as the patron saint of artillerymen and gunpowder. In Cuba, Oya is the Virgin of Candlemas, and Oshun is the Virgin of the Charity of Copper. Oba – St Catherine in Bahia, Brazil – appears in a Brazilian street festival where reference is made to her sacrificed ear.

The Ganges, the primary river of India, is closely associated not only with death – cremations take place on its banks – but with the purging of sins during life and beyond. Pilgrims travel from all over India to immerse themselves in the river at Varanasi, and Gangajal (Ganges water) is preserved in bottles and used to perform healings and blessings.

The same association is found in Babylonian myth where Nanshe, the water goddess and arbiter of judgement, presided over a festival that took place on New Year's Day. A cavalcade of boats would sail to Lagash, where the goddess awaited them in a consecrated barge, and judged everyone so that they could begin the year afresh. Nanshe was also an interpreter of dreams.

When the Irish goddess Boann – described in early accounts as the "shining" or "wisdom-giving cow" – violated a taboo that was set by her husband, Nechtan, the waters of his well chased her to the sea. The result was the River Boyne. Although this flowed from a masculine source, and was the result of Boann's transgression, she nevertheless became its patron – a measure of the extent to which rivers are mythologically linked with goddesses.

The link between river goddesses and cows – whose supply of milk is compared to the river's life-giving flow – is not restricted to Boann, but can be found in mythologies worldwide. Authumla, the divine cow of Swedish creation myths, licked the primordial salty ice-mass and converted it into four massive rivers. Hathor, one of the oldest deities of Egypt, who was associated with the rising of the River Nile, was worshipped as a cow, or as a woman with a horned head-dress (in this she resembles the Nile goddess Isis).

The sea Goddess

Venus being born from the waves, a detail from The Birth of Venus, *by Botticelli (1445–1510).*

One of the earliest descriptions of the Goddess was as primordial water (see pp.46–7). It is not surprising that, especially among coastal or island peoples, the primordial water should become identified with the ocean, and most of the great mother goddesses, such as the Egyptian Isis, were at one time described as being, or being born from, the sea. The link between the moon and the tides has led most cultures to attribute lunar goddesses with power over the ocean. The crescent-horned cow-goddess is a symbol of the moon in most Indo-European mythologies, and is typically said to be married to a bull, who is both her son and her lover (see pp.80–81). The bull is also one of the main symbols of Poseidon, the Greek sea god, and it has been suggested that this apparently strange choice of animal for a marine deity is an archaic remnant in Greek myth of an earlier cosmogony, in which a goddess ruled the sea.

Aphrodite, who is best known as the Greek goddess of love, is also a survivor from an earlier tradition. She was originally a Near Eastern goddess, possibly an aspect of the Ugaritic Asherah, "Lady of the Sea" (see p.39). In Greek

SEDNA

The myths of Arctic Canada, Alaska and Greenland abound with references to a submarine mistress of all the sea mammals. Sedna, daughter of Anguta, turned down many human suitors but eventually chose to marry a bird who promised her a life of ease in his softly feathered nest. In most versions of the myth, Anguta was furious at his daughter's decision, but was unable to stop her.

Sedna found that the bird's promises had been false, and when Anguta visited her a year later, she escaped with him in his kayak. The bird and his kindred followed, and Anguta abandoned Sedna to save his own life. He threw her overboard, and when she tried to climb back, he severed her fingers which turned into sea creatures. Sedna's home became the ocean floor. From her underworld, Adlivun, she released animals for humans to hunt and, with the help of her father, captured the souls of the dead. Women who refused marriage to their parents' choice of partner were thus held up as a terrifying example to their sex – returning to wildness through actions such as bestiality, and living lives of painful isolation.

A copy of a 20th-century drawing of Sedna, from Greenland. In different versions of the myth, Sedna may be known as Taleelayo, or Uiniguimasuittiq.

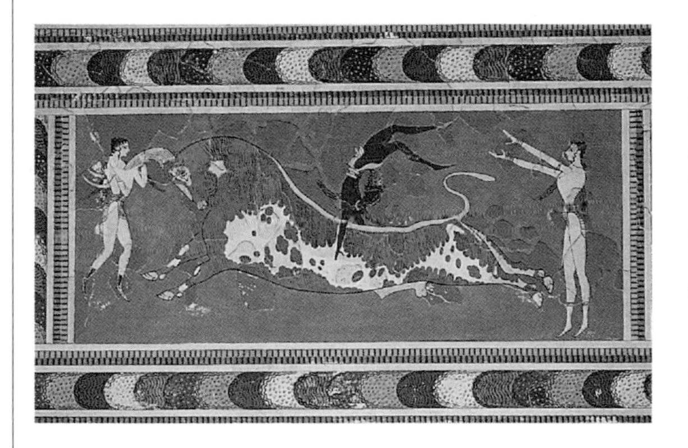

Men and women leaping over a bull, as part of a religious festival, from a Minoan fresco, c.1700–1400 BC. A bull sent from the sea by the god Poseidon was claimed by King Minos as the emblem of his right to rule Crete. However, the Cretan Goddess is frequently depicted in a bull-vaulting posture and it is likely that the bull-vaulting festival has pre-Minoan origins, symbolizing the marriage of the Goddess and her son.

myth, Aphrodite came into being when the sky god Uranus was castrated and produced a last, mighty ejaculation which foamed in the sea and coagulated into the goddess. She was blown by friendly winds until she came ashore on Cyprus, where she was clothed and venerated. She was eventually co-opted by the Greeks into the Hellenic system, but remained unruly, like her source, the sea-womb. It is possible that she became the divinity of sexual love because of a metaphorical link between the sea and desire: both are unpredictable, mysterious and potentially overwhelming.

The fate of the sea goddess in the largely oral cultures of Oceania was often determined by her male ancestors. The human father of the Melanesian sea goddess Walutahanga chopped his serpentine daughter into eight pieces. Her body was reunified after eight days of rain but she was once again dismembered, and eaten, by terrified islanders. Walutahanga once more became whole, this time at the bottom of the ocean, causing eight gigantic waves to submerge the islands and destroy nearly all human life. The only survivors were two women who had refused to eat her flesh. Walutahanga rewarded them with gifts of vegetation and the fruits of the sea.

The sea goddess survives in a debased form as water-sprites, sirens or mermaids. Probably the first mermaids were images of the fish-tailed Aphrodite – they are famously able to seduce men away from the land, and draw them down to their underwater kingdom. A reminder of their lost divinity lies in the tales of a mermaid – called Ran among the Teutonic peoples – receiving the souls of drowned men.

In European folklore, Morgan Le Fay ("Morgan the Fate"), like the water-sprites of Brittany (the morgans), takes her name from the Celtic word for sea ("mor"). Morgan was once the ninefold goddess who ruled the Fortunate Isles, where dead heroes went. She was only reduced to the status of a wicked sorceress when the Arthurian cycles were transcribed by medieval Christian clerics. Nimue, the "Lady of the Lake", is sometimes thought to be a personification of Morgan; she was the arbiter of Arthur's success as a monarch, and his saviour in death.

The cosmic egg

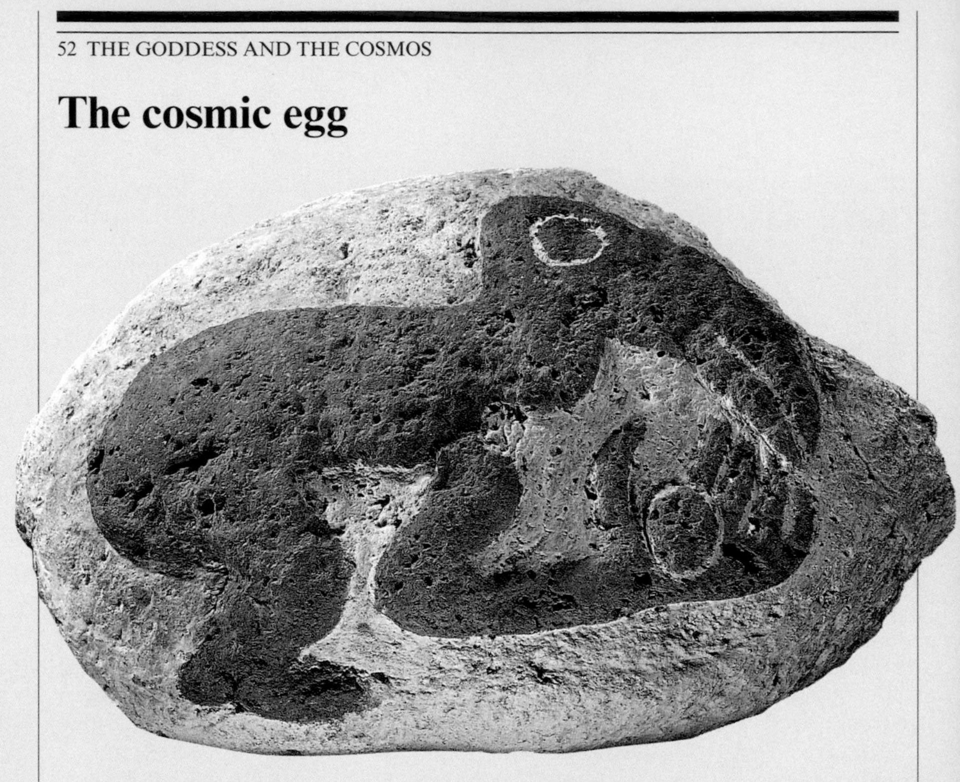

A painted rock found on Easter Island in the south Pacific. The figure is a combination of human and bird, and is thought to be holding the egg that contains the world.

Creation myths that describe a cosmic egg as the source of the world can be found on all five continents. They fall into three main categories: there is the creator-spirit, which projects itself into the primordial (see pp.46–7) waters as an egg; alternatively, the egg may be laid by a passing celestial bird; or it may be created by or given to the first individual or couple. Having come into being, it produces the cosmos and all that is contained in it, including the heavenly spheres and elements, culture, ritual and the primordial human. Sometimes an egg is described as the founder of noble dynasties. For example, according to the 4th-century Chinese *Shiti Ji*, Jiandi, one of three major goddesses, was made pregnant by swallowing a bird's egg while out walking and became the ancestor of the Yin clan. Other aristocratic families also claimed descent from the cosmic egg.

Some myths combine different motifs. The Tibetan goddess Srid-Lcam ("Lady of the Visible World", also known as the "Magical One") married a mortal in order to increase the prosperity of the earth and enhance the veneration of the gods. The union, at the dawn of creation, resulted in three eggs: a gold one produced the arrow of life, a turquoise one produced the arrow of fertility and a pure white one produced a spindle (perhaps symbolizing fate). Then from light and sea mist came a cluster of *Bon* (faith), which was woven by the wind into the male (*dmo*) and female (*g-yang*) yarns of good fortune (still worn at Tibetan marriage ceremonies by the bride and groom as they chant the tale of creation).

According to the Orphic Greeks the first egg, fashioned by Time, produced Phanes (or Eros), a bisexual, golden-winged creator being. Phanes' daughter and eventual consort, Night, was a black-winged bird, who produced Gaia, the earth (see pp.60–61). The Finnish epic *Kalevala* tells of a teal who flew over the primordial waters looking for a place to lay her eggs. The Ocean Mother raised her knee for the bird, who laid seven eggs on it. The teal brooded over her eggs until the goddess began to burn with the heat. The Ocean Mother jerked her knee, causing the eggs to fall into the waters and shatter. But from their fragments came heaven, earth, sun, moon, stars and clouds. As in many other cosmic egg myths, fecundity is here related to warmth. For example, in one Korean story, the daughter of a river was locked in a room by her husband, but the sun pursued and impregnated her. She bore an egg out of which came the sun deity Zhumang.

THE BIRD AND THE SERPENT

The depths of the earth and the vaults of the sky are represented in myth as regions that are alien to humans, but home to the gods and other supernatural beings. Two creatures that inhabit these regions – the bird and the serpent – show a widespread affinity with the Goddess: representations of bird-women, with egg-shaped bodies and long, slender necks were being made as early as the Paleolithic era, while the serpent appears in many ancient icons, either as a companion of the Goddess, or as an accoutrement – a wand or sceptre, a belt or head-dress. In addition to inhabiting the underworld, the serpent is often thought of as a denizen of the ocean, and the Ouroboros, a snake with its tail in its mouth, is a common, yoni-like symbol (see pp.18–19) of the waters encircling the earth.

Birds and serpents both lay eggs, and often appear in myths that describe the beginning of creation. The association between the two creatures is recorded in an early Greek creation myth. The great mother Eurynome materialized from a formless abyss and danced in the darkness. Her movements created a wind, which she moulded into the serpent, Ophion. He began to lust after her, and Eurynome eventually submitted to sexual intercourse with him. Finding herself pregnant, she transformed herself into a dove and brooded over the waters, until she laid an egg which the serpent took in its coils and hatched. It was from this original egg that all things were created.

A strikingly similar Guatemalan tradition tells of a sea-green, feathered serpent, brooding at the beginning of the world, her wings outstretched over the seas. She attracted the attention of the powerful wind, Hurrikan, who passed over her, dredging up land from the depths of the sea.

LEFT *A Greek terracotta figure, from the 1st millennium BC or earlier, showing a goddess in the form of a bird.*

RIGHT *A Minoan goddess clutching snakes, c.1800BC.*

The Goddess as the earth

In addition to being Mother Earth itself (see pp.60–61), the Goddess is embodied by mountains, volcanoes, rivers, deserts and other geological features. She may also transform parts of herself to form cosmic elements. For example, the Tibetan Klu-rgyal-mo ("Queen who set in order the visible world") produced the sky from the top of her head. The earth came from her flesh and mountains from her bones, the oceans from her blood, the rivers from her veins. Her right and left eyes produced the light and four planets, while her upper teeth formed the moon. Thunder, lightning and clouds came from her voice, her tongue and her tears, hailstorms and winds from her nostrils and the fat of her tongue.

Many myths of the Goddess's earthly incarnations are lost today. The Celtic Danu appears only as the mother of the Irish and Welsh deities, but her name is remembered in the Danube, the Dane Hills and numerous other physical features of Europe. Those earth goddesses whose myths have survived are usually worshipped in a human as well as a geological form. The Indian goddess Dharani was the ground that rose up to swallow the demons sent by Mara, king of evil, against the Buddha. Although this myth spread throughout Southeast Asia, Dharani is invariably personified as a young woman, who wears her hair in a twisted coil to represent a river.

The geological features that are most closely associated with goddesses are caves (which are symbolically linked to vulvas; see pp.96–7) and mountains (which tend to be viewed as pregnant stomachs or overflowing, nourishing

Silbury Hill, in Wiltshire, England, was probably constructed c.2600BC. *Michael Dames, in* The Silbury Treasure *(1976) contends that it is not, as was previously thought, a burial mound for a chieftain, but is a model, piled up from the earth, of a goddess figure lying back and giving birth.*

breasts). The myths of ancient Sumeria described a twin-peaked mountain at the end of the world, called Mashu, that reached up to nourish heaven while its mirror image hung down to nourish the underworld. The River Ganges (herself a nourishing goddess) rises in the Himalayan mountain of Nanda Devi ("Blessed Goddess"), while Annapurna is synonymous with the deity living at its peak, who is believed to provide food for all the world.

Caves such as this Neolithic burial site in India were probably the first geological features to be associated with the Goddess.

Instead of forming natural features with their bodies, Celtic land goddesses, in the form of giant hags, moved enormous stones in order to shape the mountains of Ireland and Scotland. These goddesses were the spirit of the land. In the British Isles, where their myths are most prominent, they were known as Sovereignty, and had to test all rulers to ensure that the land would be respected. Morgan Le Fay, of the Arthurian legends, is such a Sovereignty goddess, whose tests have been misinterpreted as acts of malice against Arthur and his successors.

PELE, THE LIVING GODDESS

The mainland of the Hawaiian archipelago owes its existence to volcanic activity which, as recently as the late 1980s, extended the land area by approximately 100 acres (40 ha.).

Pele, the goddess of volcanic fire, nature, disorder, ceremonies and sexuality, lives in the active crater, Halema'umu 'u. According to legend, Pele left the land of her birth because of a conflict with her sister, a sea-spirit, who pursued her and forced her into a battle in which Pele was killed. After her death she was transformed into a powerful goddess.

Although nominally Christian, many Hawaiians continue to revere Pele both publicly and privately. They regularly follow church attendances with a visit to Pele's crater, where they make offerings of gin, cakes and other objects.

Halema'umu 'u lies within the Volcanoes National Park, and the removal of lava rocks or pebbles is strictly forbidden. The museum on the site displays letters telling of the misfortunes that dogged those who disregarded the ban, until finally they were compelled to return their trophies.

In popular representations, Pele is sometimes shown either as a beautiful young woman or, as in this 19th-century image, as a terrifying hag.

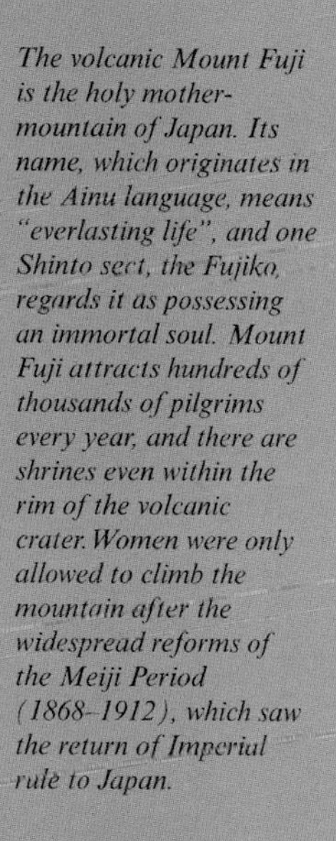

The volcanic Mount Fuji is the holy mother-mountain of Japan. Its name, which originates in the Ainu language, means "everlasting life", and one Shinto sect, the Fujiko, regards it as possessing an immortal soul. Mount Fuji attracts hundreds of thousands of pilgrims every year, and there are shrines even within the rim of the volcanic crater. Women were only allowed to climb the mountain after the widespread reforms of the Meiji Period (1868–1912), which saw the return of Imperial rule to Japan.

The Goddess in the soil

In many traditions, an incarnation of the Goddess in mortal or semi-mortal form produces the earth's flora and fauna. Usually, this incarnation dies as the result of treachery or misunderstanding, but instead of taking revenge, the Goddess transforms her dead body into foodstuff. This act can be compared to the sacrifices of mother goddesses, such as Aphrodite, who give up their lovers annually to ensure the welfare of the crops (see p.80). It also resembles the widespread tales of important plants springing up from the ashes, blood or limbs of male heroes. Elements of all these themes – illustrating the similarities, and possibly the prehistoric links, between them – combine in the Polynesian account of the origins of the coconut. The mate of the great goddess Hine was killed by people who saw him in the form of his alter-ego, the serpent. The bereaved divinity did not punish the murderers. Instead she planted her lover's head, which grew into a coconut tree, providing a source of sustenance in the flesh and milk of the coconut, as well as jute and coir.

CHANGING WOMEN

The Changing Woman of the Navajo North Americans is blessed with the gift of rejuvenating herself after she becomes senescent, which associates her with the seasons and vegetation. In one Navajo puberty ceremony, a girl who embodies Changing Woman has her face painted with an upward stroke, which promotes the growth of plants.

In contrast to the image of the nourishing goddess are the traditions of divinities who metamorphose into harmful vegetation. The Navajo Changing Bear Maiden fled the role of servant to her twelve brothers in favour of a passionate relationship with the trickster, Coyote. Like many goddesses who did not follow social ideals of womanhood, she became seen as the epitome of female wickedness. When Coyote was killed, Changing Bear Maiden assumed that her brothers were responsible. She used magical powers that Coyote had taught her to turn each of her limbs into a species of bear. Then, changing her teeth into thorns she tracked down and killed eleven of her brothers, but the twelfth escaped and eventually killed her. When she died, her vagina became, in some traditions, a porcupine, and in others the yucca fruit; her breasts turned to pinon nuts, her tongue into cactus and her entrails variously into snakes or poisonous herbs.

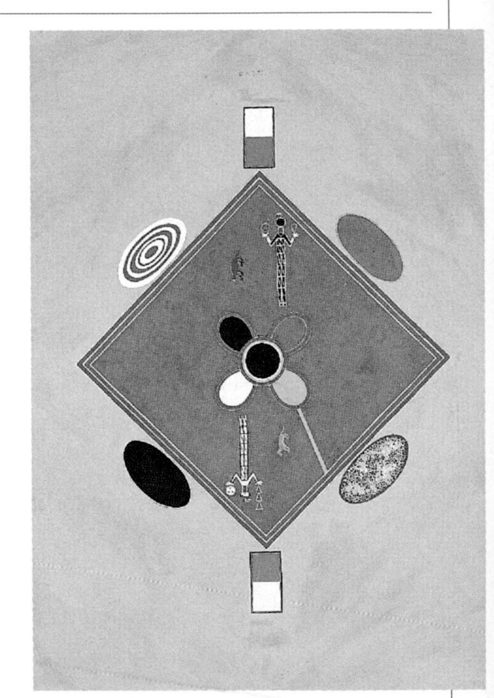

A reproduction of a Navajo sandpainting – showing a celebration of the first menstruation of the Changing Woman – which is used in the Navajo puberty ceremony, or Kinaalda.

The creation of edible animals is often a corollary to the death of the Goddess and serves to reassure a people that she continues to thrive and show benevolence, even though a particular incarnation may have been killed. A legend from the tradition of West Ceram, Indonesia, tells how the girl Hainuwele was adopted by Ameta, a man who helped her grow and emerge from a magical coconut palm. One of Hainuwele's unique attributes was that her excrement metamorphosed into fabulous objects, including china, gongs and jewels. At the time, the people of the nine races of man gathered together for ceremonies at which the women offered their men betel nuts as gifts. Hainuwele's gifts overshadowed those of everybody else and, prompted by jealousy, the other women killed her and hid her body.

The desolate Ameta performed various rituals which eventually led him to Hainuwele. He enlisted the help of a supreme divinity, the virginal Satene, who was so enraged by the murder that she decided to withdraw from the world. Before leaving she decreed that all living humans should attempt to pass through a spiral gate to reach her. Those who succeeded founded tribes, those who did not were transformed into deer, pigs, birds or fish – beings which had never existed before. Satene then withdrew to the world of the dead. The buried portions of Hainuwele, meanwhile, produced tuberous plants such as yams and taro which became the staple foods of the local population. The myth bears a striking resemblance to the story of Devi Sri in Java and Bali (see pp.70–71).

The Goddess-incarnation usually shares at least some characteristics with the plants that spring from her. The psychotropic plant, kava, has important ritual uses almost throughout the Pacific, but too much of it may cause grey and scaly skin. In Tonga, this side-effect is explained by the story that the kava plant sprang from the head of a leprous girl, who was killed by her father to feed a visiting chief.

Imberombera, a fertility goddess in the Northern Territories of Australia, emerged from the ocean, made the land, and took animals, plants and humans from her body to populate it. Her myth extends the parameters of what can be considered as nourishment to include language, which is generally a cultural prerogative of male gods. Imberombera was energetic and carried many children in her huge stomach. She asked Wuraka, the fertility god to accompany her on her travels, but he pleaded that the journey was too long and his penis was too heavy. He slumped down and turned into Tor Rock, while she went on her journey, spawning children and teaching them the Aboriginal tongues and the craft of growing yams. Imberombera was the progenitor of ten Aboriginal groups and their languages.

A 20th-century Australian Aboriginal wooden figure of a woman, used to educate youths. Each design painted on the body is interpreted as rain, plants or other life-giving elements.

Mother Earth and the cosmic order

The simplest way for a Mother Goddess to produce the elements – or to populate the universe with gods, demons, humans, animals and plants – is to give birth to them. The reproductive activities of most universal mothers are predictably epic in scale. According to ancient Indian tradition, Aditi, who is thought of as boundless space, squatted down to give birth to seven children who represent the solar elements. These included Indra, god of light and sky, Surya, the sun and Agni, fire. In later myth the number of children was increased to twelve, each representing a month and demarcating time and space. In Polynesia, the great goddess Hine gave birth to a series of divinities who represented various natural phenomena including the moon, the sea and death itself. Often seen as a huge, sleeping hag, Hine is the earth incarnate.

According to the *Theogony* of Hesiod, written in the 8th century BC,

A 7th-century BC Greek statue of the goddess Gaia, sitting enthroned and flanked by wild animals.

Gaia, the earth, immured Chaos, her own source of creation, inside her body, along with the "Great Chasm", a primeval equivalent of hell. Gaia created her own boundaries in the form of her sons, Uranus the sky and Pontus the ocean. She then chose the sky, stretched perpetually over her, to be her first son-lover (see pp.80–81) and began to give birth to the first divinities: six Titans and six Titanesses, three cyclopes and three monsters with a hundred hands each. Uranus was so appalled by these creatures that he thrust them back inside Gaia, but she refused to judge her children, and fought for their freedom. She persuaded the youngest Titan, Cronos, to castrate his father and free his brothers and sisters.

In Greek myth, this constituted the first act of violence, resulting in the law of revenge, and setting in motion a vast saga of vendetta and warfare between the offspring of Gaia and the Olympian gods, who were the children of Cronos. The Olympians lied, quarrelled and fought among themselves, and none of them could be considered the embodiment of an absolute good. However, by the time of Hesiod, and increasingly after him, the pantheon as a whole was treated as an explanation, and guarantor, of both cosmic and social order. In addition, individual, positive, abstract qualities, such as Justice, were worshipped as divinities.

The development of a common pantheon was also used to help to forge a concept of Greek nationhood, distinct from the surrounding, threatening "barbarian" races. So the Olympian gods became the champions of civilization. In this light, it is possible to see the

A 5th-century BC *Greek pottery representation of Medusa the Gorgon. The Gorgons were descended from Gaia, and although Hellenic writers referred to them as monsters, their names, Medusa, Stheino and Euryale, derive from the virtues of, respectively, wisdom, strength and universality. Far from being the monstrous offspring of the earth, it is likely that the Gorgons were a trinity of goddesses, possibly representing the moon. Pre-Hellenic mystics called the moon "the Gorgon's head".*

mythical battle between the Olympians and the children of Gaia as a way of polarizing the elements of creation into good and evil. Their conflicts were not parochial power-struggles, but established an all-encompassing, eternal differentiation between right and wrong. By contrast, the goddess advocated renewal and constant change – which implies the necessity of death – and the opportunity for all manner of life to flourish, regardless of its values or moral qualities. By instigating patricide, Gaia allowed new beings to emerge, regardless of how horrifying, cruel or destructive they might be.

THE COSMIC ORDER OF SILA

The formulation of cosmic order is a concern of most mythologies that address the necessity of death and attempt to understand the inclemency or inconsistency of natural phenomena. An Inuit myth from Greenland tells of a woman who wished for "war and disposal" to solve the problem of overcrowding, so death came to humanity. But the ways in which men fought wars and hunted animals became corrupt and cruel, so it was necessary to order the universe so that its conflicting elements could be brought into harmony through universal agreement.

To this end, the moon killed his mother for violating the sacred law of sharing the first catch of the season. Later, he had illicit sexual intercourse with his sister under cover of night, thereby violating another sacred law. When his sister realized what had happened, she cut off her breast, turned it into a flare and flew into heaven where she took her place in the firmament as Siqqiniq, the sun. Her brother followed. He is Taqqiq, the moon. Sila – the cosmic order – was thus established and consisted of "following the sun".

Everything now had a place, a period, a function and a direction. Among the social practices articulated by this myth are the incest taboo and the practice of the marital exchange of women.

Light, sun and moon

A Tibetan bronze figurine of the Green Tara, a star goddess who, in Tibet and Nepal, is identified with the sky-scraping Himalaya.

In many of the world's cosmologies, the sky is represented or ruled by a male deity, whereas the earth is the realm of a related goddess. This division may well reflect the starkly opposed character of day and night, as well as the comparatively rapid alternation between them (the diurnal cycle is much quicker than most others in nature): the sky is often described in myth as a theatre of conflict, and a home for heroes. The medieval Turco Mongols believed that Erlik (Erklik), the "Valiant One", slew the stars each night to allow the advent of dawn. Under Buddhist influence she became a demon king, god of hell and rival to the heavens.

If the sky represented to the ancients an enormous battlefield for the hostilities between darkness and light, moon and sun, then it is not surprising that major star goddesses like Anahita, the supreme goddess of the ancient Persian Empire, fulfilled, like Erlik, the function of warrior. Anahita was not restricted to a martial role, however, and also possessed the liquid and reflecting qualities of water, which coursed from her stars (which were also fountains) to fertilize the earth. By extension, she was also thought to fertilize humans, making her the patroness of semen. Like many Indo-European and Romano-Celtic deities, she combined the patronage of healing with the powers of fertility. Her children experienced only her benevolence, but she could become ferocious in their defence, when her warrior-aspect would be reawakened.

Anahita, somewhat like the male sun gods found throughout the Indo-European traditions, rode through the skies, dressed in blazing gold, on a chariot drawn by four horses named wind, rain, hail and cloud. This suggests that her sovereignty was not restricted to the night sky, and that solar activity was also subsumed under her title of "Shining One". There are traces of Anahita in Egypt and Babylon, where it is likely that she became assimilated with local deities such as Nut (who continually reproduced heavenly bodies each morning and evening, to replenish them after they had lived out their twelve-hourly life-spans), Anath and Ishtar (see pp.114–5). Other star goddesses, such as the Tibetan goddess Tara, also combined opposing natures, like the sky itself. The ferocious Green Tara lusted insatiably for death, while three-eyed White Tara revealed the beauties of the afterlife.

Stars or constellations which once had living, breathing existences as heroines, demigoddesses or minor divinities, can be found in myths from around the world: Cassiopeia and Andromeda in Greece, Mayi in Australia, Mataliki in New Zealand and the star-skirted Omecithuatl in Mesoamerica. For these and other, similar, figures, transformation into stars often represented either reward or redemption. The Pleiades, or Seven Sisters, were of special importance to many cultures. They were the focus of sacrificial New Year rites in Greece, southeastern Asia and central America, and are still associated with the Hindu festival of Diwali, the Feast of Lamps (see p.146).

Traditional cosmologies treat the sun and moon as paired opposites. They are often brother and sister or husband and wife, but the tension between them is so acute that they cannot share the skies. Although, in the most widely anthologized myths, the sun is usually perceived to be a male deity, the reverse is often the case. Baltic myth boasts a supreme sun goddess, Saule, as do the Inuit of Greenland. There are even remnants of sun goddess worship in Greek myth.

By far the most powerful of the sun goddesses past and present is Amaterasu, whose tradition has dominated Shinto belief for centuries. Her shrine was built in Ise, in the 7th century AD, and is rebuilt on the same site in

THE BELOVED MOTHER SUN

In the Baltic regions, Saule was the supreme goddess of the sun. As well as being the Great Sky Weaver, Saule governed mortal life, presided over childbirth, cared for orphans and welcomed the dead into her apple tree. Saule's consort was Menesis, the moon, whose laziness and unreliability contrasted with Saule's efficiency as she spent the day traversing the sky in her chariot to spread daylight, warmth, healing and growth. The pair separated after the birth of their daughter, the earth, whom they now take turns to watch over.

Songs known as *Dainas*, collected in the Baltic regions, including Lithuania and Latvia, frequently pay passionate tribute to Saule. Because Baltic mythology survives mainly in such songs, and other little-recorded folk traditions, some scholars question Saule's authenticity as a supreme goddess. Others, including the Latvian-born archeologist Marija Gimbutas (see p.13), defend her status as a pre-Indo-European divinity.

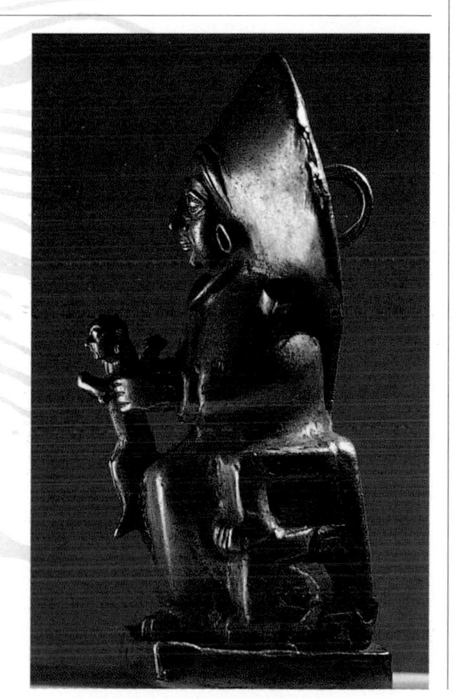

A gold pendant, c.1400–1200BC, depicting the Hittite sun goddess Arinna, who was a forerunner of the Baltic Saule.

Two panels from a 19th-century Japanese triptych of Amaterasu emerging from her cave. This story has been interpreted as a legend about the return of spring, and as a description of a solar eclipse.

exactly the same form every twenty-one years. Although in modern Japan the emperor can no longer officially claim the status of a living god, the imperial dynasty still traces its descent from Amaterasu and her festival is celebrated throughout Japan.

The tradition of Amaterasu was first recorded in AD712, in the sacred text *Kojiki* (Record of Ancient Matters) and re-attested in AD720 in *Nihongi* (Chronicles of Japan). She was the daughter of the primordial couple, Izanami and Izanagi. Because she was so blindingly bright, they sent her high into the skies as soon as she was born. Amaterasu's most famous myth recounts that she withdrew into a rock cave after her brother, Susan-o, went on a destructive rampage culminating when he desecrated her quarters with his excrement. When the horrified Amaterasu looked down to witness the havoc, Susan-o pierced her vagina with a spindle-shaft (by the time the *Nihongi* was written, it was the goddess's lady-in-waiting whom Susan-o wounded, possibly because it was already inconceivable to countenance such an indignity to the imperial ancestress).

Amaterasu's absence made the world grow dark and funereal. To woo her out of her cave, "800 myriad" gods decorated a tree with jewels, ribbons and mirrors, and placed it at the mouth of the cave, along with a large, copper mirror, prepared by the smith goddess. The shaman, no-Uzume, goddess of jollity,

VENUS – THE TWIN STAR

The planet Venus is probably best known as the morning and evening star, whose lustre outshines any other heavenly body except the sun and the moon. The planet's brightness usually links it to goddesses of love and beauty, from the eponymous Roman deity to the Afro-Brazilian goddess Oshun (see p.46). However, in some cultures, such as those of China and Mesoamerica, it is a sign of ill-omen. In traditional Chinese astrology, Venus was called "Grand White". Its appearance in the daytime sky indicated strife, punishment and revolution, because it stood for the yin principle of negativity, darkness and the female (according to Chinese thought, the whole universe can be divided up into complementary opposites, called yin and yang, with yang being the force of light and maleness).

The dual, or morning and evening, appearance of the planet also often leads to its association with twins. The Aztec plumed serpent Quetzalcoatl was identified with the morning star, and its sinister twin Xolotl with the evening star. Moreover, each of these gods was itself a twin being, indicating a primal androgyny that was gradually disguised and eventually obliterated by Aztec theology (see pp.28–9). A similar duality can be observed more clearly in one of the oldest manifestations of the planet as a goddess: the Babylonian Ishtar (see pp.114–5) was sometimes thought of as male when the morning star, and female when the evening star.

A popular 19th-century Hungarian print of Venus.

The Venus who appears in Roman myth was probably at one time a primeval goddess, like Ishtar. Although she became a tutelary deity of Rome, she had a sanctuary in Ardea long before the city was founded. The Romans thought of her as the mother of Aeneas, the Trojan general and founder of Rome. There is no myth that directly links her with the evening or morning star, and it is likely that this, along with other of her attributes, derives from the Inanna-Ishtar tradition of Sumeria. In a number of related mythological complexes from this region, the planet Venus is seen as the pole star of the axis on which the world turns.

The mythological Venus's celebrated role as the goddess of love is explained by her identification with the Greek goddess Aphrodite. By the 5th century BC, she was already turning into a minor deity, but echoes of her wider aspects, such as life-giver or divine destructress, occasionally resurfaced. In 217BC, oracles suggested that a temple be built to her at Mount Eryx, Sicily, because she had directed the Roman victory in the First Punic War against Carthage (at the time, the second Punic war was going badly for Rome). Julius Caesar built a temple to her as "Venus Birth-giver", and Pompey called her "Venus Victorious" when dedicating his temple to her.

A pre-Colombian statue of Xolotl (the deformed, dog-like twin of Quetzalcoatl) as the evening star (shining on his forehead). The axe in his hand shows his destructiveness.

then performed a dance ritual intended to restore the earth's fundamental energies. As the dance of the shaman grew more frenetic, she began to undress and make jokes. Her ribaldry brought loud laughter from the gods and when Amaterasu emerged to see what was causing such hilarity, she caught sight of her face in the mirror at the entrance. Dazzled by her own radiance, the goddess returned to the world, and banished Susan-o.

There are descriptions of "groups of villages" in Japan, controlled by female shamans devoted to Amaterasu. This personal, rural worship is described by scholars as "folk-Shinto", as distinct from the state Shinto that formed a bedrock of nationalism, or the elegant and formal Shinto practised at the many ornate shrines of Japan. In AD400, Amaterasu-worship survived an onslaught from Confucianism, and later from Buddhism, which nearly succeeded in synthesizing Amaterasu with a male sun-Buddha.

Lunar myths are usually less apocalyptic than those concerning the sun, and consistently address periodic changes in the moon's appearance. They describe goddesses who belong to different phases of the lunar cycle: deities associated with the crescent, such as the African Yemanja, who also became a goddess of the Brazilian Macumba religion; or the Greek Selene, Titaness of the full moon, whose monthly disappearance is explained as a visit to her lover, Endymion, in Asia Minor. For all its vicissitudes, the moon is reliable, continuously re-enacting a pattern that associates it with earthly currents and periodic phenomena such as the tides of the sea and menstruation.

The moon's ability to bring about such recurrent and influential processes was often equated with an ability to predict the future. According to the Araucanian people of Chile, the only beneficent deity was Auchinalgu, the moon, who protected against evil spirits and changed skin colour to convey her knowledge of forthcoming events.

HOW THE MOON GOT ITS SCARS

The moon is generally seen as a force of serenity and harmony, which regulates all natural phenomena related to the lunar month. The sun on the other hand, is marked by a fiery, aggressive nature, whose characteristic cycles are daily and yearly. According to some cosmologies, this was not always the case. One Chinese origin myth provides an explanation for the age-old problem of how the moon became scarred, and tells of a time when she was as hot as the sun, scorching the earth and its inhabitants with her harsh rays. To put an end to the suffering of the people, a man of substantial size and strength, called Qua, climbed onto a high mountain and flung a fistful of sand in the moon's face, where it stuck, melted by the heat. In pain and terror, the moon withdrew to a remote spot in the skies, since when her heat is no longer threatening to humankind. A tragic Baltic star-deity, Saule Meite "the Little Sun" was raped by her father Menesis, the moon. Her mother Saule, the sun, slashed the moon's face, scarring him forever. Then she banished him from the skies, setting in motion the battle of day and night by refusing to share the skies with him.

An early 16th-century Mexican stone head of Coyolxauhqui, who was the most important Aztec representation of the moon. She wears a moon-shaped pendant in her nose, and her ear ornaments symbolize the lunar Aztec calendar. The bells on her cheeks relate to her other common name, "Lady Golden Bells".

Themes of sibling rivalry and female competition are by far the most compelling moon myths, reflecting important aspects of human relationships while at the same time dramatizing deep, universal conflicts at the heart of human consciousness. These tales are generally tragic and savagely dramatic, as in the case of the decapitation of Coyolxauhqui, the Aztec moon, by her brother the sun, after the goddess had opposed a conspiracy by all her siblings to kill their mother, the earth goddess Coatlicue. A vast stone circle, excavated in Mexico City in 1978, which depicted the mutilation of Coyolxauhqui, so impressed the archeologists working on the site that they chanted a hymn in her praise. Later research revealed that the circle was a major religious centre during the Aztec empire.

Identification of the Goddess's head with the moon is further demonstrated in a Cambodian moon myth. A young girl, Biman Chan, married Brah Chan, lord of the skies. His other wives, jealous of their newest rival, persuaded her to ask their husband to take her higher into the heavens. There, violent winds tore off Biman Chan's head, which fell into the pond of a Buddhist abbey. The resident Buddha restored it to her body so that she became the goddess of the moon, who undertook a nightly journey, circling the three worlds during the sun's rest period. Biman Chan is unlike other moon goddesses in that she is free of any sun–moon hostility.

In another example of female rivalry, Ino, the mistress of the Boeotian king, demanded that his children Phrixus and Helle be offered as a sacrifice to restore the earth's fertility. A gold-winged ram rescued the children and carried them toward safety in Colchis, but Helle became dizzy and fell into the narrow strip of sea dividing Asia and Europe. This was named Hellespont. The 20th-century poet and scholar Robert Graves identified in Helle's tale remnants of a Pre-Ionian lunar divinity and ruler of tides. Like other moon goddesses, Helle and Biman Chan fall into the water, highlighting the ancient association of the moon with fluids (mainly sea-water and blood).

Patrons of the seasons and the elements

The seasons and elements have often been interpreted as the actions or moods of a Mother Goddess. The Etruscans, for example, explained thunderbolts as manifestations of their Sky Queen's anger. The Roman goddess Cardea, who was described by the poet Ovid (43BC–AD17) as the "hinge" of the world, on which the seasons turn, also controlled the four winds. More unusual and evocative is the Inuit story of the children who cause storms. One child, Kadlu, jumps on hollow ice to create the massive rumble of the thunder, while a second sister, Kweeto, rubs flint to make lightning, and the urination of a third sister produces the rain.

The story of the Inuit children conforms to a common pattern in which goddesses responsible for the weather occur in groups of three. Sometimes this pattern, although it still exists, is hidden, as in the case of Frau Holle, a deity who survives in a degenerate form to this day in an eponymous fairytale by the Brothers Grimm. Frau Holle is also remembered, in Germany, Switzerland and Austria, on the twelve days of Christmas, when she traverses the sky. On January 6, wheat pancakes are left for her and her sister, Perchta. Like Kadlu and her sisters, Frau Holle is associated with three, connected natural phenomena. The sun shines when she combs her hair, snow falls when she dusts her feather quilt and the water from her laundry causes rain.

Throughout history, and in many different cultures, the rain-making function of the Goddess has generally been welcomed, except when it produces storms like those brought by Lilith (also known as Ardatu Lili, see p.98), which might result in the destruction of the land. Just as she squandered the fruitfulness of the rain and the soil with her excess, Lilith was also alleged to waste potential human fertility by causing

In this 19th-century Native North American Navajo blanket, based on a sand-painting, the rainbow encloses two holy people, who in turn flank the sacred maize plant which is their gift to humanity (see p.70).

THE RAINBOW GODDESS

The seven coloured bands of the rainbow were the bright veils of Maya, the Indian goddess of appearance and illusion. The rainbow also appears in Egypt, as the seven stoles of Isis, and in the Bible, as the seven veils of Salome. Ishtar of Mesopotamia wore a rainbow necklace, which she could use as a bridge to heaven for the faithful, or as an uncrossable barrier. After the sky god sent a flood against humanity, she punished him by placing her rainbow before his altars, so that he could not receive offerings or sacrifices.

Among the Bantu peoples of Africa, the rainbow is a python, patron of both dry weather and bodies of water. Among the Bemba and Lunda, the rainbow-python is a goddess, who is sometimes the barren princess Lueji, and at other times the provocative Tshilimbulu. Whenever Tshilimbulu acquires an admirer, her husband becomes jealous and kills him, so Tshilimbulu turns into Lueji and causes the dry weather. The goddess is ceremonially killed, and her body cut into pieces and thrown into a water-filled jar, in order to bring the rains.

A detail from Primavera, *painted by Sandro Botticelli in 1477–78. The painting shows the flowers of spring falling, newly formed, from a maiden's mouth, and being scattered by the wind. The Roman goddess of spring was Flora, who was celebrated at the Floralia, an annual May Day festival. In northern Europe, the virgin goddess of spring was called Maj or Mai. The month that bears her name was the traditional season for "wearing the green", in imitation of the earth mother. It was also, until approximately the 16th century, a month during which rural men and women copulated illicitly in the ploughed fields, so as to encourage the growth of the crops (see p.40).*

men to ejaculate in their sleep. She was one of the most feared of demons, and a great variety of amulets and defensive measures were used against her.

The Goddess is often associated with spring, summer and winter, in her triple form as virgin, mother and crone (see pp.110–11), but sometimes these different aspects of her character are seen as being in conflict. The battle between the seasons is dramatized in the British and Irish myth of the Cailleach Bheur, a blue-faced winter hag, also known as the Loathly Lady, the Caillagh ny Groamagh (the "Gloomy Old Woman" of the Isle of Man) and Black Annis (in the Dane Hills of Lancashire, in England). This goddess captured the sweetheart of the Spring (sometimes identified as Brigit, see p.35), and set her the impossible task of washing a brown fleece until it was white. Spring tried to fight the hag but could not overcome her, so he asked for the sun's help. The sun cast a spear that made the terrified Cailleach take shelter beneath a holly bush, and Spring's sweetheart was freed.

It is possible that the Cailleach Bheur is a pre-Celtic divinity. She had rejuvenating powers, which suggests that the spring-maiden is her youthful and productive aspect, and that her "loathly" form merely vanishes each Beltane (April 30), and reasserts itself each Samadh (October 31), the traditional date of her rebirth.

The gifts of life and grain

The Goddess, worshipped as the earth, is usually described as overseeing the productivity of the crops sown within her. In some traditions, the Goddess appears in human form, before parts of her body transform themselves into important local plants. Dewi Sri is a southern Asian goddess of ripening rice. One Javanese myth tells how she emerged from a jewel brought up to the earth's surface by the underworld serpent, Antaboga, and died after refusing to marry the sky god Batara Guru. Her head yielded the coconut palm, her vulva bore rice-crops, her fingers provided banana crops and her teeth grew into corn. Sometimes a goddess's stewardship of crops can be more abstract: Eshara, a Chaldean goddess, represented the right of ownership of land which had been ploughed and tilled.

A Native American Pueblo Katchina doll, carved from cottonwood, representing the spirit of the corn. These dolls are given to children to help them recognize the native deities.

Throughout the world, rice, corn or wheat have always been the most essential cultivated grains. Their importance is enshrined in numerous Asian and Pacific deities like Dewi Sri, in the myths and rituals of the Greek Demeter, and in a significant body of oral mythology among various races of the Americas, where corn was often the staple crop.

A Pueblo Native American account tells how humans entreated the sun to send them more food. In answer to their prayers, six corn maidens arrived on the Pueblo. Each one was a different colour, representing a distinct variety of corn. The crops flourished until the people became wasteful, and began valuing the goddesses and their gifts too lightly. The maidens withdrew, leaving the crops to wither and die. Eventually they were persuaded to return, but in order to impress upon the people that they could never take for granted the bounty that they had once abused, the maidens refused to stay throughout the year. The Penebscott myth of the first Mother (see p.17) likewise demonstrates the need to treat the land with respect. Frequently, the corn itself is addressed as Mother Corn, a sentiment echoed on the other side of the globe in the German expression, *Kornmutter*.

In mythological thought, the sowing, growth and harvesting of grain is a metaphor for the human life-cycle: from the reception and fertilization of the seed, to emergence from the womb (or earth), to death and burial. Corn is particularly associated with the sun and the evening star, both of which, in many cosmologies, endure a journey through the underworld in order to be reborn.

In Greece, Demeter, the daughter of Gaia (see p.72), not only gave grain to humankind but laid the foundations of civilization when she made a gift of the plough and the techniques of farming to Triptolemus (a young god-king). When Hades kidnapped Demeter's daughter Kore (or Persephone), whom he bore away to the underworld, the earth became sterile. Hades agreed to release Kore, but because she ate some of a pomegranate – a symbol of the vagina – during her time in the underworld, she was forced to return there for

GRAIN RITUALS OF THE GODDESS

The Roman historian Tacitus wrote in AD 98 about a Celto-Germanic earth mother called Nerthus. Periodically, the goddess, probably represented by a crude icon, rode on a cart drawn by cows across the fields of an area peopled by seven tribes. During this time her worshippers suspended all hostilities to celebrate her coming. When her journey was over, the priest in attendance returned her to her sacred grove on an island where she was plunged along with her cart in a lake.

Although Tacitus does not mention the time of the festival, it probably took place at the end of winter or in early spring, like the festivals of most vegetation Goddesses. In Asia Minor, the worshippers of Cybele similarly drew her across the land in a cart, to bless the fields. Later they trooped to a river where they ritually bathed her to symbolize the cleansing and irrigation of the fields ready for planting.

This modern Balkan corn dolly represents the Goddess. It is kept as a lucky charm and to bring a good harvest in the coming year.

a part of each year. Winter is caused by Demeter mourning her absence.

The moment of abduction was commemorated in Athens by the all-female Thesmophoria festival (see p.41), in which sacrificial piglets were flung into a chasm full of snakes. Pigs have been closely associated with earth goddesses from Isis in Egypt to Pele in Hawaii, possibly because the animals are extremely fertile (producing many young in frequent litters) and appear to plough the soil as they root for food.

The all-female participation in the Thesmophoria may point toward the greater involvement of women in cultivating the earth during the Neolithic, at a time when the male activity of hunting was becoming less and less capable of supporting a growing human population. This view is reinforced by the discovery of female figurines in grain bins in the 6th-millennium-BC ruins of Çatal Hüyük, in present-day Turkey.

A 1st-century-AD Pompeiian mosaic, showing Ceres about to crown the newly born ear of wheat. Ceres was the Roman name for Demeter. The wheat symbolized her daughter.

The Goddess and the natural order

The Titans, giants, and other "monstrous" children of the Greek earth goddess Gaia, can be seen as personifications of all the destructive powers of the universe. The goddess did not judge these forces (see pp.60–61). Destruction was necessary to make room for new life, and was itself a part of the process that ensured the world's vitality. The battles between the constructive and destructive elements were part of the natural cycle, and the concept of one as good and the other as evil was a later innovation, based on the human understanding of threat as evil and safety as good. Zeus, the king of the gods, who was a descendant of Gaia, won power by trickery, aided by his first wife, Metis ("Cunning Intelligence"). It was only after he swallowed her that he married Themis ("Right"), the goddess of natural order, and begat the Horae, Eunomia ("Good Order"), Dike ("Justice") and Eirene ("Peace").

The story of Gaia describes her efforts to free her offspring, which a succession of male figures try to subjugate, devour or imprison within her. Gaia's actions have been interpreted in various different ways: socially, as examples of inscrutable female mysteries, or as folk memories of humankind's unregulated, pre-social state; mythically, as indomitable elements of the religions of conquered people, surviving into the new orthodoxy; and scientifically, as an analogy for the workings of the planet earth.

The Gaia Hypothesis was first suggested by the British scientist James Lovelock in 1969, and worked out in more detail in the 1970s. It proposes that the earth is a complex, self-regulating organism, at the heart of which lies reciprocity between animate and inanimate parts. The environment not only affects, but is affected by, its inhabitants. Living creatures are the sense-organs of Gaia: they detect changes (for example, the sun radiates 30 percent more heat than when life first evolved), and help the "global metabolism" to adjust and create a new balance. However, these adjustments may involve mass extinctions. Because humankind has had such a destabilizing effect on the environment, it has been suggested that Gaia may be about to leap into a new state of balance, involving the extermination of many species, including humans.

An Attic red-figure vase, c.*460*BC*, which links different aspects of the earth goddess. The upper scene shows a battle between the Olympian gods and the monstrous children of Gaia, while the lower scene shows Demeter with Triptolemus (see pp.70–71). Demeter stood for the beneficence and productivity of the earth.*

The Calumny of Apelles, *by Sandro Botticelli,* c.*1498. The naked figure on the left, pointing skyward, is Truth. From the 15th century onward, science was increasingly described as an active process that "probed" or "penetrated" Nature. At the same time, Truth, which in medieval art was usually depicted as a veiled, modest virgin, became allegorized as "Naked Truth". She was innocent because she had nothing to hide, and was the most primordial aspect of Nature.*

NATURE AND CULTURE

The 16th-century philosopher Francis Bacon expressed the view of Nature current in the 16th century: "We will put Nature on the rack and torture her secrets out of her." His words indicate that the natural world is something apart from, and alien to, the humans who investigate it. Over the next 300 years, this attitude would create a completely mechanistic theoretical framework for scientific research, in which the universe was nothing more than a machine, running according to the laws discovered by men such as Bacon, Galileo and Newton.

According to Goddess-worshippers – and a growing number of philosophers of science – the view that there is an irreconcilable duality between Nature and humankind is characteristically masculine. It is thought to stem in part from man's inability to reproduce from his own body: a lack that must be redressed by sophisticated cultural models which establish his part in the act of creation. A mechanical universe allows the possibility of a creator who is a machine-maker or inventor, rather than a creatrix who brings forth life organically, from her own being.

The tendency to treat Nature and Culture as binary oppositions continues, sometimes implicitly, in the work of 20th-century thinkers such as the French anthropologist, Claude Lévi-Strauss. He used the idea to investigate the underlying structures of traditional societies, claiming that, in such societies, if Nature was female, unpredictable and wild, then Culture was male, contained and stable.

Fertility and the Divine Couple

The divine pair – a god and goddess joined in sexual union – exists in myth and religion to bring together the male and female principles crucial to fertility, and to maintain the earth and its species in a state of equilibrium. Therefore, the sacred marriage between the Goddess and her lover is essential to the welfare of the world and, predictably, it became understood as the prototype for the human couple in societies worldwide. The sacredness of human marriage has its roots in the emulation of the gods. The association of marriage with fruitfulness survived beyond the early, Goddess-worshipping cultures. The Hebrew Scriptures enjoin people to "go forth and multiply" in marriage, while other Jewish sources say that an individual who does not marry reduces the status of God.

The sacred couple represents a whole: a perfected male–female duality, elevating divinity above mortal, gendered existence. However, it can do this only by combining elements that are intimately associated with gender. Male thus joins with female to recreate what a number of mythologies portray as the original form: the perfect, all-encompassing androgyne.

The pre-Colombian Mexican manuscript, Codex Fejervary-Mayer, *which depicts the fortunes of the maize plant. In the third year (right), the rain god Tlaloc blesses the plant, which is depicted as Chalchiuhtlicue ("She of the Jade Skirt"), a goddess of lakes and streams.*

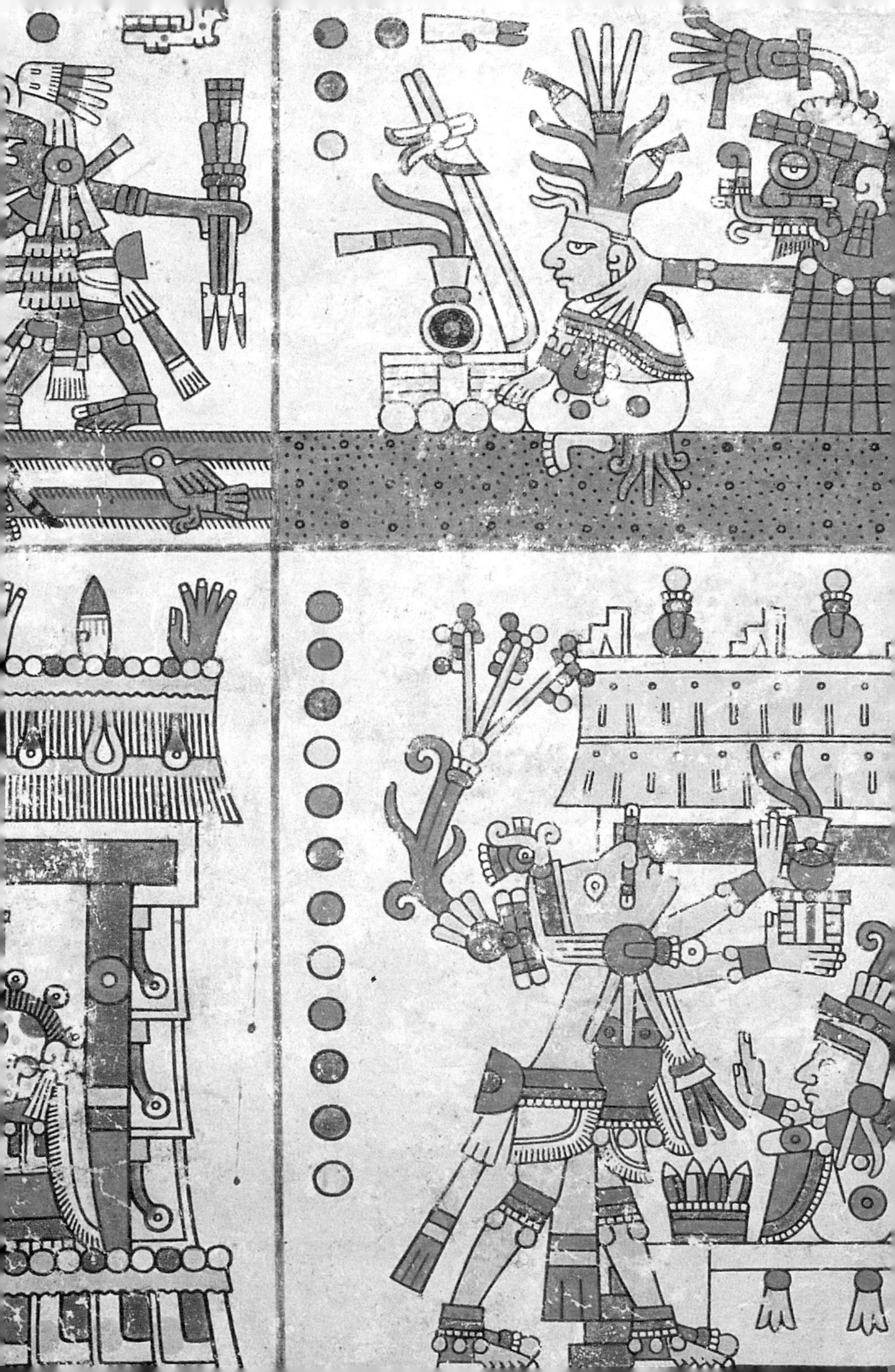

The journey into the underworld

As early humans began to settle in fixed communities, and change from a predominantly hunting and gathering to a predominantly agricultural way of life, it is likely that their existing belief systems – including the analogy between the reproductive body of the female and the reproductive body of the earth – expanded to accommodate fresh knowledge of husbandry and the seasons. The yearly, cyclical process of sowing and harvesting crops became enshrined in rituals and myths of the Goddess and her interaction with the underworld, which was at once the place of burial and new life.

The Greek Kore–Demeter myth is the best known tale of a goddess's journey to the underworld, and may even have originated in the Neolithic age, when

A Greek vase, from the 4th century BC, showing Persephone and Hades. Persephone is often shown holding either grain, as here, or a torch, symbolizing the light that leaves the world in winter.

there is evidence of two (unnamed) goddesses, joined together, who are probably manifestations of the same life source that surges through all living things. The names of the pre-Olympian duo, Demeter ("Grain-mother") and Kore ("Maiden") suggest two sides of the same essence – maturity and youth.

According to the Homeric poem of Demeter, the younger goddess (here named Persephone) was abducted by Hades, the lord of the underworld. Demeter, lamenting the loss of her daughter, travelled far and wide in search of her, eventually arriving at Eleusis where she gave the gift of husbandry to its king, Triptolemus. As her search continued, the earth began to wither and die with Demeter's mournful lamentations until there was little food

SEXUALITY IN THE HYMNS OF INANNA

The cycle of verses describing the activities of the Sumerian goddess Inanna have existed for more than 4,000 years as part of a body of work inscribed on stone tablets. According to the cycle, the young Inanna was leaning against an apple tree when "rejoicing at her wondrous vulva, the young woman applauded herself", and decided to visit her grandfather Enki (or Enlil). He welcomed her and as they feasted, handed over to her the *me,* or attributes, of civilization. Despite Enki's later efforts to recover the *me*, Inanna sailed back to heaven with them. Soon afterward, she was filled with sexual desire and "sang a song of her vulva", likening it to a horn and "the lovely crescent of the new moon". She also described it as a "fallow plot", thus establishing the basis for the agricultural myth of her marriage to Dumuzi. She cried:

"For me, open my vulva for me!

For me, the maiden, who is its ploughman?

My vulva, a wet place, for me –

For me, the lady, who will provide the bull?"

Encouraged by the response that the king would plough her vulva, she commanded:

"Plough my vulva, man of my heart!"

It was at the moment of penetration that the goddess's lover became a vital part of the agricultural process, the crucial, male element who made her fallow ground fruitful. The duty of coitus and fertilization remained sacred and elevated as well as being pleasurable to the participants. In fact it was among the attributes of civilization and Enki put it on a par with truth, death and rebirth, in the formula: "To my daughter Inanna I shall give the truth! Descent into the underworld, Ascent from the underworld! The art of lovemaking! The kissing of the phallus!"

Lovemaking was therefore practised as a sacred ritual of some sophistication. Enki's reference to fellatio shows that sex was not restricted to procreation, and the verses' mention of the sweet taste of the vulva, and of Dumuzi's face between Inanna's thighs and on her lap, clearly allude to cunnilingus. The vulva, referred to time and again, was a freely used part of the Sumerian vernacular. The cuneiform for "woman" is sometimes interpreted as a pubic triangle.

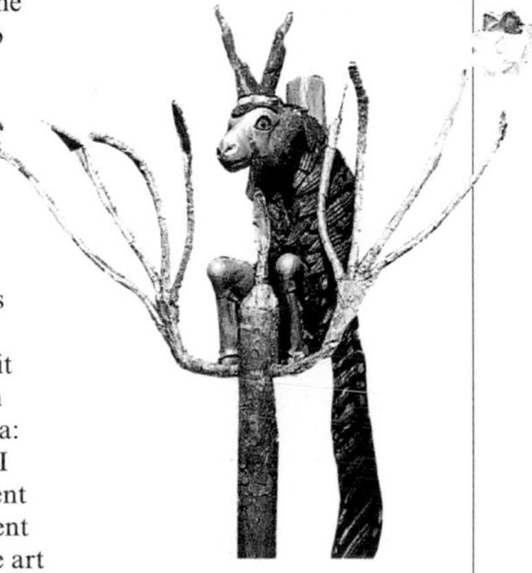

A ram, c.2500BC, *found in the royal graves at Ur, and symbolizing Dumuzi the shepherd, trapped in the thickets of the underworld.*

left for humans to eat or offer to the gods. Zeus, the king of the gods, grew alarmed and agreed that Persephone could return above ground for two-thirds of the year but was obliged to stay underground with her husband Hades, for the remaining one-third. Persephone's return to the living world – celebrated in the festivals of Demeter – symbolized the coming of spring. Her descent to the underworld marked the onset of winter.

Isis as the queen of the underworld, from the Theban Book of the Dead, *c.1150BC.*

The major elements of this myth remain the same wherever they occur, with the seasonal cycle beginning when a Mother Goddess – such as Freya in Scandinavia, Inanna in Sumeria or Aphrodite in Greece – loses her child. However, there are many regional, and historical, variations. The Egyptian Isis loses her husband, Osiris, but in recovering his dismembered body, and giving it life, she symbolically becomes his mother. Although she does not journey to the underworld, her journeys through swamps and wastelands have the same mythic character. Most goddesses, including Freya and Aphrodite, lose not a daughter, but a son (Baldur and Adonis, respectively) who goes to the underworld as the result of a violent

THE GREAT BELOW

Ereshkigal, like the Mother Goddess of most cultures, was the ruler of the underworld. Her name has been translated as "Queen of the Great Below". She is usually thought of as the sister or dark aspect of Inanna, and the pair are described as once having shared dominion of both the upper and lower worlds. This view is supported by Inanna's claim, on her journey to the underworld, that she is going to attend the funeral of Gugul-ana, "husband of my elder sister, Ereshkigal".

Ereshkigal shares many of the emblems of Inanna and other Sumerian goddesses.

However, Ereshkigal is also sometimes identified with Ninlil. This goddess, patron of the city of Nippur, was a maiden who was repeatedly raped by Enki (Enlil), Inanna's grandfather. The angry gods banished Enki to the underworld, but Ninlil, who knew she was pregnant and did not want to be alone, followed him. Later, Enki escaped and appropriated the earth, but Ninlil was held by the "Great Below" as its prize. Nevertheless, even in the underworld, she gave birth to the moon. In this way, Ninlil-Ereshkigal conformed to the primal, mythological role of a Mother Goddess by returning underground in order to bring forth new life.

death. A period of mourning follows, characterized by the devastation of the world, before the goddess negotiates the return of her son for part of the year.

The goddess Inanna did not make the journey to the underworld to rescue her child, but to experience her own death and regeneration (in a sense, this is also true of Kore and Demeter, if they are considered as two aspects of the same being). The poem known as *Inanna's Descent to the Underworld* indicates that she went voluntarily, and even eagerly. As she descended into the realm of her dark sister, Ereshkigal (see box), she had to pass through seven gates, and at each of them shed an item of clothing. In this way, her journey stripped her piece by piece of her regalia and her power. In the underworld, Ereshkigal fixed her with the eye of death, and hung her carcass on a hook. Inanna could only leave the underworld by appointing a sacrifice in her place: she sent her son and husband, Dumuzi. Like Aphrodite, she volunteered her partner (see pp.80–81) to the underworld as part of the son–lover tradition in order to ensure the fertility of the earth. The descent of Inanna also enacts the monthly phases of the moon: her body hangs on Ereshkigal's hook for three days, the period during which the moon is dark.

The child in these agricultural myths symbolizes the seed, buried in the earth, until it returns in the form of newly sprouting plants. These ripen until they are harvested and the whole process is re-enacted. In this way, a basic agricultural principle becomes an allegory for human life, and the desire to be involved in the celestial drama of the seasons

The idea of life being reborn from the dead within the ground is reflected in this vagina-like opening into the womb-grave of the Neolithic burial mound at Bryn Celli Ddu, Wales.

leads to rituals which symbolize the process of fertilization. The rites, known as the Eleusian Mysteries of Demeter (in early spring and autumn), included secret rituals reserved for initiates, in which the individual died to his or her past life and the soul returned to its source, before being reborn. This was a symbolic reliving of the descent and return of the divinity. The mystery itself consisted of the revelation that life does not end, but ceaselessly transforms itself; and that both nature and humanity, as well as the Goddess, embody this process. The grain was the symbol of this eternal life. The 5th-century-BC playwright, Sophocles, said: "Thrice-blessed are those mortals who have seen these rites and thus enter into Hades: for them alone there is life, for the others all is misery."

The Goddess and her son

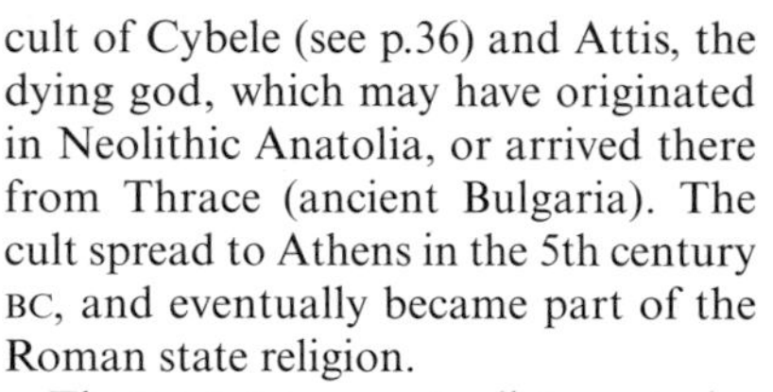

Throughout the Near East and Europe, whenever a Mother Goddess is worshipped, there is usually also a cult surrounding a god who is simultaneously her son and her lover. Such cults have existed since at least the 6th century BC, in the Çatal Hüyük civilization of Turkey, and subsequently in Syria, Iran, Egypt and western Europe. The Mother Goddess is the constant root, her son the fruit who is sacrificed, consumed and reborn. The myth complements the underworld journey of Kore and Demeter and parallels those of Aphrodite and Adonis and Ishtar and Tammuz (see pp.76–77).

One of the best documented traditions of the son–lover is found in the cult of Cybele (see p.36) and Attis, the dying god, which may have originated in Neolithic Anatolia, or arrived there from Thrace (ancient Bulgaria). The cult spread to Athens in the 5th century BC, and eventually became part of the Roman state religion.

There are many contradictory stories concerning Cybele and Attis. Probably the oldest account of Attis's birth describes an androgynous Cybele who severed his/her male genitals, which fell to the ground and produced an almond tree. The fruits of the tree gave birth to Attis. His death is sometimes ascribed to a hunting accident (he was gored by a boar, like Aphrodite's lover, Adonis). In other accounts, he falls in love with

The Pietà, *sculpted in 1546–55 by Michelangelo. The Crucifixion is a typical spring sacrifice.*

THE WEEPING MOTHER

The complicity of the Mother Goddess in the sacrifice of her son lent her, in some traditions, a ruthless quality. However, in most myths, she was portrayed as placing Nature's needs above her own, and suffering greatly for the loss of her son and her newly-wed husband. She wept eternally for the holy child that she had sacrificed for the salvation of humanity.

The ancient myth of the weeping mother who presides over spring survived beyond pantheism. Her tradition is obvious in Christianity, where the Crucifixion is commemorated at Easter. Husain, son of Fatima and grandson of the Prophet of Islam, is remembered for his bloody death, as a result of decapitation, during *Muharram*, the new year of the Islamic calendar. The greatest adoration for Husain is found in Iran, which was the home of the ancient goddess–son tradition of Attagartis and Mithra. The spring festival survives there in the form of the traditional new year, *Nauruz*.

The pagan Goddess was expelled as a sacrilegious falsehood by the strictly monotheistic religion of Islam. However she reappeared in the form of the mourning Fatima – an historical figure, to whom an increasing number of legends and divine titles began to accrue (for example, she became known as "the mother of her father"). The Goddess's ancient sacrifice of her son seems to have retained its hold on the Near-Eastern imagination.

M·D·M·I· ET· ATTINIS·
L CORNELIVS·SCIPIO ORFITVS
V·C·AVGVR·TAVROBOLIVM
SIVE·CRIOBOLIVM·FECIT·
DIE·IIII·KAL·MART
TVSCO·ET·ANVLLINO·COSS·

A Near-Eastern plaque, c. AD*295, showing Attis standing by a sacred tree, and Cybele riding in a chariot drawn by lions. The Roman poet Lucretius (95–55*BC*) suggested that a statue of Cybele really was drawn through the streets of Rome in a chariot yoked to tame lions.*

a mortal woman, whereupon Cybele sends him into a frenzy, so that he castrates himself and bleeds to death.

Cybele's festival began on March 24 with her sacred marriage to Attis – a symbolic marriage of earth (the goddess) and rain (the blood of the sacrificed god), intended to produce the child, grain. A bull, representing the dying god, was ritually slaughtered and its testicles were offered to the Earth Mother. The bull symbolism is shared by many other dying gods, including Dumuzi–Tammuz of Mesopotamia and Mithra of Persia. Dying gods (and bulls) were solar symbols – like the sun, they were believed to perish at night, red and bleeding, only to be reborn the next day. The gold of the corn as it ripened at harvest was also compared to the sun's light, and in order to emphasize the harvest imagery of the sacrifice, the genitalia of the bull were dismembered with a sickle provided by the goddess. The next morning the chief priest announced that it was time to rejoice: the god had returned. Not all son–lover sacrifices involved actual bloodshed Adonis was only killed in effigy eac spring, or in the form of "gardens Adonis": pots of herbs, allowed to and cast into the sea.

Drought and plenty

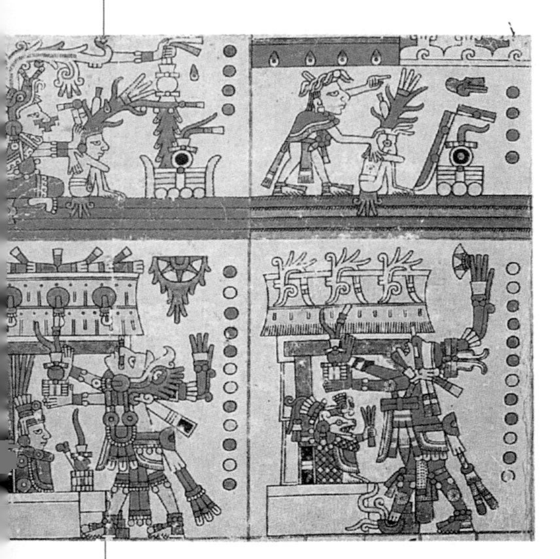

A page from the pre-Colombian Mexican Codex Fejervary-Mayer. *On the right, a water goddess irrigates a maize plant, which prospers. On the left, the following year, the maize withers under the attention of a god (the Lord of Jewels).*

Although there are innumerable goddesses of water in world mythology (see pp.46–51), there are relatively few with control over the rains. This discrepancy is based on the common symbolic pattern by which the earth is described as a mother, having to be impregnated by rain, which is therefore necessarily male in origin. For example, in the religion of the Aztecs, although there were several different goddesses associated with water, it was the god Tlaloc who dispensed rain, as well as frost, drought and lightning bolts.

Nevertheless, the Goddess is often voked as supreme deity even in rain-king rituals. Fertility and the regula- of the seasons are the central motifs e Ugaritic mythology of Canaan. The primal Ugaritic myth is the story of El, the father of Baal (see box). In different interpretations of this story, El, the creator god, either attempts to produce two women or else discovers two goddesses. In either event, his phallus becomes engorged with desire and he wants to "possess" the two beautiful females, Asherah and "the girl" Anath, who, in a subsequent myth, is the wife and sister of Baal.

This narrative forms part of a drama which was probably ritually enacted following a poor harvest, or at the beginning of every seven-year cycle in order to ensure that the next cycle was prosperous. The ritual enactment of the play has been described as being full of suspense because, the eagerness of the god notwithstanding, it was the response of the goddesses upon which the abundance of the fields depended. If they called El "father", he would have to treat them as daughters and the earth would remain barren. If, on the other hand, they addressed him as "husband", he would have intercourse with them and they would procreate – which they did abundantly, bearing him dusk and dawn, followed by another 70 "good and gracious" deities, who suckled at the breast of Asherah and thereby acquired the power to rule. These gods and goddesses would ensure the regulation of rain, dew and storms in the appropriate seasons, and agriculture would prosper.

The construction of the Ugaritic myths is striking for its human motivation – the gods shared the concerns of ordinary mortals, although these were obviously the problems and ambitions of kings rather than of commoners. The

A 14th-century-BC Ugaritic seal showing Baal and El.

THE SEMITIC GODDESS

The Ugaritic tablets, which date back to 1400BC and provide an insight into contemporaneous ideas of the Goddess, were discovered in Syria and Palestine from 1929 onward. The narratives cluster around the male divinities, El and Baal. However, while Baal ("Lord") is connected with the protection of cities, it is the Goddess who is his protector. Similarly, although El is the father of the gods, he is preceded by Asherah (also known as Athirat).

The most famous myth from the tablets tells of Baal, god of rain, dew and fertility, and his sister–spouse Anath who guides and protects him and furthers his cause. Baal strives to gain and then defend his throne against his brothers, Yam, the sea god, and Mot, the personification of death and drought.

Anath is crucial to Baal's progress, well-being and regeneration. She restrains him from fighting Yam before he is properly armed by the craft god; she ruthlessly massacres troop upon troop of enemy soldiers; and she gains El's sanction to build him the palace he longs for (although Baal lacks the courage to ask El for a palace of his own, Anath's arrival sends the father-god cowering to his cellar). When Baal surrenders to Mot and disappears underground, she locates him with the help of the all-seeing sun goddess Shapsh, then rescues him by "killing, grinding and planting" Mot so that Baal springs from the earth as grain. Thus she perpetuates the battle of the seasons in which Baal (fertility) continually confronts Mot (drought) in a cycle which ensures eternal life (see also pp.76–9).

Goddess on the other hand was more mysterious, and had an undeniably otherworldly quality. Even the ritual drama of El took place in the Goddess's domain – the "fields of Asherah". She was immanent (or all-pervading) and appeared in several different personifications, as mother, wife, sister and daughter of the various male gods. Procreation and the continuation of all life depended upon her will. The Goddess acted according to her own impulse, using diplomacy, intimidation or violence as required, but always remaining in control of the outcome. By contrast, the gods of Canaan were creatures of fate, assigned to specific functions and trapped in a cycle of perpetuity, while the Goddess stood outside it, directing the proceedings.

Divine incest

Isis embracing Osiris, her brother and husband, from the tomb of the pharaoh Seti I, who died in 1279BC and was buried in Thebes.

Divine incest occurs throughout world mythology and is linked to a number of different mythic themes. It is a recurring theme in descriptions of the underworld, or explanations of the seasons (see pp.76–81). A god raping his daughter, or a woman he has created and breathed life into, is a typical account of the origins of the human race. Incest between brother and sister is frequently linked to the establishment of the cosmic or social order, as in the story of the sun and the moon among the Inuit (see p.61). Wherever the Goddess occurs in world mythology, she is likely to be implicated in incest, whether she is aware or unaware, willing or unwilling.

Despite their apparent differences, all incest motifs are concerned with the unification of complementary opposites to create a perfect, all-containing, androgynous being. A goddess personified as the moon mates with a god personified as the sun, or a god responsible for death rapes a goddess associated with new life. Often this "unification" can only be approximated through a balance or alternation between opposing forces: the sun and moon mark day and night, Hades and Persephone signify winter and spring and Baal and Anath symbolize fertility and drought.

The Egyptian story of Isis and Osiris combines many of the mythic themes of incest. Nephthys, Seth, Isis and Osiris were all brothers and sisters, and were the product of a long chain of incestuous unions (see box, right). Isis and Osiris loved each other from the womb, and became separated for the first time when Seth tricked Osiris into climbing into an ornamental chest, which was immediately locked and set adrift on the waters. This attempt by Seth to take over his brother's kingdom initiated a typical underworld quest, as Isis went in search of her husband.

Because Isis was cognate with Nut, she represented both the mother and lover of Osiris. In her role as a divine mother, her absence from Egypt caused a barren period. Isis eventually brought Osiris back to Egypt, thus enacting the return of the dying god, common to many other underworld journeys. Isis

THE DESCENT OF GODS AND KINGS

The early part of the Egyptian creation myth shows a formless entity dividing into logical pairs of binary opposites. The latter part is more complicated, because the opposites are not the incestuous couples – Osiris is opposed to Seth, and Isis to Nephthys.

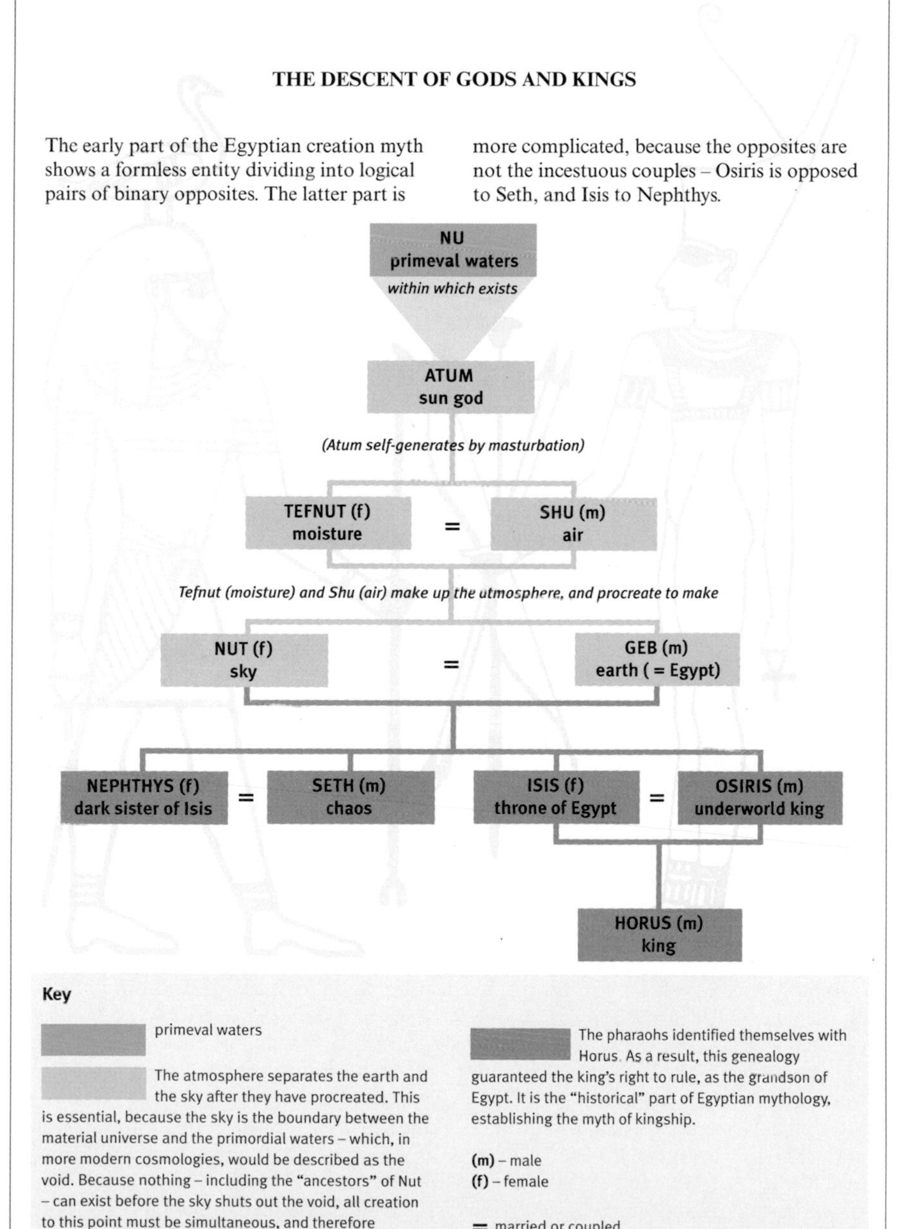

Key

primeval waters

The atmosphere separates the earth and the sky after they have procreated. This is essential, because the sky is the boundary between the material universe and the primordial waters – which, in more modern cosmologies, would be described as the void. Because nothing – including the "ancestors" of Nut – can exist before the sky shuts out the void, all creation to this point must be simultaneous, and therefore timeless. So the sky is sometimes described as the mother of Atum, and sometimes as his granddaughter. This is the cosmological cycle of Egyptian myth.

The pharaohs identified themselves with Horus. As a result, this genealogy guaranteed the king's right to rule, as the grandson of Egypt. It is the "historical" part of Egyptian mythology, establishing the myth of kingship.

(m) – male
(f) – female

= married or coupled

A 19th-century Maori house lintel, depicting the separation of Rangi, the sky, from Papa, the earth, by their son, Tane. This moment represents the first division of the primal androgynous unit into male and female. Tane went on to populate the earth by coupling with his daughter.

then took the form of a bird whose wings breathed life into Osiris, who masturbated so that his semen might impregnate Isis.

However, Seth found Osiris, chopped his body into fourteen segments (representing the fourteen sections of the Egyptian year) and dispersed them throughout the land, an act which, mythologically, establishes and explains the sequential process of the seasons. Isis again travelled far and wide collecting the pieces but could not find the penis, which had been eaten by a fish. With the help of Nephthys, she reassembled Osiris, symbolically establishing herself once more as his mother. The child conceived during their earlier union, Horus, was also Osiris reborn.

When Horus grew to adulthood, he challenged Seth for supremacy. Isis pleaded and won her son's case before a divine tribunal, but Seth, unhappy with the result, continued the struggle. A savage contest ensued, during which Seth and Horus sodomized each other forcibly. It is possible to see this mutual sexual assault as another form of divine incest, intended to merge violently opposing forces. The antithesis of Osiris (who represented order and the fertility of the Nile) was not his wife-sister Isis, but his brother, Seth (who represented chaos and the barrenness of the desert). The incest of Isis and Osiris can be interpreted as a political union, which guaranteed the divine right of succession of their offspring. On the other hand, the cosmic objective of divine incest – the unification of polar opposites – could only be achieved by the incestuous coupling of Osiris-Horus and Seth. After the gods' mutual assault, Isis dispelled Seth's semen from Horus and caused Horus's semen to infiltrate Seth, so when Seth claimed to have humiliated and tainted Horus through anal rape, the gods discovered the opposite. The vanquished Seth was made to serve Horus.

Incest between brother and sister was used to link the divine and human systems and equate the cosmic and social orders. In an act of imitation of the gods, pharaohs married their sisters to ensure divine favour, and to reinforce their claim to have descended from divine ancestors (the Inca of South America practised a similar tradition). Their performance of the taboo activity of incest also introduced the idea of an order of beings above ordinary mortals in power, splendour and wisdom, who were therefore worthy of power.

Most cultures were too fearful of the incest taboo for even kings to risk breaking it. The Maori of New Zealand believed that it was an act of incest that had introduced death into the world, when the creator figure, Tane, seduced his daughter, Hine-nui-te-po. When she discovered that Tane was her father, Hine fled to the underworld. Tane followed her and begged her to return, but she told him to go away and rear their children (the human race), while she stayed below and waited to receive them. Before this, nobody ever died. The tale is reminiscent of one of the oldest surviving myths, which describes the rape of Ereshkigal, the Sumerian queen of the underworld (see p.78).

RULES OF SUCCESSION

By the time the Inca empire of South America fell to the Spanish in 1532, it stretched from what is now northern Ecuador to central Chile. The Inca traced their origins to mythical ancestors who emerged from caves. The first Inca emperor, Manco Capac, married his sister, Mama Ocllo, and chose their son Sinchi Roca, to succeed him. From the imperial genealogy, it is possible to date this semi-legendary event to some time in the 12th century.

It is not clear from surviving accounts whether Sinchi Roca also married his sister, and incest was only adopted as a formal custom by the emperor Topa Inca Yupanqui, who took power in 1471. His aims were to reassert the divine origins of the Inca, and to ensure the purity of the royal bloodline. However, the sister and principal wife of the next emperor, Huayna Capac, died childless. In these circumstances the emperor could choose any of his sons as successor, so long as the choice was endorsed by divine portents.

An illustration from an 18th-century Peruvian genealogy, showing the Inca princess Mama Ocllo, dressed to represent the moon. She is holding a mask symbolizing the sun, which bears the features of her brother and husband, Manco Capac.

Yahweh, Shekhina and Eve

Yahweh, the Jewish deity – alone, supreme, male and perfect – was an alien being to the conquered races of Canaan (see pp.38–9), who were accustomed to a Mother Goddess who encouraged sexual activity and enjoyment as an essential part of her worship. Despite the violent attacks of the Hebrew prophets against the Goddess, she persisted in popular worship, and even found a place in the texts and traditions of Judaism. The discovery of jars and plaques inscribed to "Yahweh and his Asherah" have led Hebrew scholars to reassess a passage in the biblical book of Hosea, in which God speaks through the mouth of Ephraim, saying: "I am his Anath and Asherah," that is, the bringer of abundance and fertility. Clearly, Asherah survived in popular belief until at least 621 BC (when King Josiah reformed the religious practices of Jerusalem) and became a consort for the Jewish God. References to the Goddess can also be found in The Song of Songs and, in the book of Isaiah, when referring to Yahweh, use is made of a word that is grammatically female. There are also references to Yahweh as a mother, which are explained as a reflection of the status of God as a being who transcends gender. Gnosticism (see p.107) advances this hypothesis several steps further, suggesting that the divine combines both male and female and that the spiritual search of humankind entails a quest to unite them.

A medieval fresco from the Amagni Cathedral, Italy, showing the prophet Samuel admonishing the Israelites against the worship of Baal, Asherah and other pagan gods.

In a parody of this concept of divine marriage (see p.100), the Goddess was introduced into Jewish texts as the symbol of Israel, who was described as an evil, destructive harlot, constantly betraying her husband, Yahweh. However, the most enduring Judaic form of the female divinity is hinted at in the book of Proverbs, through which flits a shadowy woman of wisdom – a female partner who is present from the beginning. Clearly an imprint of the Goddess, this "wife" of Yahweh appeared in numerous sacred and mystical Judaic texts other than the Bible.

According to the Talmud, she was the manifest aspect of God – one whose presence was not merely felt by the people but often seen and heard as well. The Midrash acknowledged her as man's intercessor with God and the Talmud confirmed this status. However, she held a position greater than most of the hypostases (creatures who did God's bidding and conveyed his instructions):

David playing to the Shulamite Women, a 16th-century painting after Theodore Pulaki. The Shulamite is one of the descriptions of the female voice in The Song of Songs.

THE SONG OF SONGS

Estimated to be composed around the year 1000BC, the biblical Song of Songs contains a dominant female voice (the Bride) and hints at fertility rituals common in the pre-Jewish Near East. The language used by the Bride reverberates with the sexual, earth-related imagery of Inanna's own bridal song (see p.77): "... Blow upon my garden that the spices there may flow out. Let my beloved come into his garden, and eat his pleasant fruits." To which the Bridegroom responds: "I am come into my garden, my sister, my spouse: I have gathered my myrrh with my spice; I have eaten my honeycomb with my honey; I have drunk my wine with my milk." His consistent reference to a sister–wife is reminiscent of Osiris and Isis, or Baal and Anath, leading to the conclusion that the verses existed long before they were collected together in the Song.

Following the union, the Bride continues: "I opened to my beloved; but my beloved had withdrawn himself, and was gone. My soul failed when he spake: I sought him, but could not find him; I called him, but he gave me no answer." Like the son–lover, following the sacred marriage (see p.80), the Bridegroom has died and "gone down into his garden", the cradle of the next generation, where he "feedeth on the lilies".

The Song's place in Jewish scripture was confirmed only in AD100, when the council of Jamnia decided it was an allegory of the relationship between Jehovah and Israel. The verses have also been rationalized in the light of monotheism as metaphors for the union of the human soul with the divine, and the communion of Christ with the Church. However, the dying Bridegroom appears to evoke something more tangible in his question: "Who is she that looketh forth as the morning, fair as the moon, clear as the sun, and terrible as an army with banners?" This is too clear an evocation of the Near-Eastern Queen of Heaven to be a coincidence (see p.114).

as Wisdom – also known as Shekhina, Hokhma and Sophia – she stood up to God, with strong words of advice.

Her physical size extended millions of miles and her brightness caused the angels to cover their eyes, yet she could become minute and invisible. One Rabbi compared her to the sea, which did not diminish if it entered and filled a cave. So it was that the Shekhina lived in the Jerusalem Temple, yet walked with the tribes and embodied Israel and its people. She was visible only to the Children of Israel, and part of her function was to heal and comfort.

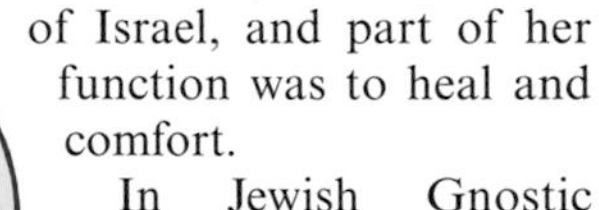

The anguipede, *an early image of Yahweh, which exhibits Goddess-like traits such as feet made of serpents.*

In Jewish Gnostic myth, it was the Shekhina who created the world and the first man, but with each successive generation of sinners, from Adam to the Sodomites, she retreated until finally she took refuge in the seventh (remotest) heaven (this recalls Inanna's journey through the seven gates of the underworld, see pp.78–9). The personification of the Shekhina has in part been attributed to the Aramaic Bible, *Targum Onkelo*, which transposes the Jewish verb "I dwell" in all its forms to "my Shekhina dwells". Essentially, she was a projection of the need for a female deity who could supply those elements that were felt to be missing in a lone male god. It has been suggested that Moses abandoned sex with his wife because the Shekhina was his lover, and not merely because he needed to keep himself ritually pure to communicate with her.

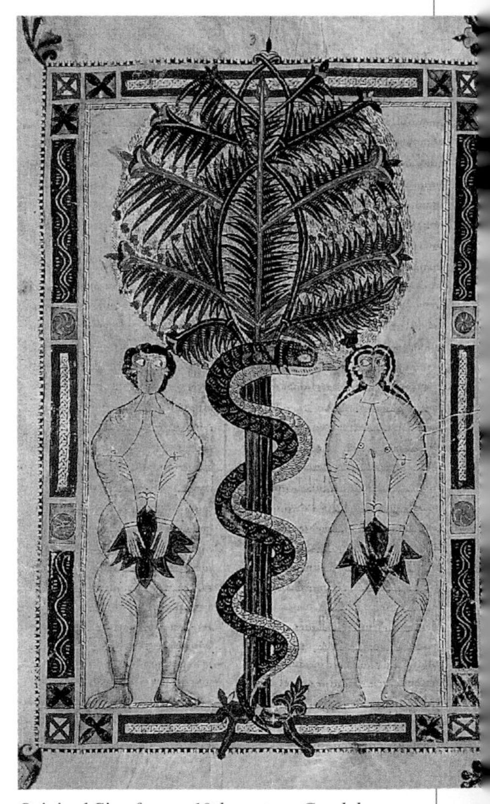

Original Sin, *from a 10th-century Guadalupan commentary on the Apocalypse. Early paintings on this theme bear a powerful resemblance to ancient Sumerian seals, depicting the Goddess and her son on opposite sides of the Tree of Life, with the serpent as a symbol of regeneration.*

As Wisdom – the unknowable, bodiless consort of Yahweh – the Goddess was revered. However, when she manifested herself in the book of Genesis as a flesh-and-blood woman, Eve, she was openly degraded and stripped of all her divinity. The story of Eve's origin from Adam's rib is probably a corruption of an ancient Mesopotamian myth, in which the Mother Goddess Ninhursag healed the rib of the water god Enki, in the process creating the Goddess Nin-Ti (both "Lady of the Rib" and "Lady Who Gives Life"). Nin-Ti became patron of childbirth, creating infants *in utero* from the ribs of their prospective mothers. Although Eve (from Hawwa), means "Mother of All Living", she was berated as the origin of all evil and the corrupter of men, qualities believed to be passed on to all mortal women, who are her heirs. Tellingly, in light of the Goddess's other biblical manifestation, as the Shekhina, Eve's sin is the longing for knowledge. The Fall is a symbol of her humanization. It was Eve's act that introduced death – not as a precursor to regeneration, as it would be in a Goddess-religion, but as a terrifying cessation of life. And because the Goddess embodied all nature, in the Fall of Eve, Nature too became a degraded ("fallen") state (see p.73).

THE MATRONIT

The possession of wisdom – or secret knowledge – has often been a source of consolation to the persecuted. The Jewish symbolic mysticism known as Kabbala arose in the Middle Ages, and became a mass movement within European Judaism after the expulsion of the Jews from Spain in 1492. By this time, the Matronit, or Matron, had become the most popular manifestation of the Shekhina, and like her alter-ego, the Virgin Mary, performed miracles and was adored for her bounty and grace. Tradition had it that when God withdrew to an inaccessible heaven after the destruction of the Jerusalem Temple, the Matron stayed on earth with her children.

According to the *Zohar*, a 13th-century Hebrew mystical text, she was the fourth element of the Kabbalistic tetragram symbolized by the four letters of the name of God, YHWH: Y representing the father/wisdom, H the mother/understanding, W the son/beauty and H the daughter/kingship. The Matronit herself has a similarly four-fold character, which can be compared to that of the great Near-Eastern Goddess in her various guises. She is virginal and wanton, motherly and destructive, and her descriptions make her into a fantasy figure: pure until the supplicant arouses her desire for the first time and turns her into a harlot for his own gratification, she returns to her chaste disposition when he is absent; she fulfils his need for reassurance and is his arch-protectress.

Boethius being visited by his Wisdom, from a 12th-century German manuscript. Boethius (c.AD470–524) was a Roman philosopher and statesman. His masterpiece, The Consolation of Philosophy, *written while he awaited execution, describes how philosophy, personified as a woman, taught him that all things, even his death, served a greater good.*

The Sexual Life of the Goddess

In an anthropomorphically constructed pantheon, there could be no creation without the sexual life of the divinity. For this reason, male and female fertility deities led lives of intense sexual activity to ensure the productivity of Nature. Nor was their activity curtailed by any sense of discrimination as to the quality or character of the beings that might result from their numerous unions. Because they had to maintain cosmic equilibrium, they were not merely entitled, but duty-bound, to produce both good and evil, and all their countless variations.

Fertility goddesses displayed no hesitation in using guile or illusion to satisfy their vigorous carnal appetites. Nevertheless, the sexuality of the Goddess was highly prized and respected: it was re-enacted in ritual drama, emulated by her priestesses, and imitated by her followers in orgiastic rituals. Furthermore, the Goddess's sexual life provided the pattern for a system of sacred prostitution in a number of societies where copulation was part of a sacramental replay of the divine act of creation.

A 6th- or 7th-century AD silk funerary banner, depicting the Chinese creatrix, Nü-Kua – known as the "Restorer of Cosmic Harmony" – and her husband, Fu Xi, coiled around each other.

The creative function

Literary, historical and archeological sources all indicate that the techniques of sexual pleasure were a highly prized part of many ancient civilizations, and that their standing was comparable in many ways to the position of art or music in modern societies. They were refined, practised and developed to such levels of sophistication that they became a basis for philosophical and religious thought. The moment of sexual union was considered to be the supreme expression of human creativity.

The civilizations, such as ancient Sumeria, that have treated sex as a complex and pleasurable activity, which is also spiritually and physically beneficial (in much the same way as the Indian discipline of Yoga), have generally worshipped an active female godhead. In the rites of this deity, copulation is an act far more important than mere carnal gratification or the urge to preserve the species. This type of sexual ethos has inspired numerous erotic texts that were not intended merely to arouse, but formed part of a religious discourse which survives to the present day. These religious-erotic works include the Sumerian tableaux framed around Inanna (see p.77), Ugaritic ritual dramas, various Japanese texts including the *Nihongi* and *Kojiki*, and diverse Chinese medico-philosophical tracts. Perhaps the most famous of all the ancient erotic texts is Vatsyayana's *Kama Sutra*, written in India some time between the 3rd and 5th centuries AD.

An 18th-century bronze Tibetan statuette of the supreme Buddha, copulating with the female source of his wisdom and power.

The notion of sex as a sin is entirely absent from this work, as it is from most early erotic writings. The *Kama Sutra* contains frank and detailed discussions of the beauty of the female form, from the eye-lashes to the toes and, crucially, the yoni (see pp.96–7), which is said to resemble "the opening lotus bud", and be "perfumed like the lily that has newly burst". Vatsyayana's *Kama Sutra* inspired the authors of many of the *Tantras*, or texts sacred to the Asian mystical philosophies collectively called Tantrism, which date back to at least the 6th century AD. Tantrism perceives the universe as a set of energy vibrations, emanating from the love-play of the god Shiva (who is passive and unknowable), and his active female principle Shakti. One of the "Five Practices" of Tantrism is *kamakala dhyana*, or meditations on the art of love. Here the devotee contemplates desire with the yoni of the Goddess as the focus of his worship.

Physical intercourse takes place in a number of Tantric traditions, as an allegory for the mystic union between the Goddess and the acolyte. In addition to assuring peace in the afterlife, this union brings *jivanmukti*, or liberation, while still in the world – a condition which is deemed desirable only in those religions

with a powerful goddess-figure. Sexual intercourse is believed to nullify all social barriers, unblocking the flow of energies essential to the divine creative function, which must be emulated by devotees of the Goddess in their rituals.

The *Tantras* and the *Kama Sutra* elevate women by casting them in the mould of the Goddess (see pp.96–7). The same process can be discerned in the West, among the rites of modern Wiccans (see pp.152–3). At the opposite extreme, in the Christian tradition, St John, also writing out of fierce commitment to his holy tradition, filled his book of Revelation with abuse hurled at the "abomination and filthiness of ... fornication". Women, cities and the Goddess – in the shape of the Whore of Babylon – were all condemned as harlots who peddled the filthy commodity of sex. However, although male-centred religions never embrace sexuality as completely as those which have a powerful, central goddess, they are not always actively opposed to sex. The Prophet Muhammad never advocated celibacy, and the Koran contains little evidence of the hatred of sex. Even the Bible includes the sensual and erotic Song of Solomon (see p.39), although this probably has pagan origins.

TARA AND *DAKINIS*

Tara, whose name means "star", is the most popular deity of Tibet, where she is also known as Dolma. For the laity, she is the supreme mother, the Great Tara – Mahatara. She has her origins in the Indian goddess, Kali, but by the 3rd century AD she was incorporated into the Mahayana Buddhist pantheon. As the ultimate creatrix, she gave life to the Buddhas and *bodhisattvas* themselves. Tara is also goddess of asceticism and the journey to wisdom. Her 108 names are regularly invoked on prayer beads.

The importance of the female principle in mystical Tibetan Buddhism is demonstrated by the fact that even the male *bodhisattvas* all have their female consorts (often referred to as their "energies" or "powers"), called *dakinis*. These females are, like Tara, initiators. They lead men to a state of esoteric knowledge, usually by passing on their divine energy through sexual congress. In recent Tibetan literature, they have become fantasy-figures, called *Kha-do-mas*, or sky-goers.

A 17th-century Tibetan statuette of a dakini. *In some branches of Tantric Buddhism, an acolyte is initiated by having a statue of a* dakini *placed in his lap in an act of symbolic intercourse.*

The yoni

The inverted triangle, representing the vulva of the Goddess, appears to have been worshipped since prehistory. Evidence exists of its use in the Paleolithic era, as a pendant, a fertility symbol or a charm to ward off danger (see pp.12–15). It was emphasized on Venus-figurines and stylized in diverse forms of art and in the cuneiform scripts that comprise the earliest writing.

The genital triangle of the Goddess, widely known today by its Sanskrit name of yoni, and symbolized as a lotus in bloom, is the entry and exit to the world-womb. However, the Goddess's yoni is not only life-giving. The path by which life enters the world is also the path by which it departs, and the yoni has, in various cultures, been portrayed as a fearsome, hungry, independent entity with snapping teeth – the *vagina dentata*. The Navajo and Apache tell many tales of detached, walking, biting female genitals, which were chastised by culture heroes such as Monster-slayer, son of Changing Woman (see p.112). Highly sexual, phallic imagery is applied to the overthrow of vagina women: Monster-slayer kills Filled Vagina (one of the more ferocious of her species, who mates with cacti) by driving a club into her to break her sharp teeth. The Pueblo and other Native North Americans re-enact the smashing of a vagina woman's teeth with a carved wooden phallus. Mythologically, this is often the point at which menstrual and birth taboos are also imposed on the vagina woman. Her vaginal bleeding, which was once under her own control, and an important aspect of her power, is restricted to a monthly cycle, and parturition.

An 18th-century Indian ritual yoni-vessel. Dishes like this would have held oil, to be poured as a libation.

The fear of the devouring vulva is strikingly absent from the dominant

SHEELA-NA-GIG

Images of the Sheela-na-Gig, sometimes known as the Sheela-na-Cloich, stand out as rare examples of Goddess iconography to have survived from the ancient Celts. The Sheela appears in churches throughout Celtic Britain, but is especially common in Ireland, where her presence has been justified as a reminder of the evil and profanity that existed before the introduction of Christianity. However, an equally compelling rationale points to her as a reminder of a past in which she was so dearly loved that her absence from the new religion would have discouraged any potential converts.

Some scholars link the Sheela to the goddess Brigit (see p.35), who presides over the spring festival. It could be that she is the split off, sexual aspect of this otherwise virginal goddess (who was absorbed into the Church as an emblem of chastity: a nun who became a saint).

A Sheela, or "exhibitionist figure" from above the Priest's Door of Buckland Church, Buckinghamshire, England.

Indian images of yoni worship. Here the Goddess, generally personified by Devi or Kali, is shown lying on her back, legs splayed, or stands, legs apart, releasing her vaginal fluid, *yoni-tattva*, a divine elixir which her worshippers take into their mouths.

An event from a mystical text called the *Yoni-tantra* tells how the god Brahma chopped pieces off the goddess Sati's corpse to lighten the burden of her husband Shiva as he carried her around in a state of grief. The vulva fell to earth in Kamakhya, Assam, and a temple was erected in its honour. Inside the temple, the yoni is represented by a cleft rock, kept moist by a natural underground spring which runs red with iron-oxide once a year, at the onset of the monsoon. This annual "menstruation" is interpreted by worshippers as Nature's way of confirming the veneration of the female vulva and the processes to which it is subject, and as proof that the Goddess is the earth.

Yoni-like rock formations, caves and dolmens are worshipped all over India, and pilgrims will often crawl through the aperture, if it is large enough, and crawl back out again in an imitation of divine rebirth – the entry and return from the celestial womb. Where such structures do not exist naturally, they are constructed in the form of triangular ponds outside temples. The altars of Hindu temples often have red-stained or painted triangles attached to them to symbolize the yoni. Sometimes the yoni has a black, erect phallus in the middle. In this case it is known as the yoni-lingam, and symbolizes the union of the lord Shiva with his female principle, Shakti. At other times, the symbolic yoni is itself upright, particularly when placed directly opposite an altar.

The entrance to this community house on the Northwest Coast of America represents the yoni of the bear-totem mother of the Tlingit people.

The yoni-fluid is frequently confused with menstrual blood in the mystical texts of Tantric Hinduism, when it is called "blood-food" (see p.139). It is highly venerated, and is said to contain special potency for healing and magic. The yoni-fluid is also designated *pushpa*, or flower, because "like the blossom of the tree" it announces its potential to produce fruit.

Handmaids of the gods

Sacred prostitution was a widespread, honourable form of religious worship in many ancient European civilizations, such as those of Greece, Rome and the Near East, and remnants of the practice survive in modern India, where Goddess worship has never been eradicated. The terms for the prostitutes, such as *devadasi* in India and *hierodule* in Greece, suggest a "servant of the divinity". However, the nature of the service – and the nature of the divinity – has varied from culture to culture. In ancient Mesopotamia, the *qadishtu* were thought of as servants of Ishtar, and would sleep with any worshipper for a fee. The *devadasis* of Puri, in India, are servants of the lord Jagannatha, and are supposed to sleep only with the *brahmin* priests who officiate at Jagannatha's temple.

Nevertheless, in all her manifestations, the sacred prostitute was essentially the embodiment of a goddess. Most love goddesses patronized such a tradition, and although little evidence

The marriage of Hera and Zeus, depicted on a 5th-century-BC Greek vase.

HERA AND ZEUS

The *hieros gamos* – or sacred marriage – of Zeus and Hera was formally established in the Bronze Age and subsequently celebrated in many parts of Greece. Although later Hellenic myth makes Hera the inferior of her husband (she gains her glory from "lying in the arms of Zeus") it is likely that she was once a supreme goddess in her own right. As such, in the early celebrations of the marriage, she would have been perceived as honouring Zeus by choosing him as consort. The 5th-century-BC Greek historian Herodotus believed that Hera was much older than any of the Olympian gods, and was appropriated by them from the indigenous Pelasgians of northern Greece.

In Knossos, the sacred marriage was remembered in rituals enacting the wedding of heaven and earth, which made the world both beautiful and fruitful. Similar bridal festivals were held in numerous Boeotian cities every half century or so, when a cow and a bull were ritually burned as an offering to the wooden effigies of Hera and Zeus.

Homeric theology defines their union as the blueprint for the human marriage ceremony, and lyrically describes a thick, golden cloud which veiled the lovers as they consummated their marriage on an earth spilling forth its bounty. In this way, Homer contributes to the undermining of Hera's ancient autonomy as a triple goddess (see p.110): in the Classical period she became redefined as simply Hera the wife. Even in her ancient temples at Stymphalos, in Arcadia, the three phases of Hera's nature came to be understood solely in terms of her relationship to Zeus: she was venerated as the Child before marriage, as Full and Completed in consequence of marriage and as the Widow when separated from him.

Hera's role became confined to the sacrament of marriage, and her fiery, intolerant attitude to her husband's sexual liaisons was attributed to her doctrine of fidelity. However, it could be interpreted as an expression of the conflicts between the old, matriarchal religion and the new patriarchal one.

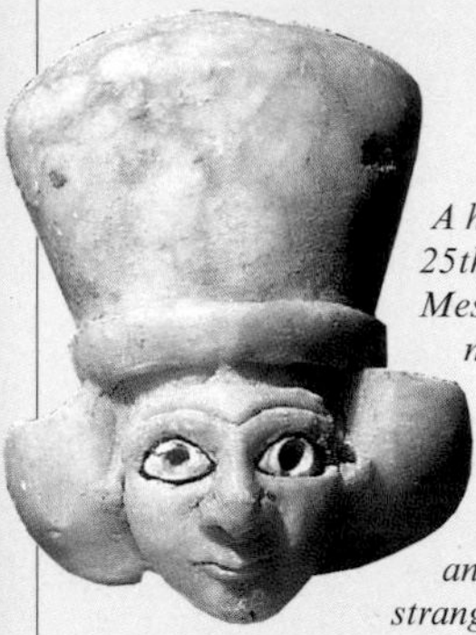

A head of Ishtar, from 25th-century-BC Mesopotamia. As the mother of harlots, Ishtar decreed that all Babylonian virgins should serve in her temple and perform sex with strangers, at least once in their lives. Sacred prostitutes could gain immense power. According to the law they were entitled to inherit from their fathers and brothers and participate in the selling and running of family property. They were generally well-educated and considered the equals of men.

At the Corinthian temple of Aphrodite Pandemos, men queued up to choose a young woman. The rite began when the woman, trained by priests and priestesses, bathed the man and together they made obeisance. The man placed money on the lap of the prostitute as an offering to the goddess. Sexual intercourse, with the couple representing the divine male and female principles, completed the process of purification. According to a Greek commentator, "the sacred whores ... mellowed the nature of man".

has survived about the origins of the practice, theories abound. It is possible that the sex act of the Goddess in the sacred marriage with her son–lover was being emulated by her worshippers and consecrated to her. Alternatively, victorious generals in antiquity may have dedicated their female prisoners to temples of the Goddess. It is also possible that the tradition grew out of a tribal system incorporating *jus primae noctis*, whereby a chief had the right to take the maidenhead of a new bride.

Chiefs were often representatives of the deity, in which case the process was believed to be a form of ceremonial purification, an idea which recurs in the custom of the sacred prostitute. The historian, Strabo, writing in Rome in the 1st century BC, described how "a very beautiful virgin of most distinguished heritage" was offered to the god, and then had sex until "the natural purification of her body was accomplished".

As a rule, a young girl was offered to the temple after she had passed puberty, and had to have sexual intercourse with at least one man before she could leave.

A young girl dancing in worship of Krishna, at the Trakamba temple in India. Dance is a traditional form of Hindu worship. A devadasi *has to dance for her temple god on certain ceremonial occasions when he is being fed, and the dance itself can be seen as a symbolic form of sexual congress.*

From creatrix to harlot

The concept of a supreme Goddess has attracted the special enmity of those religions that make absolute distinctions between the spirit and the flesh, and believe that salvation must be attained by denying, and ultimately abandoning, the latter. These transcendent creeds posit a divinity who is separated from nature, and abhor one who pervades it. One of the ways in which the priests of such religions chose to denigrate the female divinity was by dividing her essential nature and assigning her spirituality, wisdom and virginity to an abstract male principle, and her physical qualities and appetites to a female principle, which they considered to be all too concrete.

The most obvious way of attacking the female divinity was by attacking her priestesses, who were often prostitutes (see pp.98–9), and by denying the sanctity of sex, which played such an important role in Goddess worship. Often this also involved denying the possibility that any woman could be holy. The 6th-century-BC Greek philosopher, Pythagoras, for example, decreed: "There is a good principle which has created order, light and man; and a bad order which has created chaos, darkness and woman." Much later, the Christian St Paul exemplified the attitude that sex was a regrettable need within humankind, which was best avoided, and stated that it is preferable for "man not to touch woman".

When the Hebrews invaded Canaan (see p.38), they passed laws that robbed the sacred prostitute of her previous

LILITH

The Sumerian Lilitu was absorbed into Judaic folklore and scriptural commentary as Lilith, the essence of depraved sexuality, created either as the female half of Adam or from "filth and impure sediment instead of dust or earth". She fell foul of Yahweh when she demanded to mount Adam during sex and refused to accept that she was his inferior. She discovered Yahweh's secret name and demanded wings which enabled her to fly away from heaven and live in freedom in a cave by the sea. However, she had to leave her children behind.

In her new existence she became the mistress of the sea demon Ashmodai and produced hundreds of monsters by him each day. She also crept into men's beds and caused them to ejaculate in their sleep, wasting their semen, or else she stole their emissions to inseminate herself and produce more demons, in revenge for the loss of her heavenly children.

A relief of Lilith-Inanna, wearing a lunar crown, from Mesopotamia c.*2000BC.*

status, including the rights of inheritance that she had enjoyed since the very first records were kept in ancient Sumeria. Gradually, the temples came to serve precisely the opposite of their former function. Men prayed for spirituality and release from the pleasures of the flesh in the same locations where they had once venerated the act of sexual congress. Temples were no longer places of joyful worship, but of penance and fear. The sexual activity of the female ceased to be treated as a process of purification, and the union with the divine was attenuated to an exclusively spiritual procedure. The Goddess and her representatives were condemned as being profane.

In India, by contrast, the sacred prostitute is merely regarded, at least by the government and the educated elite, as an embarrassment – an archaism that has no place in a modern state. Sacred prostitution thrived in India until it came under attack from British colonial powers, and later from Anglophile Indians. The first law against sacred prostitution was passed in Madras, in 1947, but most Indian states are content merely to discourage the practice, which is gradually dying out.

A necklace worn by the prostitute-priestess of Inanna in the city of Ur in the 3rd millennium BC.

Even after the female embodiment of the divine had supposedly been purged from the temples of Judaism, traces of her remained in the form of Sophia (wisdom), who had at one time been known as *prunikos* (unclean, or prostitute). In the biblical book of Proverbs, Sophia speaks about the creation of the world and reminisces about her nearness to the male deity "rejoicing in the habitable part of his earth", and continues that "my delights were with the sons of men". This could be a veiled reference to sacred prostitution, although elsewhere in the same text the sexual rites of Ishtar are identified with wickedness and corruption. Ishtar is named the Great Whore, as is Babylon, the city of which she is the ruling deity. She is condemned as the worst kind of temptress, seducing men ruthlessly: "But if he go wrong, she will forsake him and give him over to his own ruin."

Eve in the garden of Eden, a Turkish miniature c. AD1595. The early Christian Church credited the first woman with the introduction of sin in general – and sex in particular – into the world.

The Goddess of love

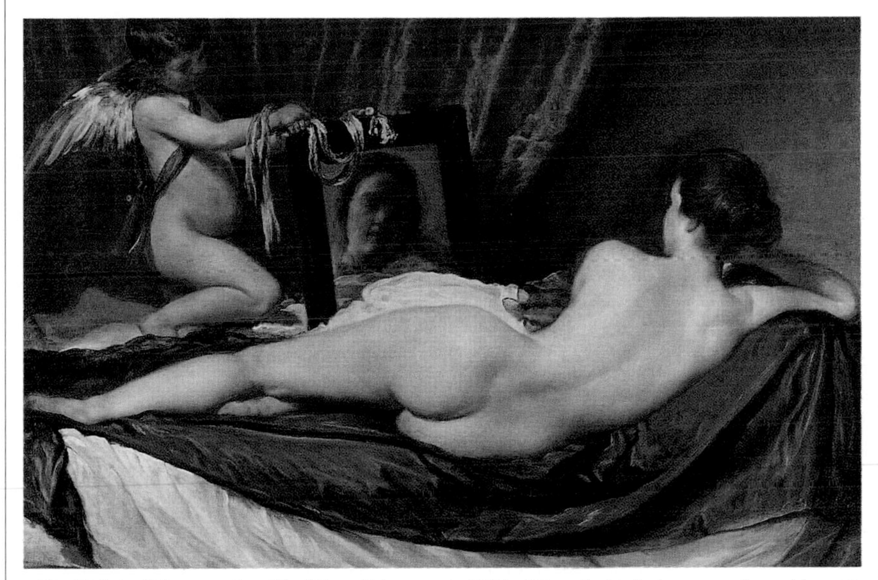

The Toilet of Venus, *painted by Diego Velasquez in 1651. Although chiefly known as the goddess of sensual love, Venus was also the goddess of growth and the beauty of orderly nature.*

Love goddesses have historically tended to be the best known, most popular and most frequently petitioned divinities of any pantheon. The largest temple in Rome belonged to Venus, and stood on the Circus Maximus. Love goddesses typically share a number of common features: they are generally connected to water and have a particular fondness for bright or colourful objects, especially flowers. One of the most famous composite flower/love goddesses is the Aztec Xochiquetzel, known as the "bitch-mother", who encouraged sexual freedom and survived a great flood, after which she and her mate peopled the world. Love goddesses are often swathed in jewels: for example, the Indian Lakshmi as she emerged from the churning of the ocean, or Oshun, wife of Shango (see p.48) with her penchant for precious metals, gems and self-adornment. The Voodoo goddess Erzulie's long and elaborate toilette includes adorning herself with flowers, jewels and numerous other forms of decoration. A certain degree of narcissism and the enjoyment of flattery are part of the love goddess's character, and she is usually also a goddess of beauty and sex.

The Indian goddess Lakshmi was originally called Sri, and was a manifestation of Devi-Shakti, the sexual principle that, by its exertions, generated the universe. However, through successive incarnations she was increasingly bound to her husband, Vishnu the Preserver. As Radha, she was a married woman who entertained an immense

passion for Krishna, the avatar of Vishnu. Some of the most highly-charged erotic poetry of India is about Radha stealing away from her mortal husband to meet Krishna.

In these poems, Radha's adultery reflects her original character as a fickle goddess of luck, and an indiscrimate goddess of fertility to whom, when aroused, fidelity mattered little. Most love goddesses were indiscriminate in their carnal pursuits, although generally they loved one partner above all others. For example, Freya, whose lovers included virtually the entire Scandinavian pantheon, remained inwardly faithful to her preferred mate and brother, Frey, just as the Canaanite Anath did to Baal. The Greek goddess Aphrodite was, according to some accounts, married to Hephaestus the ugly, crippled artisan, whom she regularly cuckolded. Her passion for the beautiful youth, Adonis, was celebrated annually (see pp.80–81). Her attachment to Ares the warrior was widely known and her union with the wine god Dionysus resulted in the birth of Priapus, the god with the perpetually engorged penis. Eventually, fed up with her constant infidelities, Hephaestus snared her in an invisible mesh while she lay with Ares, and invited the rest of the gods to watch. Aphrodite gave birth to Eros and several other children as a result of this enmeshed mating.

The Roman love goddess Venus also had frequent liaisons with the war god Mars and according to some traditions was even married to him. Love and war

AVATARS OF THE GODDESS

A Babylonian seal c.2000 BC, showing a politician being led to the king by the priestess of Ishtar. Congress between the king and a woman who represented the goddess was a magical guarantee of the fertility of the land.

The priestess of a love goddess was very rarely just the deity's servant. On certain ceremonial and ritual occasions she could embody the goddess, and bestow her sexual favours on male worshippers so as to ensure the prosperity of the land, the city or the kingdom (in ancient Sumeria, a king established his right to rule by sleeping with the high priestess of Ishtar).

Because ancient love goddesses were imbued with the responsibility of creation, they were frankly sexual. However, the definition of their love had always been wide, including mother love and *agape*, the love of a friend, as well as *eros*, or sexual love. As female promiscuity gradually became increasingly taboo in many societies, the love goddess suffered some redefinition, although her immense popularity ensured that no single aspect of her could be dispensed with.

The Greek philosopher Plato, among others, distinguished between Aphrodite Urania whose love was spiritual (or divine) and Aphrodite Pandemos who represented secular (or profane) love and was known in Corinth as Porne. Sacred prostitutes (see pp.98–9) became the servants of only the profane aspect of the love goddess.

The temple of the Vestal Virgins, which was said to be the oldest place of worship in Rome.

VESTAL VIRGINS AND SACRED WHORES

The Vestal Virgins of Rome (see pp.116–17) at first appear to be the antithesis of the sacred prostitute. They were subject to a strict code of conduct and fulfilled a number of temple duties, including keeping the fires burning in the goddess Vesta's inner sanctum. They were scourged for most transgressions, but the loss of their virginity was punishable by death.

However, the *hierodule*, or sacred servant of goddesses such as Aphrodite or Inanna (see pp.98–9), was subject to a similarly stringent code of behaviour, living by her goddess's laws, tending to the cleanliness of the temple and participating fully in its ceremonies. Vesta was a hearth goddess, and the hearth was the altar of many temples, around which *hierodules* danced as part of their duties. The 20th-century scholar and poet Robert Graves has speculated that the Vestals were originally whore-priestesses, who took part in royal orgies to procreate children, from whom the king of Rome was chosen. According to Graves, the law obliging the Vestals to retain their virginity was introduced by King Lucius Tarquinius Superbus in the 6th century BC.

also have an affinity in the myths of other cultures. The love goddess Erzulie originated in Benin, West Africa, but was transported across the Atlantic on slave ships to become a dominant divinity of the Voodoo pantheon. Erzulie's official consort is the sea god Agive but her constant companion is Ogoun, the god of war.

In Voodoo, the creative principle is shared by the male and female divine and the goddess therefore does not receive sole credit for the genesis of the world. She does, however, represent the difference between humans and animals. She is the constant possibility of perfection which can never be achieved, the impossible dream which fuels endeavour. Erzulie is famous for her attraction to handsome men, even among humans, and she insists that they dress and dance flawlessly and are impeccably clean. The men she chooses become lovesick, and will not look at any mortal woman.

In common with her counterparts, Erzulie has a passion for jewellery, flowers and clothes and takes great pleasure in singing and dancing. But beneath the gaiety lies an enduring rage, personified by a terrifying supplementary manifestation as Erzulie Ge-Rouge. Voodoo worship in Haiti includes a ceremony in which the *loa*, or divinity, of Maitress

(an aspect of Erzulie, also known as Erzulie Freda Dahomey) possesses a chosen woman. The ritual begins with an extended and complex ceremony in which the possessed woman purifies herself and, after satisfying the goddess's high standards of cleanliness, begins slowly to anoint herself with perfume and powder, helped by assistants. After dressing herself in a leisurely manner she drinks wine and eats from among the sweet cakes and other delicacies that have been presented to her. When at last she is ready, she emerges among the people. The males in the audience are clearly her favourites and receive far more of Erzulie's attention than the women. She chooses the most attractive men as her dance partners, but anyone who has imbibed hard liquor is automatically ineligible. Her devotees among the women merit a little attention but the rest are acknowledged only by a wave with the crook of her little finger.

Among the merriment and the sometimes frenetic dancing, the ceremony reaches a startling climax. Erzulie Ge-Rouge, the grief-stricken aspect of the goddess, takes over the individual and weeps copiously about the things that have gone wrong in the world, complaining that she is unloved and lamenting her unfulfilled dreams. The transformation of the possessed individual is astonishing and unexpected. The self-loving, ecstatic figure of moments before transforms into someone whose fists are rolled into balls so tight that the nails cut into the palm and draw blood. She cries herself into a paroxysm of rage which ultimately paralyses her. This is the archetypal,

Greta Garbo imitating an Asian slave-priestess in the film Mata Hari *(1931).*

savagely weeping Goddess lamenting the death of her son–lover (see p.80). In the Voodoo of Haiti, the Christian version of the weeping goddess, the lamenting Virgin Mary, has been absorbed into Erzulie-worship.

It has been argued that the love goddess has also survived into the 20th-century in the female cinema stars of India and the West. These "screen-goddesses" have devoted cult followings, from whom they repeatedly receive gifts and requests for favours (if only of autographs). They are revered entirely through their images, and spawn thousands of secular "priestesses", desperate to imitate, and thereby embody them.

Mary Magdalene

A detail from the Issenheim altarpiece, by Mathias Grünewald (1455–1528), showing the Virgin Mary and Mary Magdalene praying together at the foot of the Cross.

Mary Magdalene seems to be the antithesis of the mother of Christ – the embodiment of the sexual element entirely excised from the nature of the Virgin (see pp.122–3). However, there is a profusion of women called Mary throughout the New Testament, and it has always been unclear how many of them were actually the Magdalene. She is identified by name in the Gospel according to Luke as one of the companions travelling with Jesus after he set out from the house of the Pharisee, Simon (it is mentioned that earlier "seven demons had gone out" from her). The Magdalene is usually equated with the "sinner" who was rebuked by Simon for washing the feet of Christ in rich ointments, although this woman is not named in any of the Gospels except that of John, where she is described as Mary of Bethany, the sister of Lazarus. The theologian Origen (*c*.185–254) distinguished between Mary of Bethany, Mary Magdalene, and the unnamed sinner, and the Greek Orthodox Church gave each of these women a different feast day. In the Western Church, since the 6th century, the three have been combined under the name of Mary Magdalene, with a feast day on July 22.

Mark states that the risen Christ appeared first to Mary Magdalene, "out of whom he had cast seven devils". John also describes the Magdalene as the first person to meet Christ after he rose from the tomb, although at first she mistook him for a gardener. These are perhaps the first hints that the Magdalene may have entered Christianity from an older tradition in which she was a goddess. Inanna and Ishtar of Mesopotamia both passed through seven gates of hell on their way into and out of the underworld; and "gardener" was a common title for the son–lover of Inanna after he had returned from the land of death. The 20th-century scholar Geoffrey Ashe cites ancient Coptic texts in which the Magdalene appears to a dreamer to say that she is one with the Virgin – so that the pair are merely aspects of a composite Mary, who combines the dual nature of virgin and whore in the same way as Ishtar, Inanna and numerous other goddesses.

GNOSTICISM

Mary Magdalene is a central figure in Gnosticism, an ancient mystical philosophy that both drew from and profoundly influenced Christianity in the 2nd and 3rd centuries. Its followers believed that *gnosis*, or knowledge, was the only way to approach the divine.

As a penitent whore, the Magdalene was steeped in worldly knowledge, and as a confidant or, in some traditions, consort of Christ, she was a vessel of spiritual wisdom. The 4th-century scourge of heretics, Epiphanius, alleged that certain break-away sects of Christians placed Mary in a sexual trinity with Jesus, and another woman whom the Messiah had produced from his own side. In the *Pistis Sophia*, an Egyptian text written in the 3rd century, Jesus repeatedly praises Mary's understanding, and states that "Mary Magdalene and John, the virgin, shall tower over all my disciples and over all men who shall receive the mysteries in the Ineffable".

Each of the 60 or more Gnostic sub-sects offered its own account of the Creation, the Fall and Redemption, but, in general, Gnostics aimed to unite with God through intense learning and a passionate devotion that was tantamount to sexual love – hence the veneration of the sexual act condemned by the ecclesiastical fathers. To most Gnostics, those who aspired to the Divine were spiritual and good. Those who desired physical pleasure as an end in itself were materialistic and evil. The individual with most spiritual potential was the one who sought the Divine through experience of the physical. The Magdalene was the archetype of such a person.

The Magdalene, *painted by Antonio Correggio (1489–1534).*

In the popular imagination, Mary Magdalene is indelibly connected with carnal sin. The seven demons exorcized from her are thought to represent her sexuality, and wherever she is named in the Gospels she is the embodiment of the passionate penitent. According to the 13th-century Italian hagiographer, Jacob of Voragine, Mary meant "bitter tears" and "Magdalene" meant "remaining guilty". Nevertheless, it is the Magdalene's forbidden sexuality that makes her such a potent figure in Christian thinking. Christ loved her for, rather than in spite of, her immense sins, and as his regular companion she aroused the envy of the Apostles. Her post-biblical tradition cites her as being inseparable from the Virgin Mary until she was cut adrift on a boat and found herself on the shores of France, where she pursued an illustrious missionary career filled with conversions and wonders. Her body miraculously appeared in the crypt of St Maximin's church in Aix-en-Provence in 1279.

Mary Magdalene has not just been remembered for her renounced sexuality. Voragine, in his *Golden Legend*, described her as the mother of kings, and the pre-Charlemagne rulers of France, the Merovingians, claimed descent through her. Because they also believed that she was the consort of Christ, they were in effect claiming descent from God.

Virgin, Mother and Crone

In the mythology of a number of cultures, and in modern pagan feminist thought, the Goddess represents three phases of the female lifespan, which correspond to the lunar cycle. The new moon is the virgin, the full moon is the sexually productive woman, usually described as either a mother or whore, and the old moon is the crone. Goddess worshippers have given this three-fold manifestation the title of triple Goddess. Each of her aspects serves a particular and separate need in society, and the possibility of invoking only one of them makes the Goddess more accessible and less complex.

The triple Goddess exists in most cultures. Each manifestation may itself have three aspects, so that the triplication of the Goddess is sometimes further magnified into six, nine, twelve, and so on, earning the Goddess the description of the "One of a Thousand Names". Celtic goddesses often appear in groups of three or nine, while the Norse warrior-maids, the Valkyries, appear in multiples of nine and their compatriots the Norns embody three-fold time as Past, Present and Future.

In this Apache puberty ceremony, a girl (shown on the left), becomes a woman. She is sponsored by an older woman (shown on the right) who teaches her practical and spiritual lessons.

Cycles of the Goddess

The Goddess, like Nature, has many qualities, which often succeed each other in cycles of three. She is recurrently fallow, fertile and productive, mirroring the female cycle of menstrual bleeding, ovulating and child-bearing. Alternatively, her changing forms may reflect the entire span of a woman's life, which can be conceived as having three phases: the pre-pubertal maiden, who is not yet fertile; the woman who is fruitful and, ideally, prolific; and the post-menopausal, autonomous figure who has attained wisdom and the right to command the respect of others.

This three-fold female cycle finds expression in many cultures through the manifestation of the Goddess as virgin, mother and crone. In this form she may be related to other sets of cosmic triplets: the three stages of the continuum of existence (birth, life and death); the three points of time and space (past, present and future; and heaven, earth/sea and underworld); and the phases of the moon (new, full and waning). Female trinities are perhaps most conspicuous in the legends of the Greeks, whose goddesses and monsters regularly appear in threes – for example, the Fates, the Horae and the Gorgons. Hera, the wife of Zeus, was worshipped at Stymphalos as child, bride and widow, and Demeter, Kore and Hecate are often described as forming a trinity. The earliest known representation of what appears to be a triple Goddess dates back to 13000BC. It was carved from the rock of a cave in Angles-sur-l'Anglin, France, and consists of three huge female figures standing on a bison.

According to a number of the Shakta (Goddess-worshipping) traditions of

Transitions between the phases of a woman's life are often marked by rituals of initiation, as in this New Guinean puberty ceremony.

THE ONE AND THE MANY

The complex multifaceted nature of the Goddess often creates confusion in the reading of myths, and debates rage over the relationship between, for example, Kore and Demeter (see pp.70–71). In the opinion of some, the first is the virginal daughter, the second the sexually experienced mother. Others hold that the one is the young form of the other, so that both are aspects of a single being. Some scholars argue for the diversity of goddesses – particularly those from different waves of a heterogeneous culture, such as that of India – claiming that each goddess originates as the expression of the cultural needs or aspirations of a different people. However, the most complex cultures yield the most eloquent arguments for oneness, with examples such as the multiple forms of Kali (see pp.138–9).

Hinduism, the all-male Trimurti (Brahma the Creator, Vishnu the Preserver and Shiva the Destroyer) is merely a reflection of the absolute power of Devi, who contains these three functions within herself.

The Goddess-as-maiden is usually identified with the crescent moon. She is simultaneously titillating and intimidating, and often displays a virgin–warrior dualism (see pp.140–41), in which innocence threatened is transformed into defensive ferocity, characterized by the weapons of warrior and hunter goddesses such as Athene and Artemis. In these figures, chaste innocence is linked to wild, unharnessed instinct, which extends to the patronage of uncontrolled sexual activity.

The relationship of the Goddess to the male in her second phase (the full moon) may be expressed as that of either mother or whore. In many myths of the Goddess, both these expressions of mature sexuality are seen as equally valid acts of creation: the activities of the divine prostitute help to ensure the fertility of the land. However, the mature Goddess can also be sexually predatory, and suck the vital energy out of her lover to gratify herself, or as a sacrifice (see pp.80–81).

Finally, in her crone phase, she is the dark, disappearing moon which plunges the world into obscurity. She combines the opposing roles of ruthless judge (see pp.48–9) and unstinting guide to the mysteries of the underworld (see pp.70–71). The crone retains a powerful appetite for sex and, like Hecate, Circe and the Cailleach Bheur, copulates with young men by deception, coercion or sheer charisma.

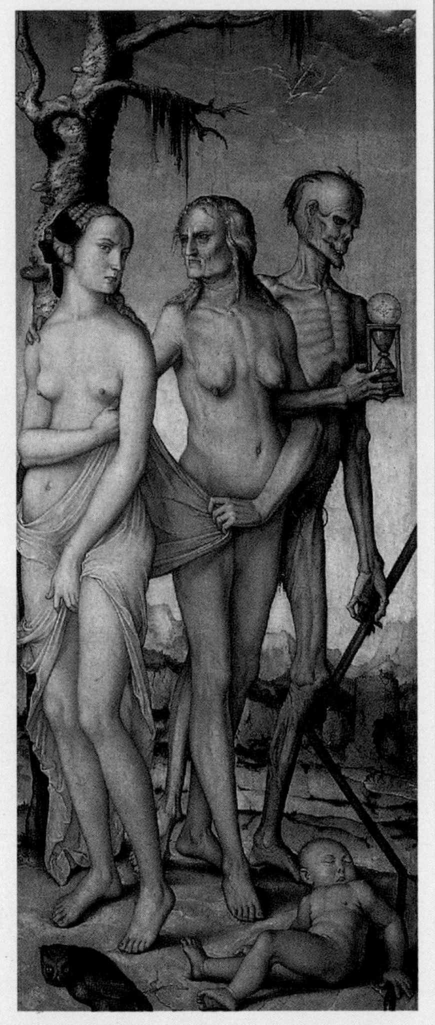

The Ages of Life and Death, *by Hans Baldung (1484–1545). Like many Renaissance painters, Baldung portrayed the aging of a woman specifically in terms of her sexuality and fecundity. Comparable representations of the Three Ages of Man tend to concentrate more on the passing of beauty or innocence into strength, and the mellowing of strength into wisdom.*

The changing woman

The onset of menstruation – the moment when a girl changes into a woman – has become a focus of rituals among peoples worldwide. Often these involve women acting out mythical stories, whose precise meaning and significance remain a closely guarded secret. The women of the Pitjantjatjara Aborigines of the Western Desert of Australia perform a seven-act ritual drama, whose first stages depict the discovery of food, water and shelter. The third act portrays the first menstruation of the initiate, whose older sister advises her on the art of sex. In the last four acts, the the pubertal adolescent, recognizing sexual desire, seeks and finds a man of her choice (played by a postmenopausal woman). In a variant of the ritual, one of the young women is abducted and raped, after which all the women apprehend and mutilate the rapist. The finale in both versions consists of celebratory songs and dances. The ritual is a source of great enjoyment to all the participants.

The Changing Woman of the Navajo and Apache Native Americans is a Nature deity known by many different names, including White Shell Woman, who brought light to the earth, or White Painted Woman, who in Chiricahua Apache tradition mothered monsterslayers. In myths of the Navajo, once a branch of the Apache peoples, she is Estsan Atlehi ("Mother of All") who changes her clothing four times a year as she emerges from the four doors of

THE PUBERTY RITUAL

Changing Woman is a living divinity, and her worshippers feed her, speak to her and give her gifts. She is venerated through storytelling, song and discussion. The most vivid and important tribute to her is made in the form of the ritual that marks the onset of menstruation (*na ih es* in Apache).

According to a Chiricahua tradition, at one time all the Apaches lived together at Hot Springs, where they received their sacred laws before they dispersed across the southwestern USA. It was here that White Painted Woman (Changing Woman) gave them the menstrual rite, in the form of explicit instructions that are still followed to the present day.

her heavenly abode to create the seasons. She rises with the spring flowers, matures with the summer, ages with the autumn and goes to sleep with the winter. Changing Woman represents all the phases of the female, but most particularly the moment when a girl turns into a woman. This transition is believed to be beneficial to the entire group, and is marked by feasting and ritual.

It was from Changing Woman that humans received knowledge and wisdom, the lunar and menstrual cycles, songs, celebration and the concept of the quest. She also taught the Navajo how to build the dome-topped huts called *hogans*. The dominant divinity of the Navajo pantheon, she was propelled into the world along with other holy people by the force of an underground flood. She then created the Navajo ancestors, and taught them how to live in harmony with Nature. In one variant she was found on a mountain-top by First Man and First Woman who brought her up as their daughter. When she was approaching womanhood, her adoptive parents took her back to the spot where they had found her and performed the first puberty ritual. In all her traditions, she then married the sun and gave birth to the twins Monster-slayer and Child-of-the-Water, who rid the world of all monsters. Changing Woman offers security against misfortune, as well as sustenance in the form of food, shelter and clothing. Today she lives in a splendid "western mansion".

During the four days of her puberty ritual, the girl receives the undivided attention of an older woman who pampers her and gives her massages and advice. One of the purposes of the ritual is to charge up an amulet with magical energy that the initiate can use when she in turn loses her child-bearing powers.

The feast begins at the onset of the first female bleeding and lasts for four days, during which the medicine-man chants prayers appealing to Changing Woman to infuse the girl with her essence so that she might be transformed into a productive and caring woman, to be honoured and venerated by her people. In response, and "travelling on his chants", Changing Woman's spirit comes to reside in the adolescent, who becomes the embodiment of the goddess for the four sacred days.

On the first and fourth day, the initiate walks clockwise, accompanied by the high-pitched wailing of women, around a basket containing pollen, feathers, paint and grain which are counted among the sacred elements of the ritual. At various stages there may be feasting, storytelling and dancing, initiated by masked dancers called *gahe*. Changing Woman's intercourse with the sun is enacted by the initiate during the course of the ceremony. By its conclusion, she has become a woman and a symbol of peace and prosperity for her people.

The many faces of Ishtar

Inanna–Ishtar was a goddess of war. One of her names was Labbatu, or "lioness", and a Sumerian poem addresses her with the words: "Like an awesome lion you annihilated with your venom the hostile and disobedient."

Ishtar, more than any other goddess, demonstrates the multiple character of the female divinity, and it is probably for this reason that so many of the major and minor goddesses of Greece, Egypt and the Near East were subsumed into her. Ishtar was Assyrian and Babylonian in origin. She is usually equated with Inanna, the multiple goddess of ancient Sumer (which lay to the south of Babylon). However, some scholars contend that she is more closely related to the Semitic goddess, Astarte, and eventually assimilated Inanna only because the two figures shared so many attributes.

In Babylonian mythology, Ishtar's parentage is uncertain: she could be the daughter of either the moon or the sun, although she eventually replaced the moon god in the pantheon and ruled the lunar calendar, which associated her with seasonal growth and the harvesting of crops. Her patronage of the stars linked her to other virgin–warriors, such as Anahita (see p.140), and to divine mothers such as Hathor the Heavenly Cow. In the form of the morning star – when she was known as Zib – she was said to govern human desire.

Ishtar features in two major Mesopotamian myths. Firstly, in a tale similar to that of Inanna (see pp.76–9) she made a journey to the underworld. In Ishtar's case this was to redeem her son–lover Tammuz, who was sacrificed following their holy marriage. Her quest is described in *The Descent of Ishtar to the Underworld*, composed at the end of the 2nd millennium BC. Whereas Inanna was respectful and patient on her quest, Ishtar threatened her way through the gates of the underworld: "If thou openest not the gate so that I cannot enter, I will smash the door, I will shatter the bolt ... I will raise up the dead, eating the living, so that the dead will outnumber the living." In Ishtar's absence, plants withered and the urge to mate

An 8th-century-BC figurine of Astarte or Ishtar playing a tambourine, possibly in her role as sacred harlot. Ishtar's prostitute-priestesses worshipped her through song as well as sex.

The face of Ishtar, mistress of the night, on an ivory plaque carved in the 8th century BC, which was unearthed in the Assyrian palace in the city of Nimrud, in ancient Iraq.

MAGIC AND THE LAW

The zodiac was known as the girdle of Ishtar. The idea that the movements of the planets affect life on earth can be traced back to the earliest known astrological calendars, which were created in Sumeria in 3200BC. Because Ishtar was the queen of heaven, she ruled the stars and planets that, in turn, governed human behaviour. As a result, Ishtar was also giver of the law, which in ancient times was closely associated with magic. Throughout history, the commandments of kings and governments have been issued with taboos and curses attached to them. All forms of magic have at various times been the subject of rigorous and detailed legislation.

Divination was a standard part of Mesopotamian courtly life, as were the magical rites and bloody sacrifices intended to divert sinister prognostications. Astrology was only one of the forms of divination governed by Ishtar. As mistress of the night, she also formulated dreams and planted omens in them, or entered them in order to communicate details of the future.

died away in humans and animals, until the goddess rescued her lover and returned to earth with him. Ishtar was forced to sacrifice her son–lover annually, in order to uphold the laws of Nature and regrowth. She maintained a weeping vigil in his absence, and plunged repeatedly down into the world of the dead to save him.

The second great myth of Ishtar appears in slightly varying forms in the earliest Mesopotamian tablets of the *Epic of Gilgamesh* and the Akkadian variant generally known as the *Standard Version* (written some 1,000 years later). As goddess of love, Ishtar offered herself to the hero Gilgamesh, who responded with scorn. His invective disguised his fear of death on the goddess's bridal couch: each of Ishtar's lovers became the personification of Tammuz, and was eventually sacrificed by her. Ishtar was incensed by Gilgamesh's behaviour, and, with her father's help, sent a gigantic heavenly bull to gore him. However, the bull was killed by Gilgamesh's friend, Enkidu. While Gilgamesh and Enkidu boasted about their prowess, Ishtar collected together her priestesses and mourned the animal. In revenge, she sent Enkidu a sickness that caused him a slow and lingering death. As the horrified Gilgamesh watched the indignities suffered by his friend's decaying body, he vowed never to die, and embarked on his great, unsuccessful quest to find immortality (see p.45).

The virgin as classical ideal

Athene and Odysseus, by Guiseppe Mantua (1717–1784). The virgin Athene guided Odysseus as he voyaged home from Troy and evaded numerous magical seductresses, such as Circe and the Sirens.

The goddesses of ancient Greece and Rome who were personified as virgins did not always require a similar chastity in their devotees. Although the virgin–warrior aspect of Athene was revered at the Parthenon in Athens, the nearby Erechtheion was a temple to a warmer, more domestic face of the same goddess. A statue of Gaia, the mother goddess, rose from the soil near Athene's altar. It was rumoured that, in parts of Greece, priestesses of Athene conducted orgiastic celebrations while wearing Gorgon masks. Artemis also used to preside over orgiastic festivals. In general, the priestesses of the Goddess emulated her whorelike, rather than her virginal, nature (see pp.98–9).

A notable exception was the Roman goddess Vesta, who corresponds to the Greek Hestia. Both were fire incarnate and therefore formless, so they were not represented by anthropomorphic icons. This may in part explain why Vesta is less conspicuous than the other goddesses with whom she shares a place as one of Rome's twelve great divinities.

Vesta's was the most important of the hearth-cults vigorously practised by the royalty of the time. In the Senate, the social and magical merits of Vesta's hearth earned her the accolade "She of the Senate". Vesta received the first sacrifices of the season and was first to be invoked in prayer and oath. Her priestesses were the Vestal Virgins. It was their job to keep the sacred fire alight until they ceremonially doused it on the

first day of March. The Vestal Virgins represented the daughters of the nobility and were regarded as the "essence of Rome". The chief Vestal acted as an ambassador at times of war.

The Virgins were chosen by the Pontifus Maximus – the high priest and only male official of Vesta – from up to twenty candidates of between five and ten years old. Two to six of these girls were appointed for a term of approximately five years, although historical records show that they served as long as thirty years. During this time they remained virgins. Although free to marry once they had discharged their religious duties, they rarely did so, either from a continued commitment to the temple or because it was considered an ill omen. The punishment for a serving Vestal Virgin who broke her oath and lay with a man was to be imprisoned without food or water until she died. On June 15 every year, the temple – in the Forum of Rome – was swept and the refuse thrown into the Tiber. This was the last day of the festival of Vesta, and represented the symbolic purification of the goddess.

Diana and her Nymphs Surprised by Actaeon, *by Andrea Vaccaro (1598–1670). Because he saw the naked form of the goddess, Actaeon was turned into a stag and torn apart by hounds.*

TEMPLES OF THE VIRGIN

The Roman virgin-goddess Diana is identical with her Greek counterpart, Artemis. Her cult was extensive and generated a number of major temples, the most famous and important of which was the temple of Ephesus (see p.126).

In Capua the goddess was Diana Tifatina, Mistress of the Woods, who drew her name from the "holm-oak grove". She was, however, intimately linked to the city – according to legend, she possessed a sacred hind, with whose well-being the preservation of Capua was bound up. Her bond with wooded places continues in Aricia, in perhaps her most famous cult-centre at Speculum Dianae on the shores of Lake Nemi, where her temple was set in the middle of a grove. It was here that she is said to have resurrected her devotee, Virbius, as a monster, in which form he became chief priest at the sanctuary.

The presence in Rome of an icon resembling the multi-breasted Artemis of Ephesus suggests an attempt to exploit the fabled antiquity of the Ephesian temple, and transfer the headquarters of the cult from Aricia to the centre of the Roman Empire.

No myths concerning Vesta have survived to the present day, except for a fragment in which a donkey, her sacred animal, saved her from the attentions of Priapus, the ithyphallic (permanently erect) Roman god of gardens. However, her place of worship still exists in the Forum Romanum which was burned down in Nero's fire in 64BC and subsequently rebuilt in various stages. Inside was a veiled chamber, the *penus*, in which the sacred and magical objects of the goddess were stored and where Vesta's fire was kept continually guarded by the Vestal Virgins.

Virgins and lovers

The Rebirth of Aphrodite, a marble relief from the Ludovisi Throne, c.470BC. Despite her role as a love goddess, Aphrodite was ritually washed clean and reborn as a virgin once a year.

The virgin is only one part of the divine female trinity (along with mother–whore and crone), but her chastity is unaffected by the intense sexual activity of her other aspects. She is able to renew herself in a pristine state, either at will or as the result of ceremonies or festivals. This makes her the Ever-Virgin, a title shared by Ishtar, Anath and others who were nevertheless known for their numerous amorous ventures. Aphrodite, although described as a virgin, was Aphrodite Pandemos (of the people) whose temple in Corinth housed sacred prostitutes, any one of whom could embody the goddess while lying with a man (see pp.98–9). Among the few virgin goddesses who were steadfastly and literally chaste are the Greek goddess Artemis; her Roman equivalent, Diana; and Athene, daughter of Zeus, who were all associated with violence and action.

The repressed sexuality of the virgin is often described as a potential source of great energy, which may be extremely dangerous or destructive. This energy

THE LADY OF THE WILD THINGS

The virginal Goddess is often surrounded by animals which symbolize her unsocialized, pure and natural state. These may be creatures that are powerfully associated with sexuality, such as the goats of Aphrodite Pandemos. The mythical unicorn could only be approached by a virgin, and was often depicted in medieval Christian art in the presence of Mary.

The virgin is linked with animals in three main ways. As goddess of the hunt she may be surrounded by hounds, but she combines the function of hunting game with the task of protecting it. In addition, she may herself be an animal. The ancient Greek Kalligenia festival, in which young women put on bear-skins to worship Artemis, suggests that the goddess may once have been a bear. Artemis was also associated with a hind, which legend said would live as long as Athens.

Primeval myths reveal many other animal-shaped forms of the Goddess (see p.161). As Eurynome she is "fish-bodied" and as Echidna she possesses the body of a snake, like many nymphs. Ancient sources refer to Artemis and the Sumerian Lilitu as "owl-faced" and doves have also been closely associated with the Goddess since antiquity. The joining of two doves around an *omphalos* (navel) at Delphi represents to some scholars a depiction of the vulva (it has been described as "a clitoris between feathery labia").

The Goddess is also sometimes the mother of animals. For example, the Indian light-goddess Sanjana gave birth to the twin horses or Ashwini which towed their father's sun-chariot.

An 18th-century Indian miniature, showing Shiva and Parvati. Shiva's lingam *(penis) is thought to be a source of cosmic power, caused by the retention of semen, which is equated to the stuff of the soul. However, it is matched by an equal and opposite power generated by the rigour of Parvati's asceticism.*

is harnessed to positive effect by the warrior–virgins who act as guardians of all female mysteries. In this role, they are often the patrons of activities or events from which their virginity would seem to preclude them. For example, as the guardian of Nature, Diana was also a goddess of fertility and eventually became associated with childbirth and the cultivation of seed. The sexual fulfilment of women is another part of the female mysteries, and this may be why Diana patronized orgiastic festivals despite the fact that she herself shunned sex.

Athene was stricter: she was the personification of chastity and spurned natural motherhood. She turned down the marriage proposal of Hephaestus, the craftsman god of fire and volcanoes, although it had been sanctioned by Zeus. In the scuffle that followed, the god's sperm fell on her leg. Disgusted, Athene wiped the sperm away. It fell on Gaia, the earth, who was immediately fertilized and produced the hideous Ericthon, a future king of Athens. Athene brought him up as her own son, thus attaining a form of motherhood.

The Indian virgin Parvati became an ascetic only in order to acquire a mate in the form of Shiva, her male half. She starved and isolated herself until the male principle, in grieving for her, allowed the world to die, an event that underscored Parvati's own importance as a fertility figure. Indian myths that describe sexual abstinence all convey a sense of the vast and combustible energy that is conserved in the virgin or the ascetic.

Mothering the gods

In the earliest surviving mythologies, which derive from the Near East, the importance of the Goddess's procreative function was usually connected with the birth of a son, brought into the world as a saviour (see pp.80–81), who delivered humankind from extermination by ensuring the return of seasonal crops. In these myths and their associated ceremonies the Goddess was the instigator of her own son's death and the focus of the resulting rituals, but in later myths of a similar type her role became confined to conception and birth. The idea of deliverance came to dominate the legends, which now centred on the salvation of the human soul (as in the case of Jesus and Mary) or the quest for a homeland or empire (as in the case of Alexander the Great, whose mother, Olympias, was said to have conceived him after being visited by a god).

In this later tradition the Goddess was made human, and only her lover was divine. Her child was therefore often described as half man and half god. The confusion of history and myth helped to popularize the characters in religious legend, by making them seem real, while at the same time investing historical kings and heroes with an aura of divinity.

The Venus of Willendorf, c.*23000*BC. *The Paleolithic Venuses, although apparently fertility figures, are depicted without accompanying males, which may suggest that Paleolithic humans thought that men played no part in reproduction. If this is the case, to the people of the Paleolithic, every birth would have been an example of parthenogenesis.*

It is often assumed in the modern West that the idea of parthenogenesis – or virgin-birth – is confined to the Christian faith (see pp.122–3). In fact the origin of the myth is ancient, and may even date back into prehistory. Typically, a virgin (*parthenos*) conceives, often without knowledge of the father's divine identity. The child grows to be the saviour of a people, is killed (usually in the prime of his youth) and is then resurrected. The virgin is separated from her semi-divine son at a very early stage – possibly so that he is not influenced by her and remains free to receive the exclusive imprint of his holy father, and carry out his will.

The *modron–mabon* (mother–youth) motif prevalent in Celtic myth follows this pattern more obviously than most. For example, Arianrhod was the daughter of the Welsh goddess Danu. Her uncle, King Math, was compelled by a taboo to keep his feet in the lap of a virgin whenever he was not actively engaged in battle. After his first "footholder", Goewin, was deflowered, Math asked Arianrhod to take her place. She had to step across a magic rod to prove her virginity, but when she did so, twin boys dropped from between her legs. The second of these was taken away by Arianrhod's brother Gwydion and raised in a magic forest. Arianrhod, incensed by the calumny she had suffered, laid a curse that the boy, Lleu, would have no surname, could not be armed and would never have a human wife. Through elaborate magic and

BECOMING SACRED

The Buddha was born to a human couple, King Suddhodana and Queen Mahamaya. He was not divine, but because of his patient progress through a long succession of previous incarnations, he was born already bearing the marks of a great being (such as wheels or *cakras* on the soles of his feet).

Mahamaya knew she was giving birth to a hero because of a dream in which she was taken to a plateau by spirits, and a white elephant entered her womb. The birth itself was a magical event: it happened while the queen stood upright, grasping the branch of a tree. In fact, early depictions of the birth resemble ancient Indian images of tree spirits, suggesting that Mahamaya originated as a goddess figure in a pre-Buddhist Nature cult.

In later accounts of his birth, the Buddha sprang fully formed from Mahamaya's side. This legend may also be borrowed from an older tradition. Parsvanatha, the 9th- or 8th-century-BC Jain *tirthankara* (or saint) – the first *tirthankara* for whom there is historical evidence – was sometimes described as emerging from the side of his mother.

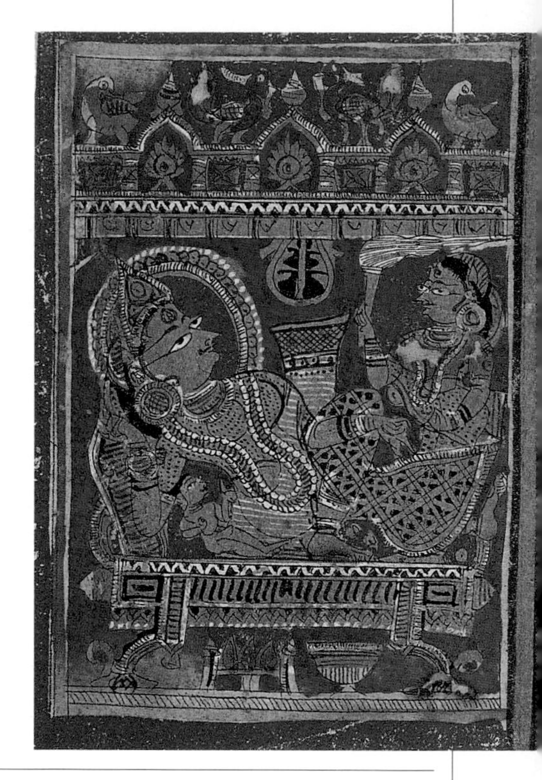

The birth of the Jain saint Parsvanatha, depicted in a 15th-century miniature from Gujarat, India.

trickery, Gwydion deceived Arianrhod into breaking the first two curses herself. To break the third, Math and Gwydion created Blodeuwedd, a woman made from flowers, to be Lleu's bride. Blodeuwedd, who appears to be the embodiment of a fertility goddess, betrayed her lover, Lleu, to his death, but his spirit hung on a tree and was resurrected on the following day.

The dying and reborn son often becomes a solar figure in many mythologies worldwide. In Ireland, St Patrick is said to have referred to Jesus as the "perfect Sun-Christ". Among the Aztecs, Coatlicue was the creatrix of all living things. She conceived the saviour Huitzilopchtli (the sun, who was the resurrection of the hummingbird god) when a bundle of feathers fell on her one day as she swept her temple. Her daughter Coyolxauhqui (the moon), infuriated by what she assumed was a sexual transgression, led her brothers, the stars, in a revolt against the goddess. The sun emerged from her womb to protect her, clad in armour and carrying weapons. He outshone his siblings, and became the saviour of the Aztecs, leading them in search of a homeland.

The Virgin Mary

The mythic prototype for the conception and birth of Christ was well-established in the Near East for many centuries before the Christian era. Mary, like many mother goddesses before her, such as Demeter, Isis, Astarte, Cybele and Atagartis, gave birth to a god incarnate who died for the salvation of humankind and returned, resurrected, on the third day.

The massive past and present Catholic veneration of the Virgin Mary (sometimes called Mariolatry) is certainly not justified by the Bible, which relegates her to the subsidiary position of the vessel which contained the Saviour. The Virgin is first mentioned at the Annunciation, when the angel Gabriel informs her that she will conceive the son of God. St Luke's Gospel includes a song known as the *Magnificat*, which exalts and praises Mary, but after describing her travels with Joseph, the birth of the baby Jesus and his veneration by shepherds and kings, the biblical narrative ignores her, except for brief encounters with her son and an appearance at the Crucifixion.

With her maternal role thus drastically minimized, her most famous appellation – that of mother – is something of a misnomer. Some theologians of the early Church tried to restrict her role to that of *Theotokos*, or God-bearer. However, the countless prayers, songs and paintings that celebrate her motherhood suggest the powerful influence of the ancient mother–son dyad (a pair of beings who are also one substance, see pp.80–81). The biblical account alone could not have inspired a popular love that amounts to deification, and it is much more likely that the Mother Goddess central to Celtic and Mediterranean worship permeated the new theology and perpetuated her own ancient tradition.

The Black Madonna of Notre-Dame-aux-Neiges, Aurillac, France.

Uniquely, the sexual interaction that is found between mother and son in the ancient prototypes is missing because, in order to meet Jewish criteria of womanly goodness, Mary had to be innocent of sexual experience. She also had to be docile and completely guiltless, which meant the eradication of her chthonic, or darker, side. Ironically, to many of the early Church fathers, it was Mary's lack of conventional Goddess attributes that guaranteed her divine status.

However, the ancient aspect of the Virgin-as-Goddess could not be expunged from popular consciousness, and Mary was soon credited with numerous pagan attributes and miracles, which helped to stimulate her increasing elevation. Mariolatrous cults proliferated and abound to this day within the safety and sanctity of the Catholic Church. The lack of biblical testimony has inspired many theologians to try to snuff out Mariolatry, but to no avail. The first relics and icons of the Virgin are usually dated back to the 5th century. The Roman Empress Eudocia (408–450) reportedly acquired Mary's shroud, and

in 438 sent her sister a portrait of the Virgin, thought to be painted by St Luke. The power of such objects to heal the sick is still widely reported throughout the Catholic world.

Some of the most extravagant miracles have been claimed for the so-called Black Madonnas. There have been many explanations for these figures: that they have been darkened by candle soot; that they are folk memories of ancient African idols; that they are pagan images brought back from the Crusades; and that they reflect the aspect of the ancient Goddess that is the dark ruler of the underworld.

THE IMMACULATE CONCEPTION

In the 4th century, the Virgin Mary was described as unspotted (*amiantos*) by St Gregory Nazianzen and as undefiled (*acheantos*) by Marcellus of Anycra. The Western Church already considered her incapable of sinning. The Greek theologians, by contrast, although they considered her exceptionally pure, attributed several sins to her, including vanity. St Augustine (354–430) declared Mary to be free of the Original Sin committed by Eve (see p.91), which was transmitted to every human in the womb. However, he stopped short of claiming that Mary had been conceived without sin – that is, without sexual intercourse.

The first suggestion that Mary herself was the product of a virgin birth was probably contained in the 2nd-century apocryphal *Book of James*. This suggests that Mary was a miraculous child, born to Anne and Joachim in their old age. Despite great theological controversy, the idea that the Virgin was immaculately conceived gained widespread popular acceptance, and the feast of the Conception of St Anne was probably celebrated from at least the 7th century. The Immaculate Conception became doctrine in 1854, in a bull issued by Pope Pius IX.

The Immaculate Conception, *by Zurbarán (1598–1664). Such paintings were part of a propaganda war between the Jesuits, who upheld the Immaculate Conception, and the sceptical Dominicans.*

Mary, Queen of Heaven

The death of the Virgin Mary is not mentioned anywhere in the Bible. There are no contemporary accounts of her burial, and there is no record of the whereabouts of her grave. The lack of any scriptural authority provoked feverish speculation among the faithful, and by the 4th or 5th centuries there were a number of texts that mentioned the circumstances of Mary's death. These texts were all heretical. Nevertheless, some of them became the basis for the medieval tradition of the Assumption: the belief that Mary ascended bodily into heaven.

Perhaps the earliest reference to the physical Assumption is in the anonymous *Obsequies of the Holy Virgin*, written in Syriac (an Aramaic dialect which is still the language of the Syrian Christian church) some time between the early part of the 3rd century and the middle of the 5th century. The *Obsequies* describes an argument between the saints, Paul, John, Peter and Andrew "before the entrance of the tomb of Mary". Jesus appears with the archangel Michael to decide between them, and then orders that the Virgin's body be carried up to heaven. The body is taken "to the Tree of Life" – a common goddess-symbol, dating from ancient Sumer – and is reunited with Mary's soul. In other 5th-century accounts of Mary's last days on earth, she does not die at all, but is carried into heaven while still alive, by Jesus, the Apostles, a host of angels and the prophets Moses, Enoch and Elias.

As the tradition of the Assumption became increasingly accepted, Mary's identity was irrevocably confirmed as divine. Like Isis, Ishtar and others before her, she was now the Queen of Heaven (at the evening service of Compline, when the sun has set, Mary is addressed: "Hail, Queen of Heaven ... whence the light of the world has arisen"). She also acquired the appellations of other supreme goddesses, including Star of the Sea and, most significantly, Mother of God.

In AD754, Emperor Constantine the Iconoclast urged the compulsory worship of Mary, barring the entry of Heaven to anyone "who does not confess the Holy Ever-Virgin, truly, properly the Mother of God, to be higher than any creature whether visible or invisible, and does not with sincere faith seek her intercession, as one having confidence in

A statue showing the Assumption of the Virgin Mary, by Pierre Puget (1620–94). In the first ever account of the Assumption, Mary was taken into heaven by the archangel Michael. However, most artists chose to represent her being lifted by a heavenly host.

her access to God". St Anselm of Canterbury (1033–1109) described Mary in the same terms as he might a goddess of Nature: "By you the elements are renewed, demons are trampled down and men are saved, even the fallen angels are restored to their places. O woman, so full and overflowing with grace, plenty flows from you to make all creatures green again."

The Immaculate Conception placed Mary above the sinful race of Adam and the Assumption exempted her from the Adamite law of death. However, because there was no biblical evidence that justified either the Virgin Sinless or the Virgin Assumed into Heaven, the church did not officially sanction these doctrines for centuries. The Immaculate Conception became an Article of Faith in 1854 and the Assumption as late as 1950. Both papal decisions were based on a recognition of the overwhelming passion demonstrated by Catholics the world over for the Madonna (the 1950 decision was made by Pope Pius XII as a direct result of a petition signed by 8 million people).

In 1954, the Catholic Church officially declared Mary "Queen of Heaven", centuries after this had become one of her most commonly used titles. Since at least the 5th century, the Virgin has been seen as a co-redemptress, and humankind's intercessor with God. She performs blessings and miracles, inspires mass pilgrimages and commands her own body of worship (although, whereas God is owed *latria*, or adoration, Mary is only entitled to *hyperdulia*, a superior form of the *dulia*, or veneration, that is the right of the saints).

THE WEEPING MOTHER

The weeping statue of Our Lady, at Maasmechelen in Belgium.

The Roman Catholic world is filled with images of the Madonna that seem to shed real tears. Not all of these are in churches: mass-produced figurines hanging in houses or flats have often become the focus of regular pilgrimages, or widespread cults, after appearing to cry. Sometimes the tears are not water: a small, weeping porcelain statuette was tested in Santiago, Chile, in 1992, and the coroner's office declared that it was shedding type-O human blood.

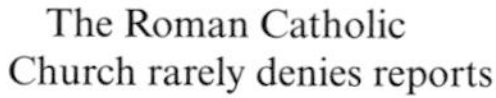

The Roman Catholic Church rarely denies reports of weeping Madonnas, but always officially distances itself from them. However, this does not prevent local priests and worshippers from acclaiming the appearance of a crying statue as a genuine miracle. When a plaster of Paris plaque depicting the Virgin cried for four days in Sicily in 1953, the Archbishop of Syracuse wrote to reassure his flock that the tears were a blessing, and not a reprimand: "Mary has wept! ... Weeping is fecund. There has never been a sterile tear. As the rain that falls from on high irrigates the countryside and prepares it to receive, in all fertility, the crops and seed and fruit ... so it happens in the realm of the spirit. A woman who weeps always becomes, in the very act, a mother."

The archbishop's words acknowledged the link between Mary and the early earth goddesses who also wept for their sons (see p.80). The cult of the mourning Mary probably arose in the 6th century, with a Good Friday lamentation written by the poet, Romanos Melodos, for the Emperor Justinian. At the time, the last of the temples of Isis were being closed by the same Emperor, and it is likely that the imagery of the Egyptian goddess, weeping bitterly for her dead husband Osiris, was appropriated by Melodos and the poets, priests and artists who followed him.

Nourishing mothers

The power of the mother archetype (see pp.18–19) is revealed in the abundance and variety of Mother Goddess representations throughout the world. Among these are the nature goddesses: indiscriminate parents to the gods, humans and vegetation. Other, more personalized figures resemble the *matres domesticae* of Celtic-Roman times: mothers to a people, a place or a country. Most Celtic goddesses were not named, and were referred to simply as mother, followed by the name of the site at which they were believed to appear. Britannia, the female embodiment of British military power, is a vestigial relic of these sorts of mother figures.

Perhaps the most enduring and widely represented mother goddesses are those, such as Isis or the Virgin Mary, whose mythology emphasizes their relationship with a single child. These goddesses are often depicted suckling their offspring, and the ability of the breast to nourish, comfort and protect is one of the most important and frequently cited attributes of the Goddess. This power of primal sustenance is so important that it has also been claimed for supreme male deities. St Ambrose (AD339–397) was one of many Christian commentators who referred to "the nourishing breasts of Christ".

Mythologically, mothers' milk is a powerful source of creation as well as sustenance. An Indian creation myth has the great mother, in the form of a milky ocean, churning to produce curds, which were

ARTEMIS

The Greek goddess Artemis seems to be a paradox: a remorseless virgin huntress who was also a universal mother and patron of childbirth (according to one myth she was born before her brother Apollo, and helped her mother Leto to deliver him). In her virgin aspect she demanded chastity of her devotees. When her close friend and companion, Kallisto, was seduced by Zeus (who was disguised as Artemis), the goddess punished her by turning her into a bear. This was also Artemis's cult animal, and young girls wore bear-masks to dance in her worship. For the Greeks, the bear was a symbol of motherhood and creation.

Although she was a huntress, Artemis was addressed, in the *Agamemnon* of Aeschylus, with the words: "Lovely you are and kind to the tender young of ravening lions. For sucklings of all the savage beasts ... you have sympathy." As the queen of all nymphs and goddess of the wild, Artemis possessed productive and generative energy, similar to that of ancient earth mothers. This aspect of her being, along with her embodiment as the moon, was celebrated with dances and orgies.

A drawing of the multi-breasted Artemis by Benvenuto Cellini (1500–71).

The Temple of Mother Artemis, at Ephesus, was one of the seven wonders of the ancient world. Inside, the goddess was represented by a vast, blackened statue, whose body was covered with many egg-like breasts and images of animals. It was probably the presence of the animals that led to this statue being identified by generations of worshippers as Artemis. In fact, its description tallies more closely with the great Anatolian Mother Goddess, Cybele, who, according to legend, gave birth at Ephesus, and who would almost certainly have had a shrine there. The name Artemis itself is not originally Greek, but occurs first on tablets from Pylos, linking her to the ancient Cretan Mother Goddess. The springtime festival at Ephesus included a running of the bulls, reminiscent of Minoan rituals (see pp.50–51).

The Birth of the Milky Way, *by Pieter Paul Rubens (1577–1640). Heracles was born to the Greek god Zeus, from his liaison with the mortal, Alcmene. Zeus secretly laid the child next to his wife, Hera, so that Heracles could become fully immortal by drinking her divine milk. Heracles bit the breast and sucked so powerfully that the milk spilled across the sky, forming the Milky Way.*

the first matter. The stars have been widely described as milk, spilling from the breast of Hera (in classical Greece), the udders of cow-goddesses such as Hathor (in Egypt) or Io (in ancient Ionia), and from innumerable other goddesses throughout the world.

Milk is also a medium for the transference of divinity, or other holy power. Isis is often shown suckling not just the child Horus, but also Horus as a man. From the first dynasty, pharaohs had themselves represented at the breast of Isis, imbibing their divine right to rule.

The image of the nurturing mother predates even Isis. A figure, from the 5th millennium BC, of an enthroned woman suckling a child was discovered in Thessaly, and the ruins of Ur, in ancient Sumer, contained a suckling, serpent-headed goddess, made in terracotta between 4000 and 3500BC. The Thessaly figure also has a serpent motif – it seems to be covered with snakes – and both these images could possibly relate to an even more primal form of mother-nourishment than breast-feeding: it has been suggested that the common association of ancient goddesses and serpents may have derived from the appearance of the umbilical cord, which resembles two snakes intertwined.

RIGHT *A 19th- or early 20th-century carving from Zaire, which idealizes woman's nurturing role in society so as to aid, by magic, the growth of the kingdom.*

OVERLEAF Tatei (Mother) Urianaku, Goddess of the Earth Ready for Planting, *a 20th-century Mexican Huichol yarn painting by Cresencio Perez Robles.*

The makers of fate

"In the myths of many societies, human destiny is routinely connected with trinities of goddesses. A common feature of such trinities is a capricious attitude, which is used to explain the seemingly random vicissitudes of fate. The trinities are extremely powerful, but rarely receive prayers or sacrifices like other gods and goddesses, because they are generally thought to be inflexible, and it is considered impossible to propitiate them. By contrast, whenever fate is thought to be controlled by a single goddess, such as Lakshmi (see p.146), she becomes the object of great and often extravagant devotion.

The trinities that control fate are often described as virgins. A typical trinity of maidens were the Norns of Norse mythology, who exceeded all the gods in power because they exemplified the inevitability of past, present and future. The Aesir, or heavenly deities, were unable to countermand their rulings on collective or individual fate, because the Norns tended the World Tree and through it controlled the living earth. The Roman Tria Fata – also named the Parcae after the Roman goddess Parca (from *parere*, "to give birth") – comprised another powerful trinity. They attended every birth and spun the thread of each individual's destiny.

In European mythology, the fates were usually weavers. The Greek Moirae, the forerunners of the Tria Fata, comprised Clothos the spinner, Lachesis the measurer and Atropos the cutter of life's thread. However, the Greeks had numerous other fateful

The three Fates foretelling Marie de Medici's future, by Pieter Paul Rubens (1577–1640).

trinities, such as the vengeful Furies, the wise but evil Graeae, who shared one eye between them, and the Gorgons. The Gorgon Medusa was veiled because she was the unknowable future, and to look upon her face was to see one's own death, or be "turned to stone" as a funerary statue. Ultimately, however, she was subjected to her own fate when the goddess Athene gave her shining aegis (or shield) to the hero Perseus, and he caused Medusa, fatally, to see her own reflection. Medusa probably had a pre-Hellenic history as a Libyan goddess, whose status was defiled and reduced by the Hellenic reconstruction of her as a beautiful, vain young woman, raped in Athene's temple by the sea god Poseidon (see pp.50–51) and turned into a hideous monster by the angry, virgin goddess.

The influence of the maiden trinity on human life is also recounted outside the Indo-European language areas. A Native North American legend that occurs from northern California to Washington tells how humans begged Coyote to bring them fire. Three ancient, withered sisters called the Skookums took turns to guard the fire, each alerting the next as her own vigil finished. Coyote invoked his own sisters – another trio, who lived in his stomach in the shape of huckleberries – and on their advice he surrounded the area with fleet-footed animals. As one Skookum handed over to another, he ran up and stole a firebrand. The three hags chased him, but Coyote handed over the fire to Squirrel and it was passed successively to several animals until eventually it was swallowed by a tree, and the Skookums were forced to abandon the pursuit.

The Wheel of Fortune, from an English psalter illustrated by William de Brailes, c.*1240. Fortuna, the Roman goddess of chance, was often depicted balancing on a ball, or a wheel, to demonstrate the uncertainty of fate. Her wheel became secularized as the carnival wheel of fortune, and Fortuna herself became known as Lady Luck, the patron of gamblers.*

THE THIRD PARTY

In *Prolegomena to the Study of Greek Religion* (1991), the writer Elizabeth Jane Harrison suggests that the fate-related goddess-trinities evolved from a mother maiden dualism, such as that of Demeter and Kore (see p.70). The possibility of – or even the impulse to – death exists in both the mother and the maiden, for example, in Kore as she descends to hell, and in Demeter as her lamentations ravage the world. However, on a day-to-day basis, the human mind is uncomfortable in associating death with images of purity or nurturing.

A third aspect of the Goddess is useful in sequestering this death impulse. By creating death as an entity apart, the worshipper can ignore the threatening quality of both mother and daughter. So death, an inevitable part of human destiny, becomes personified and is invested with the universal fear of the unknown. Together, the trinity subsumes all the negative and positive aspects of fate.

The bringers of death

Hecate, *a print by William Blake, c.1795.*

Although the Goddess is capable of killing in any of her aspects, she is most closely associated with death when she appears as a crone. This is reflected in the numerous cultures in which it is customary for old women to take care of the dead – dressing them, anointing them and watching over them until their funeral. The crone is also closely linked with witchcraft (see pp.134–5), mysteries and secrets, and when a woman is past her child-bearing age, she may be described as "drawing in her blood", or sometimes as "withholding". Her womb, although no longer obviously productive, may now become a vessel of regeneration, like the cauldron of the Celtic goddess, Branwen, in which she could boil up the dead so as to resurrect them. Nevertheless, because of her command of womens' mysteries, the crone's womb often becomes synonymous with the tomb – a place that represents the terrors of the unknown.

Perhaps the best known of all crones, unifying the domains of death and witchcraft, is Hecate. This oldest of Greek goddesses was probably derived from the Egyptian Heqit [illegible] or Heket, goddess of midwives (th[illegible]archetypal keepers of womens' sec[illegible]who were usually crones, and comb[illegible] the roles of caring for the dead an[illegible]nging forth new life). Hecate was incorporated into the *Theogony* of Hesiod (see p.60) as a being worthy of great praise. She was a scion of the dark moon, ruler of the dead and control[illegible] ghostly swarms, who prowled [illegible]treets at night, especially nea[illegible]ss-roads. Evening meals were dedicated to her, and the remnants left outside for her to eat. Hecate helped Demete[illegible] search for Persephone (see p.70), and sometimes becomes synonymous with Demeter, as arbiter of souls.

As the bringer of deat[illegible]he crone is also the ultimate judge[illegible]e[illegible]accoutrements often include bo[illegible] of records, like those of Erishkigal (see p.78) and her Semitic counterpart Hus[illegible]g. In this role, her name is used to swear the most solemn oaths, and deat[illegible]bringers from Tellus Mater in Rome to Yabme-Akka in Scandinavia a[illegible]la in Africa have become the most f[illegible]dable guarantors of truth and goodness.

Nevertheless, the que[illegible]death is usually perceived as preda[illegible] She may be a drinker of blood, lik[illegible]the Aztec Coatlicue, or a devourer of bodies, like Hine of Oceania (see p.26[illegible]M[illegible]he Polynesian mistress of th[illegible]three innermost circles of the underworl[illegible]stands to one side as the souls [illegible]newly dead journey to their an[illegible]rs, and casts out her net to snare t[illegible]The evil souls are pushed into th[illegible]onsuming flames of her oven, while th[illegible]good ones live a life much like the one they had on earth, except without fear of an end.

This man, taking part in a sacred dance of Kerala, India, is possessed by the goddess Machilottu, one of the many aspects of Devi-Kali. Machilottu was a young girl who was wrongfully accused of licentiousness, and driven from her village. After pleading her case with Shiva, she built her own funeral pyre, and roared into the sky on a pillar of flame, as a new-born goddess.

KALI – THE BEGINNING AND THE END

The goddess Kali, either under her own name or as Shakti (the embodiment of female energy, see p.94), is the form in which the great goddess Devi is most often encountered in Indian iconography, art and literature. Kali's titles include Shyama ("the Black One"), Chandi ("the Fierce One") and Bhairava ("the Terrible One"), and it is in these forms that she receives blood sacrifices of male animals. Human sacrifices were made illegal in 1835, but are still occasionally reported.

Kali's most common depiction is as a towering black goddess whose tongue lolls from her mouth, dripping blood. She is heavily garlanded with snakes and skulls. Her skirt is made of the hands of evil-doers and the corpse of an infant dangles from each ear. She brandishes a sword in one hand, while the other holds up a skull. She uses her third and fourth arms to bless and acknowledge worshippers.

As Mahakali, the mistress of time, Kali occupies both the time and space of the mortal dimension and a still point at the centre of infinity. Hindu cosmology describes a universe that undergoes a series of cycles, or ages. At the end of each age, all creation crumbles into Mahakali and returns to seed, from which the next age arises. According to the sacred text *Devibhagavata*, the Goddess at the end of time has no tangible form or quality and represents absolute Truth.

The witch Goddess

Witches are strongly linked to the Goddess, particularly in her crone phase. They often share her qualities of age, darkness, mystery and a connection with death. The child-killers and devourers, such as Hansel's and Gretel's witch, who has her origins in goddesses such as the Melanesian Likele and Kalwadi (see p.23), are creations of popular folklore – one-dimensionally evil characters, whose cruelty is devoid of reason. Medea of Colchos, who helped Jason in his quest for the golden fleece, is such a character, sacrificing excessively and indiscriminately for the sake of love. She dismembers the body of her younger brother and scatters it in the sea merely to divert her father, and later kills her own children in revenge for Jason's infidelity.

However, where myth is a living part of worship, and has not degenerated into folklore, the death-related activities of the Goddess are still perceived as part of a long-term, life-perpetuating cycle.

A page from the pre-Colombian Mexican manuscript Codex Fejervary-Mayer, *showing a witch goddess expelling magic from her vulva.*

Circe transforming the crew of Odysseus into swine, by Camillo Paderni (d.c.1770). Odysseus was protected by the magical herb, moly.

Isis, who was intimately linked with death and rebirth (see pp.84–7), was a great exponent of magic and the prototype for countless sorceresses. Although all goddesses embody witch-potential, a few stand out as exceptional. The most potent and multifaceted embodiments of the female divinity – such as Isis, Hecate and Kali – are especially prone to being degraded by unbelievers into the one-dimensional stereotype of the witch-figure. It can be argued that such an approach makes these dangerous, unpredictable beings more easily manageable in the human psyche, so that it feels safer to ignore or attack them without fear of penalty. To the Native North American Cochiti, the Yellow Woman is a predatory witch, ruthlessly pursuing her quarry. But among neigh-

HATHOR, THE EVIL EYE

The Egyptian goddess Hathor was once probably as prominent as Isis in some parts of Egypt. She was either the daughter or the mother of Ra, and was sent out in the form of a large, all-seeing eye by the sun god to spy on the human race, whose ways she found deplorable. When she was too fiercely aroused, the goddess became savage and began to destroy humanity, until the other gods became alarmed and found ways to stop her (see see p.139).

Hathor's malevolence toward the human race (which, as the Winged Cow of Creation, she brought into being) was the result of her fragmentation: during her history she moved from being a composite creator-destroyer, and patron of life's pleasures – including singing, dancing and music – to a solely destructive figure.

She was the origin of the concept of the "evil eye", which survives in many societies, representing the transformation of deeply felt or malign jealousy into actual adversity. Countless witches have been persecuted because death, illness or the failure of crops was attributed to their use of the evil eye, which they were supposed to have cast out of resentment as much as evil.

Today, the Egyptian cross (ankh), which may derive from Hathor's eye, hangs on walls as a symbol of good luck. It is placed so as to look inward, keeping fortune inside the dwelling.

Hathor placing a magic collar on Seti I, from Thebes, Egypt c.1314–1200BC.

bouring peoples she may be a bride, a benefactor or a heroine. To the Keres, her name means All-Woman, because yellow is the ceremonial colour that belongs to women.

Circe of the *Odyssey* and Morgan Le Fay of Arthurian legend are two examples of witches who, although inconceivably old, appear as beautiful and sexual young women. Enchantment is represented here as a deceitful way of acquiring love, with harmful consequences for the lover and those dear to him. The romantic epics of the Middle Ages frequently contain the motif of the Loathly Lady who lures the hero with her youth and beauty, but is in fact old and ugly. Her shape-changing is often a touchstone with which to gauge the suitability of a future king – whether he can endure the onerous ("ugly") part of his duties, such as war and the subsequent grieving, as wholeheartedly as he embraces its privileges.

Germanic fairy tales include moralistic witches like Frau Trude and Frau Holle, the latter a watered-down version of the goddess Hulde. Frau Holle summarily punishes a lazy, rude girl but is bountiful toward the girl's hard-working sister. The witch Baba Yaga, of Russian folklore, similarly rewards the good, kindly Vasilissa, but breaks up the bones of her sister.

Warriors and Guardians

When the deathly aspect of the Goddess is emphasized to the exclusion of other, more life-enhancing manifestations, the result is a warrior goddess, such as Kali, Sekhmet or Anath. As a warrior, the Goddess is portrayed as both a fierce fighter and the protector of the universe. She is the hunter who simultaneously protects the wilds, and to illustrate this dual function she is usually accompanied by a wild animal such as a lion or a stag and, in the case of Artemis and various Romano-Celtic divinities, a hunting hound as well.

The Goddess is probably at her fiercest when protecting women's mysteries, as epitomized by her own virginity: the concentrated power of her unused sexuality makes her an invincible foe. For this reason she often becomes the patron of warriors and soldiers, venerated by kings and glorified by victory monuments in kingdoms as far apart as India, Africa and South America.

In this traditional Balinese dance, the powerful and destructive witch Rangda tries to destroy the kingdom, and kills half the population before she is defeated by a holy man.

The divine destructress

In religious thought, the force of good also has a terrible side, which can be unleashed against evil and moral transgressors. The Abrahamic God sends floods, fires, plagues and other catastrophes to annihilate cities, nations or even the entire human race when it becomes corrupt. However, since images of the one male God are forbidden in Judaism (as they are in Islam), his rage cannot easily be personified.

The opposite is true of the Indian goddess Kali, whose most popular representation shows her standing huge and upright, her tongue lolling blood-red from between her teeth, and her many arms brandishing weapons and trophies of her blood-lust – human skulls, severed heads and dismembered hands. She dances so feverishly that she risks grinding the world to destruction, until her husband, Shiva, lies among the corpses at her feet. When she recognizes him she emerges from her trance and returns to normal consciousness.

The Indian myth of cataclysm begins when the gods approach the Goddess and appeal to her for help against demons who are threatening the world with their evil. From a shining mountain formed from their thoughts and prayers emerges Mahamaya, the manifestation of the cosmic presence. She assumes the form of Durga, armed and riding on a lion, and vanquishes one demon after another. At various stages of the fighting she multiplies into different war-like goddesses, until finally she is left, in the form of Kali, facing Riktavij, a demon general whose every drop of blood turns into a hundred fresh demons as it touches the ground. Kali foils this tactic by catching the blood-drops in her mouth, before finally slaying Riktavij.

There are remarkable similarities between the Indian and Egyptian myths of cataclysm. Sekhmet, like Durga, has leonine associations (see p.15) and derives from a more sedate goddess, Hathor, just as Durga does from Mahamaya. Both use their protective forces against a dangerous and evil enemy in defence of the gods (Ra and the Indian pantheon, respectively), and both are invincible.

Sekhmet evolves from the goddess Hathor, daughter of Ra, after she hears about a plot by the human followers of

A 13th-century carving from Mysore, India, of Durga slaying demons. Durga was the patron goddess of the Rajput warrior-princes of India.

Seth against her father. After a day of massacre, she withdraws to rest, and the gods, fearing the eradication of the human race, prepare 7,000 jars of wine dyed red with ochre. Sekhmet wakes to see this blood-like liquid swilling over the fields, and drinks deeply to satisfy her still-raging blood-lust. The wine makes the goddess fall into a deep sleep, and humankind escapes destruction.

A stone relief of Sekhmet from the 3rd millennium BC Temple of Horus, Edfu, Egypt.

In each case the goddess's destructive frenzy emerges temporarily to deal with enemies of a god (or gods) of righteousness, and it is a male positive energy that restores her equilibrium. By avoiding force himself, the god is able to direct the goddess back toward passivity, by mirroring her own gentle aspect until she realizes her anger has outgrown its use.

The blood that is shed by the goddess during her battle-frenzy is not merely a peripheral side-effect of destruction. It is significant as the primal matter of both life and death, which can be transmuted by divine alchemy into a new being. In purging the world of evil, the goddess is also preparing the space for the new generation or race which follows all cataclysms and peoples the world afresh.

BLOOD WORSHIP

Ever since the Paleolithic, blood has had close associations with ritual and worship. It was symbolized by red ochre (used to stain icons, and also found on corpses, folded into the foetal position to be returned to the earth-womb, ready for rebirth), and by red wine.

Blood is the basis of clan, kingship and inheritance, and it has been suggested that women were accorded a high status in ancient societies because they were guardians, and transmitters – via the act of giving birth – of the clan's blood, and therefore its spirit.

Menstrual blood was once considered beneficial in many ways. It was poured over fields as a fertilizer and used for healing and promoting power. It is described in the mystical Indian Tantras as "blood-food". Men have frequently attempted to imitate menstrual bleeding for ritual purposes, through acts such as circumcision, the subincision of some Australian Aborigines and the nipple-piercing that takes place during the Sun Dance of the Sioux.

It is sometimes claimed that priests invented menstrual taboos and sacrifice in order to eschew the use of female blood in rituals which were at one time confined to priestesses. Rejected as unclean, menstrual blood had to be replaced in sacred ceremonies by blood from the sacrifice of humans and animals.

A mid-19th-century Indian Tantric painting. The goddess Chinnamasta stands on Shiva and Shakti, while the blood flowing from her neck nourishes her disciples.

The Goddess in arms

Goddesses of war are often connected with the sun and stars. In the legends of animistic peoples, the millions of stars in the sky can easily be transformed into a glittering army of soldiers, fighting darkness with the incandescence of their bodies. In Slavonic myth the dawn goddess Zarya is personified as a great warrior who appears armed at birth to dispel the forces of the night. Dilbah, the morning star of Babylon, likewise banishes darkness. It is probably for this reason that Dilbah, along with many other war goddesses, is depicted either heavily clad in shining armour or decked with jewels, gold and silver.

For example, the multiple goddess Anahita is described in the Zoroastrian religious text called the *Avesta* as being extraordinarily tall and strong, with a commanding appearance, and heavily jewelled "according to the rule". Anahita was the divine energy for good which was thought to flow through the kings of Iran, whom she encouraged and protected against invaders from the north. This did not prevent evil-doers appealing to her for help, although in general she refused.

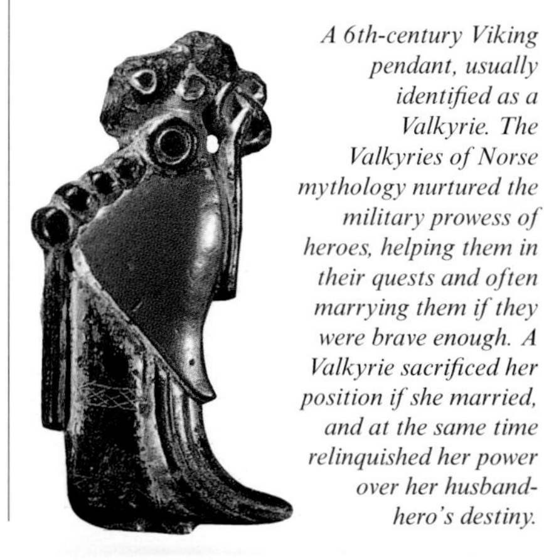

A 6th-century Viking pendant, usually identified as a Valkyrie. The Valkyries of Norse mythology nurtured the military prowess of heroes, helping them in their quests and often marrying them if they were brave enough. A Valkyrie sacrificed her position if she married, and at the same time relinquished her power over her husband-hero's destiny.

The Greeks equated Anahita to Athene. The Greek goddess too, was tall and imposing and took an interest in the deeds of heroes (see pp.142–5). She supported Achilles against Paris in the Trojan war, assisted Herakles in his labours and guided the voyages of Odysseus. Her favourite bird was the mysterious, night-hunting owl, but this was not generally seen when she was engaged in battle.

In contrast, the battle-crow of the Irish war-trinity collectively known as the Morrigan was constantly in evidence as a harbinger of death. The Morrigan had a loud, shrieking laugh, which is said to have frozen the hearts of the bravest men. The pure warrior, however, recognized that he had no need to fear her. In one of her most famous conflicts, she challenged the hero Cuchulainn in various animal forms after he had turned down her offer of sex. Although determined to teach him a lesson, she acted judiciously, giving the hero fair warning of her intentions and never employing magic during combat.

As an aspect of the land goddess, the Morrigan stood for territoriality and for "the protection of her people's general interest". She helped her favourites, the people known as the Tuatha de Danaan, to conquer Ireland in a battle with the indigenous Fir Bolg. The Morrigan was often seen washing the shrouds of warriors who were soon to die in battle, at which time she appeared as a giant hag standing astride a river, or as a tall woman wading knee deep in water which ran red with spilled blood.

Pallas Athene, painted by Gustav Klimt in 1898. Athene was born fully armed from the head of her father, Zeus. She carried a spear and a goatskin shield, which is usually depicted bearing the Gorgon's head and encircled with Fear, Strife, Force and Pursuit. She killed Pallas – variously reported as a giant or a goat-like, Priapic god – in Zeus's war against the Titans, and used his skin for a breast-plate. His name – which probably meant either "maiden" or "youth", and suggested he was an androgynous deity – was appended to hers so that she became Pallas Athene.

THE SUFIS

The Sufi school of Islamic mysticism emerged in the 8th century AD in Iraq and other Arabic countries. Its devotees opposed institutionalized religion and the corruption that accompanied it, but were persecuted as heretics and forced to emigrate to Iran.

Gradually a body of Sufi verse emerged, which was ostensibly love poetry, but which actually described, in a coded form, the mystic's thirst for the divine. The "Beloved" spoken of in the poems symbolized the divinity, and the "lover" was the mystic himself. What was believed to be a male divinity was nevertheless represented as female. As one saint–poet wrote: "The Beloved is like a fairy, cypress-statured, tulip-cheeked / From head to toe, dread-inspiring."

The Beloved possessed the same war-like mien as the ancient Iranian goddess Anahita. Her eyebrows were compared to swords and bows, her glances to spears, her eyelashes to daggers. She was the quintessence of a virgin–goddess, fierce and life-threatening one moment, soft and alluring the next. She usually remained invisible or appeared behind a tantalizing veil. She was unavailable, mysterious and flirtatious like the idealized, unattainable women of medieval Islamic societies, and these qualities combined to magnetize the acolyte, drawing him on in the hope of a vision or a meeting.

Eventually, an encounter with the divine Beloved became the sole purpose of the mystic's existence and his life was lived in anticipation of the moment of union, symbolized by death, when he would merge with her. During the course of his devotions he had learned that *Fana* (annihilation) results in *Baqa* (eternal life), which was the Beloved's final secret.

The Goddess of the quest

The Judgement of Paris, *by Pieter Paul Rubens (1577–1640). This beauty contest, between Hera, Aphrodite and Athene, led to the Trojan War, in which each goddess championed her own hero.*

The Goddess is linked to the heroic quest at many levels. She may be present at the very beginning, as initiator of the hero's journey, or she may appear at a later stage, helping, guiding or throwing obstacles in the hero's way in order to test him. Sometimes the Goddess herself is the final obstacle, as in the case of the Gorgon, Medusa, who had to be killed by Perseus before he could consider his quest complete. He could not have killed Medusa without the help of another goddess, Athene, who provided a burnished shield for the purpose (and who was herself, in her pre-Hellenic form, identified with the Gorgon). To a large extent therefore, the hero is a pawn in a celestial game between different aspects of the Goddess.

The quest, which is usually undertaken by a male, may be interpreted as a psychological voyage of discovery that

THE INNER QUEST

In *The Transformations of Lucius*, otherwise known as *The Golden Ass*, written by Lucius Apuleius in the 2nd century AD, the central character seduces a slave girl in order to steal her mistress's magic so that he can transform himself into a bird – the symbol of the Goddess. The attempt goes wrong and Lucius ends up as an ass, leading a life full of toil and misfortune. At the culmination of the tale, Lucius encounters Isis, initiates himself into her mysteries, is transformed in the goddess and becomes her priest. This central, coherent narrative is interspersed with shorter stories, which the Jungian analyst (see pp.18–19), Marie Louise von Franz, interprets as dreamlike structures which seek to bring Lucius's inner life to the surface. As his inhibitions are lowered, Lucius experiences the interaction of his physical and psychic energies and confronts the buried strata of his personality.

"*The Golden Ass* is the modern description of the development of a man's *anima* or feminine, unconscious personality," writes von Franz, and adds that it also "gives form to a deep process of evolution of historical dimension: the coming back of the feminine principle into the patriarchal Western world."

is essential to his full development. The first stage is the call to the quest, when the hero decides to undertake the journey. This is comparable to his first ever separation from the female matrix, or womb. The aim of the journey may be understood as the need to seek out the female elements within himself – both positive and negative – and integrate them so that the conflicting impressions he has of the mother are reconciled. Success in this task is symbolized by the "prize", which is generally a desirable young woman. Before the hero can achieve this, however, he must face and vanquish a dragon (see p.51) or some other kind of monster, perhaps a giant or witch, or an excessively powerful, evil man or woman. He is helped or hindered in these encounters by one or more females in whom the Goddess is incarnate. In these encounters she variously represents the Good Mother and the Terrible Mother (see pp.18–19), and part of the hero's challenge is to deal with each manifestation as appropriate in order to achieve a sense of inner balance. Thus, killing or outwitting the witch on the one hand, or seeking her help on the other, will be a crucial stage in the acquisition of his goal.

On another level, the quest is a metaphor for initiation into manhood or a spiritual life. Various, seemingly distinct, goddesses may appear at different stages of such an initiation – firstly as the psychopomp (that is, the motivation for the quest), then as the hero's tester/helper and finally as paramount opposer/prize. However, all the goddesses can generally be established as aspects of the same immanent (or all-pervading) divinity.

The Trojan War had numerous apparent causes and psychopomps. The goddess Eris, or Strife, upon finding herself excluded from a heavenly feast, threw a golden apple among the participants. It was intended "for the fairest", so Hera, Aphrodite and Athene all claimed it. Zeus refused to choose between them, but compelled Paris, as the most handsome of men, to do so. Each of the goddesses offered Paris a bribe so that he should choose her. Hera promised him power, Athene promised him wisdom

PRACTICAL QUESTS

Among Native North American peoples, magical female protective power often manifests itself in non-heroic, everyday tasks. Micmac women – of what is now New England and northeastern Canada – had to make beautiful clothing for their husbands-to-be, to demonstrate their practical skills. However, the resulting elaborate designs were also a source of magical protection.

Women of the Cheyenne undertook sacred porcupine quill- or bead-work as a form of prayer to ensure the welfare of their relatives. The task of making the object, rather than the object itself, was considered magical.

A Navajo sandpainting showing Changing Woman and six footprints which represent her mind. It is a source of power, which is used for preparing men to go to the mountains and pray for rain.

and victory in war, and Aphrodite promised him Helen, the most beautiful woman in the world. However, the choice presented to the Trojan prince was an illusion: he was acting out a destiny planned by Zeus to depopulate Greece through war. Zeus had fathered Helen to this specific end. Paris duly chose Aphrodite, but in preferring one element of the divine female principle over the others, he activated the inherent oppositions between the different aspects of the Goddess. When he chose love and beauty he rejected motherhood, as well as chastity and protection. In the Trojan war, Hera and Athene both aided the Greeks.

The Goddess may also appear in legends in the form of mortal or semi-divine warrior women, such as the druidess Scathach, mentor of the Irish hero Cuchulainn. Such women are part of the same mythic heritage as the great Goddess Sovereignty (see p.55), who in her various guises, including that of Morgan Le Fay, tempted and tested the worth of heroes such as King Arthur and his knights.

The Welsh tale of Cullwch and Olwen is a complex example of the Goddess appearing in many forms throughout a quest narrative. The hero Cullwch is born in a pig-run (the pig is sacred to ancient goddesses such as Demeter and Artemis) to a queen who dies soon afterward. The queen's name, Light-of-the-Day, suggests that she represents nature and the sun. Having fulfilled her single function by mothering the hero, she withdraws and is replaced by a queen who remains unnamed in the narrative, and who initiates the quest when she sets a curse on Cullwch – that he will never marry anyone but Olwen, daughter of the evil giant Ysbaddaden. In direct contrast to his mother, who displays elements of the sun, Olwen stands for the moon, and she immediately becomes the goal of Cullwch's life. The hero embarks on thirty-two missions. During these he acquires a cauldron from Annwn ("the underworld"), signifying the womb (sec p.35), and defeats the king-turned-bull, Twrch Trwyth, which symbolizes the conquest of his own animal power. Cullwch's

THE AMAZONS

The Amazons are believed to have received their name (*a-mazos*, or "breastless") from their practice of removing one breast from their infant girls, so that when they grew up they could more easily shoot an arrow or throw a lance. Although the Amazons were armed warrior–maidens, they were not divine. They fought on equal terms against the Greek heroes with whom they came into conflict. They were devout worshippers of Artemis and are sometimes claimed not only to have constructed the Temple of Artemis, but also the city of Ephesus.

The Amazons lived in northern Africa, Anatolia and around the Black Sea, on the very fringes of the civilized world. They used men sexually in order to become pregnant, then discarded or killed them. They also disposed of any male progeny at birth.

These military super-women were obviously threatening to men, and the surviving myths that tell of the Amazons depict battle encounters in which a male hero is invariably triumphant. When Queen Penthisilea led her warriors to the aid of King Priam in the siege of Troy, she was killed and her corpse raped by Achilles (in a magical attempt to conquer her angry soul). Queen Hippolyta was murdered by Herakles, during his quest to steal her magic girdle.

It has been suggested that the defeat of the Amazons by the Greeks is an allegory for the setback the Goddess received when Indo-European conquerors introduced their male gods into their newly vanquished territories.

A frieze from the tomb of Mausolas, who ruled Caria, in Asia Minor, from 353–337BC. The frieze was made c.*350BC, and this detail shows an Amazon striking down a Greek soldier.*

final mission is the slaying of a black witch, who is herself the daughter of a white witch. He is now free to reunite with his *anima*, or sister–self, Olwen.

At the conclusion of his journey, the hero or initiate, helped and guided by the Goddess, may attain a goal that is material, psychological, or spiritual. These three are not mutually exclusive, because, unlike the spiritually questing mystics from the Abrahamic religions, the pilgrim in search of the Goddess is entitled to enjoy the world of the flesh and matter. Once Isis had revealed herself to Lucius Apuleius (see p.143) and accepted him into her world, he went on to combine his priesthood with the practice of law and lived a full and happy life, contented and confident of the bounties of his goddess.

The Goddess of mercy and fortune

At Putuo, on the island of Zhoushan in central China, is the sanctuary of China's best-loved deity: Kwan-yin, the goddess of mercy, who is especially protective of women and children. She is known as "the One who hears prayers/sounds/weeping". Her birthday falls on the 19th day of the second moon of the lunar calendar, and meditating on her name is a powerful form of devotion. Her popularity is enhanced by one Chinese legend which identifies her as an indigenous princess called Miao Shan. She was the third daughter of a king and suffered terrible punishments after refusing to marry anyone but an ordinary physician.

She was eventually condemned to public execution, but her body was taken by the spirits and preserved for resurrection. When the underworld blossomed into a garden of paradise because of her presence, she was quickly accorded divine status. As a divinity she would meditate regularly on the plight of humankind and extend mercy in answer to every prayer, but she continued to assume physical incarnations, moving among people in order to help them physically and spiritually.

However, historically, Kwan-yin (sometimes known as Guanyin, or Kwannon in Japan) is an import from the Indian subcontinent, brought to China by Buddhist missionaries in the form of a *bodhisattva,* or Future Buddha. According to Buddhist theology, a *bodhisattva* was an Enlightened One who, through generations of meditation and contemplation, had learned how to escape the endless cycle of death and resurrection that afflicted the rest of humanity, but who, as an act of compassion, regularly chose a body in

HOMAGE TO FORTUNE

Lakshmi, the goddess of good fortune has an enormous following all over India. She can ensure human well-being and prosperity on earth, and every household hopes that a new daughter-in-law will bring Lakshmi, or luck. Her name is interchangeable with material wealth, but she is widely courted and flattered not merely for her bounties, but also because she is thought of as alluring and capricious. Lakshmi's altars are richly fed with oil, milk and flowers because she is fickle, and easily enticed by an impassioned worshipper, a whispered endearment or a sumptuous offering. Her tendency to be easily offended is reflected in the common proverb, "Don't shun visiting Lakshmi."

Although she is the Universal Female who floated on a lotus flower at the creation, Lakshmi only joined the gods when the primordial ocean was churned to obtain an elixir which would rid the world of evil. As she rose from the foam, rivers changed direction to flow toward her, and celestial elephants scooped up the waves to wash her. The goddess then chose Vishnu as her eternal partner, of both previous and successive generations.

The greatest homage to Lakshmi comes during the festival of Diwali, the Hindu New Year, when families light lamps in the hope of attracting her to their homes. Small terracotta lamps fed with edible oil, or ghee, surround houses and shops and are sometimes floated on water. In parts of India they are flown on kite-strings.

In her iconography, Lakshmi is depicted as a beautiful, smiling woman with black hair which rolls down her back in waves. She is swathed in jewels and has a pale, golden skin. Although she is said to have four arms, she is almost invariably represented with two. She holds a lotus flower in one hand, and performs blessings with the other.

A statue of Kwan-yin, in Hong Kong. She has been portrayed in more than thirty different ways, as both a male and a female, but is mostly depicted in flowing garb with jewels or a willow branch in her hands. By the 4th century AD, *ceramic icons of the Goddess were popular enough to justify mass production. Ceramic Kwan-yins were found in every Chinese household before the Revolution, and still adorn many homes and shops in modern China.*

which to be reborn so that he could help others to reach salvation.

Kwan-yin was originally Avolokiteshvara, the male *bodhisattva* of compassion, and her transformation into a goddess may appear to be something of an enigma in a religion where women were regarded as less perfect beings than men. However, when Buddhism was introduced into China under the Han Dynasty in the 3rd century AD, it soon syncretized with Taoism and Confucianism. These religions may have caused the metamorphosis of Avolokiteshvara by confusing him with an indigenous female deity. The germinal Kwan-yin may have been the ancient mother goddess, Nü-kua, who was a guardian of humankind, or the Taoist deity called the Queen of Heaven. A *bodhisattva* combines the attributes of knowledge and compassion, and in this light it is perhaps not surprising that the male Avolokiteshvara should be assimilated to the Goddess, who often exercises mercy in her role as the all-knowing judge of the dead (see p.49).

Liberating the Goddess

The history of contemporary Goddess revival movements probably begins in 1861 with the publication of *Mother Right*, by the Swiss historian and anthropologist, J. J. Bachofen (1815–1887). In this book, Bachofen proposed a scientific theory of the family as a social institution, and suggested that the rights and powers of mothers had once taken precedence over the rights of fathers. This idea immediately raised the possibility that if society had once been shaped by women, then religion and its objects of worship would also have been formed in their image.

Another important book for the development of the Goddess movement was *The Witch-Cult in Western Europe* (1921), by Margaret Murray, which claimed that an organized pagan religion, whose priestesses were witches, had existed continuously since the Paleolithic. Although Murray's theories were later discredited, they inspired many people to establish their own covens, or neo-pagan groups. In modern Goddess worship, the construction of a glorious female past, however historically inaccurate, is seen as a legitimate exercise in fantasy and myth-making for the purpose of self-empowerment – a role that myth and the power of the imagination have played since the dawn of human consciousness.

In the Candomblé rites of Brazil, women are often possessed by their goddesses. Cults such as Candomblé, are rapidly spreading throughout modern, urban North America, under the collective title of Santeria or Macumba.

The Goddess today

Grapceva Neolithic Cave: See For Yourself, *a photograph taken in 1977 on Hvar Island, in the then Yugoslavia. The photographer, Mary Beth Edelson, made a pilgrimage to this Neolithic ritual site after reading* Gods and Goddesses of Old Europe, *by Marija Gimbutas* *(see p.13)*.

Throughout the world, numerous traditions of Goddess worship have flourished unbroken to the present day. The female divinity is popularly worshipped as Kali throughout India. The great goddess Devi incarnates in many different forms across Southeast Asia and in Tibet. In Oceania, Australasia and Africa, various groups continue to worship the Goddess despite the evangelical efforts of Christian missionaries. Catholic countries, especially in South America, worship the female divinity in disguised forms, as saints and in the shape of the Virgin Mary.

In the period after World War II, Western society began to turn its attention to the Goddess. The war had emphasized the disparity between women's inferior social status and their contributions in all areas of life. The gender imbalance had become glaringly obvious, and mainstream religion appeared to endorse it. At the same time, post-war re-industrialization and a growing materialism in society alienated an increasing number of people who were looking for a spiritual alternative to technological progress. The Goddess provided that alternative, offering not

FOLLOWERS OF THE GODDESS

There is a vast international network of modern pagans, most of whom worship aspects of the Goddess that can be traced back to the ancient traditions of Egypt, Mesopotamia, Greece, Scandinavia, India and North America.

The majority of pagans are not people who have decided to opt out of conventional society, but are middle-class people, living in the Western world. They include scientists, educators, politicians and media figures, all drawn by paganism's holistic message – emphasizing the oneness of humankind with Nature – and its accent on freedom of belief and religious practice.

International pagan groups help each other to organize major festivals such as the first Pagan Festival of Europe, held in West Germany in 1988. The Pagan Federation includes members from Latin America, India, Africa and Europe, from religions as diverse as Shinto, Christianity, Buddhism, Judaism and Hinduism. In the early 1990s there were some 100,000 pagans in the United States. Approximately half of all practising pagans would describe themselves as witches, and in 1996 the Wiccan Church of the United Kingdom numbered close to 12,000 members, worshipping alone or in covens.

In accordance with a tenet of Goddess worship – the interdependence of all elements of the cosmic organism – pagan groups recognize no barriers of race, education, profession or class.

The Coronation of Isis *(1996), a modern version of a pagan ritual, illustrated by Stuart Littlejohn.*

only the liberty to choose a different style of worship, but also a concept of the human being as a part of Nature.

The various groups that fall under the ecumenical banner of neo-paganism, although not centrally organized, tend to believe in the interdependency of the cosmos and all its different species and resources. In her seminal account of neo-paganism, *Drawing Down the Moon* (1979), Margot Adler describes the three central beliefs of the new generation of Goddess worshippers as polytheism (the many aspects of Nature are seen as emanating from the same divine force), pantheism (the Goddess's presence in Nature leads to its deification and to the principle of taking only what is essential from the earth, and replacing it in some form) and animism (objects as well as plants and animals are perceived to possess the universal life-energy which binds everything together in the cosmic whole).

Pantheism in particular led to a fresh way of looking at the female body. As likenesses of the Goddess, women are containers of the divine and their bodies are worthy of veneration. The perception of the female body as the temple of the Goddess was a reclamation of an ancient tradition, and did much to raise female self-esteem. The use of the body in worship was reinstated and various rituals developed around it, some inspired by ancient religious practices, such as those of Egypt, and others constructed from contemporary mores.

Searching for the Goddess

In her book, *The Witch-Cult in Western Europe* (1921), the anthropologist and author Margaret Murray posed the contentious theory that the mass persecutions of witches that marked the 14th–17th centuries were aimed at the destruction of an organized pagan religion. Murray claimed that this religion had its origins in Paleolithic times, and defined it as the Dianic cult because of its apparent devotion to the Roman moon goddess. Her theories made a great impression on Gerald Gardner (1884–1964), the English civil servant who is widely credited with popularizing the idea of witchcraft as a religion.

Gardner had been a member of a Masonic occult group for several years before he joined a coven of "hereditary witches" in 1939. He formed his own coven in 1951, after the repeal of the witchcraft law in England. Although Gardner claimed that he was following the "Old Religion" of pagan antiquity, most of the ceremonies, spells and rites that he quoted seem to derive from the self-styled "Great Beast", Aleister Crowley (1875–1947), and through him from the French occultist, Eliphas Levi (1810–1875). Gardner insisted that the male God was the Supreme Being, and believed that women should be subservient to men.

The pre-eminence of the Goddess in modern witchcraft can probably be traced to Doreen Valiente, who was initiated into the Gardnerian group in 1953, and became its High Priestess.

MAGIC

The witch Doreen Valiente once described magic as a knowledge of Nature and its workings so profound and thorough that it could be used to communicate with the elements to bring about some desired occurrence. This change, if it was performed with due regard to all relevant factors, could substantially alter the course of an individual life without having any significant effect on the overall Divine Plan.

The magician's knowledge had to be accompanied by a sincerity and a sense of responsibility that would not allow him or her to belittle witchcraft, or bring it into disrepute. This is somewhat at odds with the definition of the occultist Aleister Crowley who said magic is "the science and art of causing change to occur in conformity with the will", which may include acts contrary to interests of Nature (Crowley's most famous dictum is, "Do what thou wilt shall be the whole of the law ..."). Magic may be classified as black (designed to do harm), grey or white. However, essentially it is neutral, and can only be defined according to the way it is used.

Mainstream religions contrast magic with prayer. The first, they allege, requires the individual will to be imposed over that of the deity, while the second calls upon the deity to bring about some desired effect. However, if practised thoughtfully – as defined by Valiente – magic is performed through the grace of the Goddess. It differs from prayer only in that its effects may be much more obvious and immediate.

Witchcraft is generally performed in concert with lunar movement. For example, spells connected with beginnings, abundance or elimination are most effective during the crescent phase, the waxing phase and the dark phase of the moon, respectively. Modern witches combine magic from a variety of sources, using meditation, chants, colour, perfume, crystals, symbols and body movements. A witch's spells are recorded in his or her personal *Book of Shadows*, which includes procedures the witch has developed independently, as well as those acquired from elsewhere.

A corn dance, performed by Native North Americans of the Santa Clara Pueblo, intended to promote the fertility of the earth, and encourage the growth of corn. The practices of Native Americans have had a major influence on Goddess movements in the USA.

She rewrote much of the group's lore and was the major figure in formalizing the philosophy and practice of magic in the 20th century. The Gardnerian system was undoubtedly the most influential well-spring of modern witchcraft. It was soon carried to the USA, where similar religious experiments were taking place. The charismatic Fred Evans, for example, founded an association in 1957 which became known as Ferefaria, "the festival of the wilderness". The Goddess was the focus of worship, and the group's salutation, "Evo-Kore", and its emblem, the tree, both symbolized the creed that humans are inextricably linked to the environment, in a relationship described as "eco-psychic".

One of the foremost pagan groups is the Dianic Wicca of the Hungarian refugee Zsusanna Budapest, who claims to be a hereditary witch with a pedigree that dates back to AD1270. Budapest espoused a female-centred *thealogy* (a newly coined word for the worship of the Female Divinity) which had its first meeting on the winter solstice of 1971. Her most famous initiate, the American feminist witch Starhawk, stresses the ambivalence of the Goddess who is "love and anger, which refuse to fit comfortably into the social order". She also states that in witchcraft there is no distinction between material and spiritual needs, but that a spiritual yearning may survive once material needs have been satisfied. This longing can only be resolved through the worship and nurturing of the Female Divinity within ourselves, defined as Goddess.

Wicca

Diana the moon goddess, queen of the witches, in her chariot and surrounded by the signs of the zodiac, painted by Lorenzo Costa the Younger (1537–83).

It is usual for Goddess worshippers to refer to their religion as witchcraft, the Old Religion or the Craft. Wicca, the best known Goddess-worshipping cult, derives its name from the old Anglo-Saxon word for witch. It claims roots in the paganism of antiquity, on which it bases much of its contemporary practice. Its followers worship a bipolar (male and female) divinity, in the form of the triple Goddess and the horned God. The Goddess, who is the moon, controls birth, life, death and regeneration. The God, as the sun, is subordinate to her, and complements her activities. The ultimate aim of worship is to achieve individual and universal wholeness by connecting with the multifaceted Goddess intrinsic in the human psyche. This leads to a sense of equilibrium, attained through faith in the value of all creation.

Wiccans place individual freedom above almost all else, enshrining it in the Wiccan Rede (or code): "Eight words the Wiccan Rede fulfil / An' it harm none, do what ye will." Some witches believe that this makes free will inviolate. They consider it wrong to use magic to curtail another's actions, however harmful or criminal they may be. Other witches may cast a spell to "bind" such detrimental activity, but would not undertake rituals which could in any way be thought of as revenge or punishment. However, the Dianic Wicca of Zsusanna Budapest (see p.153) sanctions a certain amount of "grey" magic as an antidote for the evil present in society. For example, the cult performed a public hexing ritual against a serial murderer and rapist in San Francisco who had been at large for more than three years. Within three months of the ritual, the rapist was arrested.

Paramount among the Wiccan rituals are those which celebrate the tenet of rebirth and continuity. The Wiccan

ARADIA

Aradia, the daughter of the moon goddess Diana, is invoked today in many rituals. She is known in the Western world solely through the translation of a manuscript published in 1899 by the folklorist Charles Godfrey Leland, under the title *Aradia, the Gospel of the Witches*. The manuscript was given to Leland by a Florentine witch whom he called Maddalena, and who became a close friend of Leland in his last years.

Leland never produced the original manuscript of the *Gospel*, later even denying that he had seen it. Although this undoubtedly brought its authenticity into question, its importance among witches has grown steadily since its first publication. According to the *Gospel*, Diana, the queen of witches, was the first created being, who projected from herself both light and dark. The former personified the male principle, with whom she mated in the shape of a cat. Aradia (a corruption of the name Herodias) was the product of the union, and was sent to earth as a prophet of the religion of witchcraft. Aradia's main following was apparently among the oppressed, whom she exhorted to fight against feudalism through the use of spells and poison.

Aradia is celebrated for perfecting the magical arts, which included healing and divining through cards and palmistry, taming wild beasts, communing with spirits and understanding the language of the elements. When Aradia returned to her mother, she charged all witches to worship at full moon and left behind a formula for invoking her. This requires the witch to go into a field at midnight with a small red bag filled with salt and implore the goddess to grant her favours.

---

myth of the Goddess describes how Death was overcome with the Goddess's beauty. He hailed her with the Wiccan greeting, "Blessed Be" and kissed her feet, knees, womb, breasts and lips (this is the "five-fold kiss", which features in many Wiccan rites, especially initiations). Death explained: "To be reborn you must die and be ready for a new body; to die you must be born; without love you may not be born, and this is all the magic."

The Great Rite re-enacts the sexual union of the God and Goddess. It can be performed by a priest and priestess, either in reality or in a symbolic form, by plunging the *athame* (witch's knife) into a chalice. "Drawing Down the Moon" is an important ceremony that allegedly derives from ancient Thessaly. In this ceremony, the High Priestess, who invokes the Goddess by asking her to come down from the full moon, becomes a medium for the Goddess's presence.

Zsusanna Budapest, whose Holy Book of Women's Mysteries *has been one of the most influential Wiccan texts.*

Some Wiccans believe that their bodies are the Goddess's instrument of healing, and however adept a Wiccan may be with magic she or he will generally avoid interfering with Nature because of a deep reluctance to upset the balance of the universe. The curb on malevolent magic is strengthened by the "three-fold rule of unsure origin" which warns that anything sent out by a witch will return magnified three times.

The female essence

In 7th-century AD India, mystical texts called *Tantras* began to promulgate the idea of Shakti: raw, female energy, the primordial power without which the gods (in particular Shiva) could not function. One *Tantra* states "women are divinity; women are vital breath". For almost the first time since the establishment of Indo-European, male-centred systems of worship, the supremacy of the Female Divinity was reasserted.

According to the Tantric vision, Shakti emanates from the central, universal force or Great Power, defined as Mahakali, the Great Kali. She is the container of the cosmos, including the gods. One painting shows Shiva sitting in her skull, Vishnu at her breasts and Brahma at her vulva. In addition to believing that the Goddess is the essential, universal energy who activates and protects the male divinities with her prodigious strength, many *Tantras* also define the Goddess as Mahavidya – Great Wisdom.

Women have increasingly turned to Shakti as a positive and powerful female force to emulate and possess. Perhaps the most famous images of Shakti, in which she is mainly personified by Kali, are those of sexual supremacy. She appears with her foot on the chest of Shiva, her husband, as she whirls in her dance of destruction, or else she rides his body in sexual ecstasy. The sacred text, *Kalika Purana*, is full of fantastic tales of Kali's sexual combats with her spouse. It indicates her enjoyment of erotic games and her determination to assert her own will in this area. Her vulva, or yoni, is worshipped by the Shaktas (devotees of Shakti) as the Great Womb. Some male Shaktas castrate themselves to emulate Shakti's appearance. The sect known as the Vamachari Shaktas drink menstrual blood in some of their rites in order to imbibe Shakti's cosmic energy.

Although in many images Kali is portrayed as bloodthirsty in character and

---

THE RIGHT TO CHOOSE

Assertiveness is one of the most obvious qualities of women or deities who embody the female essence, and is the main theme of the Arthurian legend of Gawain and Ragnell. Sir Gawain was one of the most beautiful and popular knights of the age, but he agreed to marry a loathsome hag called Ragnell in return for the answer to her riddle: "What does a woman desire most?" The answer was "Sovereignty".

Most of the retellings of this myth that survive today have been corrupted to convey the frivolous view that a woman must always have her way, but the true significance of the riddle, however it is worded, goes to the heart of female self-realization – the right to choose. When, on the night of their marriage, Gawain kissed the hideous, putrefying Ragnell out of a sense of pity, she immediately turned into a beautiful woman. Secretly, she had wanted Gawain to kiss her in her ugliness because the kiss would release her from a curse. Gawain unintentionally fulfilled her wish, but because he had not acted out of desire, the curse was only partially lifted.

Ragnell offered Gawain a choice: she would stay beautiful either by day – when the pair would appear at court – or by night, when they were alone. He told her that he could not decide, and that the choice was hers. In this way he gave her sovereignty over herself, which was the true meaning of her riddle. Gawain passed the test of manhood and chivalry and Ragnell rewarded him by remaining perpetually beautiful.

Swayambram *(1996), a gouache by Gogisaroj Pal. This is a modern artist's vision of the ancient Indian warrior tradition, whereby men would travel great distances to gather before a woman, who would freely choose her mate from among them.*

appearance, her activities were never wantonly destructive. On the contrary, at her most fearsome, her aim was to wipe out demonic forces before they could endanger the cosmic order. As a symbol of empowerment for women she is, therefore, the perfect model of female balance: powerful, active and assertive, rather than pointlessly aggressive. She returns to women the three virtues that have historically been denied to them in most cultures – strength (moral and physical); intellect and knowledge; and sexual sovereignty.

Contemporary pagan festivals

The pagan calendar has eight annual festivals, and is sometimes known as the Witch's Wheel. There are four major festivals, or Greater Sabbats – Imbolg (also known as Imbolc or Oimelc) on February 2; Beltane on April 30; Lughnasadh (also known as Lammas) on August 1; and Samhain on October 31. The four Lesser Sabbats mark the yearly solstices and equinoxes – Ostara on March 21, Midsummer on June 21, Mabon on September 21 and Yule on December 21. Although the Sabbats can be traced to the Druidic rites of the Celts, they also have clear parallels in ancient cultures throughout the world. They have all been absorbed into Christian custom, in the form of feasts such as Christmas and Easter, or as days dedicated to particular saints.

A page from Raphael's Witch or Oracle of the Future, *a popular 19th-century manuscript, based on the pagan calendar.*

Yule marks the winter equinox, the time of year when mother goddesses – like Astarte of Canaan, Ishtar of Mesopotamia, Isis of Egypt, and Myrrha of Greece – traditionally gave birth to the sun. The feast of Imbolg ("in the womb") signifies the Goddess as Mother Earth, full with child. It was during this feast that the Irish Celts welcomed the goddess Brigit ("the Shining

The Four Witches *(1497), an engraving by Dürer, inspired by the* Malleus Maleficarum *(1486), a book used by witch-hunters to try their victims.*

DANCING SKY-CLAD

Ever since the 15th century, the image of witches dancing naked – sky-clad – under the full moon has been associated with orgies and Satanic worship. For this reason, many older orders of witches now shy away from nakedness in rituals. Nevertheless, nakedness is generally accepted as an important part of ceremonies, and the decision as to whether to dance sky-clad is left to the preference of the individual or coven. As worshippers of the Goddess and her earthly bounties, many witches shed their clothes as a way of integrating as closely as possible with their surrounding environment.

The goddess Aradia (see p.155) enjoins her followers to meet naked at each full moon to offer worship to her, and promises that "ye shall be free from slavery; and as a sign that ye be really free, ye shall be naked in your rights; and ye shall dance, sing, feast, make music and love, all in my praise".

The witch Starhawk states that nakedness represents "the truth that goes deeper than social custom" and that witches worship naked "as a way of establishing closeness and dropping social masks, because power is most easily raised that way, and because the human body is itself sacred. Nakedness is a sign that a witch's loyalty is to the truth before any ideology or any comforting illusions."

Murs, in Provence, is one of the oldest villages in France. Its inhabitants have recreated what they claim is an ancient pagan festival, which includes men and women wearing each other's clothes.

One"), whose spirit was thought to permeate an effigy that had been specially prepared for the festival. Brigit then journeyed throughout Ireland, blessing fields and forests. In ancient Greece, early February marked the lesser Eleusinian festival of Demeter and Kore (see pp.70–71).

Ostara is the pagan festival that approximates to Easter. The popular Western custom of exchanging eggs at this time may have originated with the Magians or ancient Iranians, among whom the eggs were stained red and symbolized the origin of the cosmos (see p.52). Beltane is best known as May Eve or Walpurgis Night, when the May Queen marries the sun god and the universal male and female principles are in perfect harmony. The Dionysian rites of ancient Greece were performed at the spring equinox. Midsummer's Eve is when magic – particularly love magic – is considered to be at its most potent.

In Ireland, Lughnasadh was variously believed to be in honour of the sun god, Lugh, or to have been instituted by him for his foster-mother Tailtiu. Games were held, royal treaties signed and the reigning High King was symbolically married to the goddess of the land (see p.34). Mabon, the autumn equinox, and Samhain are festivals of death. At Samhain, supernatural beings may walk the earth. Traditionally, the hearths of Scotland and Ireland were extinguished on Samhain night and relit from great sacrificial fires in which the sins and trials of the previous year were thought to have been consumed.

Documentary Reference

The Goddess and the animals

In most of the surviving mythologies of Europe and the Near East, goddesses rather than gods are overwhelmingly associated with the welfare and patronage of animals. A goddess might routinely manifest herself as an animal. For example, the Greek goddess Artemis was sometimes worshipped as a bear, by women called *arktoi*, or "she-bears". At the temple of Artemis in Despoina, the statue of the goddess was clothed in a deer skin. By contrast, on the numerous occasions that a male divinity has taken on animal form, it has usually been as a ruse (as in the case of Zeus, disguising himself as a swan, an eagle or a bull in order to rape someone undetected by his wife), or as a form of sacrifice (for example, Christ the Lamb, whose blood was spilled to wash away the sins of humanity).

It is possible that the association of the Goddess with sacred animals dates back to humankind's first systematic attempts to map its own spirituality, on the walls of Paleolithic caves. Although the representations of human females in prehistory vastly outnumbered representations of human males, by far the most numerous images of all

LEFT Medusa Asleep, *by Fernand Khnopff (1858–1921). Both Medusa and the owl were closely associated with the goddess Minerva.*

BELOW *A line drawing of a Boeotian animal goddess, copied from an 8th-century* BC *bowl.*

SITES OF VENUS FIGURINES AND PREHISTORIC CAVE-TEMPLE COMPLEXES IN EUROPE

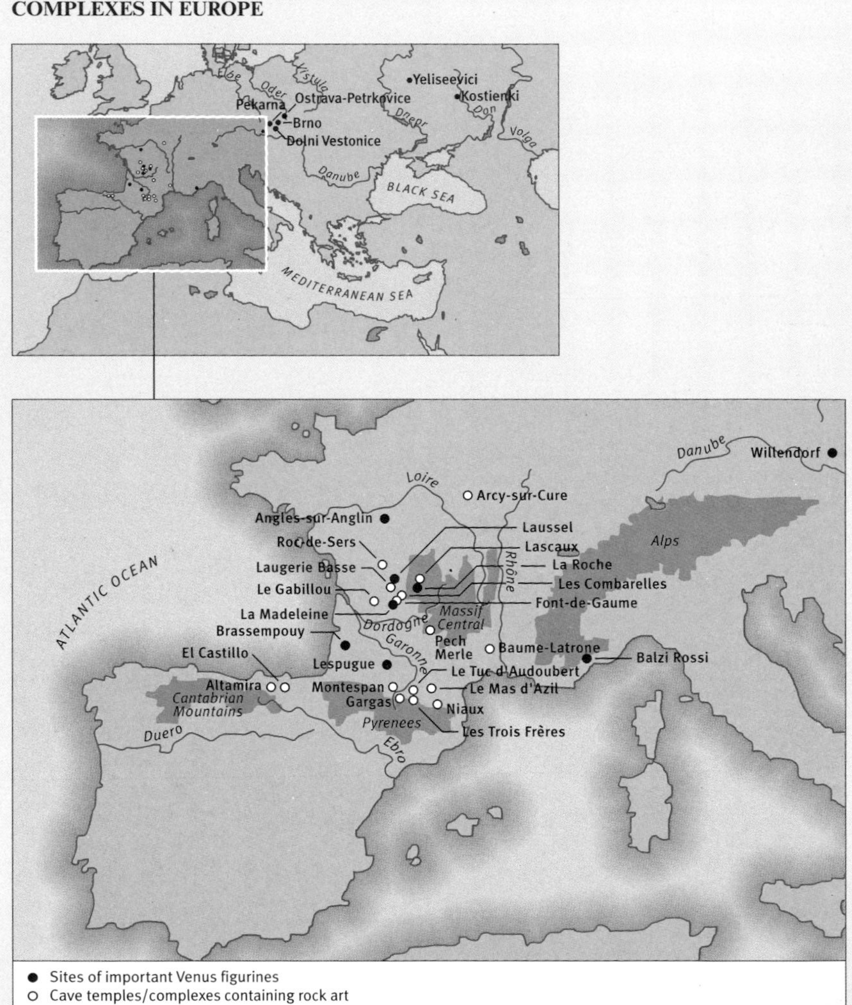

The first cave paintings that were recognized as being the work of prehistoric people were those discovered on the ceilings of the caves at Altamira, in Spain, in 1879. Most of the known caves were unearthed at the beginning of the 20th century – unfortunately, they were treated primarily as tourist attractions and sites for treasure hunters. As a result, many, such as the great complex at Lascaux, France, suffered more damage in decades than they had in millennia.

depicted animals. The larger, grass-eating animals – such as bison and horses – are most common, with dangerous creatures such as lions and rhinoceroses occurring only rarely. However, the Paleolithic caves do not merely record the eating habits of prehistoric peoples. The creatures they hunted most regularly were not the most popular subjects of their paintings. For example, reindeer fragments make up 90 percent of the food-remains in the caves of Lascaux, in France, but there is only one painting of a reindeer in the entire underground complex. Instead of the "hunters' shopping lists" that they were once believed to be, Paleolithic caves seem to be the prehistoric equivalent of holy books – containing coherent, schematic arrangements of symbols, forming the basis of a lost ideology.

In 1959, the French archeologist, André Leroi-Gourhan, began the most extensive analysis to date of more than 60 Paleolithic caves. He identified a set of abstract signs that always seemed to accompany painted animals. The "full" signs were schematic shapes that evolved from depictions of vulvas, wombs and other female images. The "thin" signs, often single or dotted lines, had evolved from sometimes very lifelike representations of the phallus. Leroi-Gourhan claimed that paintings of animals were arranged on the cave walls in very specific patterns. The full signs were associated with bison (or in some areas with female deer, or mammoth), linking them to a female power or potential. The horses were surrounded by thin signs. Of the images, those which were male were far more likely to be in outlying positions. The archeologist James Mellaart, who supervised the excavation of Çatal Hüyük in the 1960s, observed the same arrangement of images there: a central female, surrounded by satellite, subordinate male symbols.

Some of the most spectacular paintings in the Paleolithic underground complexes are in the most cramped, inaccessible locations, leading to speculation that the caves may represent the womb of the earth, from which all animals are born. This view is supported by the tendency of the cave artists to augment any natural rock formations, such as clefts and fissures, that resembled vulvas. These were daubed with red ochre so as to accentuate the similarity. However, Leroi-Gourhan's theories suggest more complementarity between the sexes than some advocates of the prehistoric Goddess would allow: the fissures are surrounded by clusters of multiple thin signs, indicating that Paleolithic humans were fully aware of the need for the male in reproduction.

The terracotta Venus of Malta, c.*3400–3000*BC. *The Neolithic temples of Malta were built between 3500 and 2500*BC *by settlers from Sicily. They are made from blocks of stone, and extend out from cave-like tombs cut into living rock. The ground plans of the temples strongly resemble the outlines of Maltese goddess figurines, such as the one shown above, indicating an identification between earth, temple and deity. Several temples are decorated with red-ochre paintings of trees and animals, including fish, bulls and suckling pigs.*

Males as females

Ritual transvestism was a feature of many ancient priesthoods, and can still be found today among a number of traditional peoples. Perhaps the best-known examples of priestly transvestism among the ancients are the priests of Cybele, who castrated themselves at their initiation and thereafter wore only women's clothes. The Roman historian Tacitus (*c.*AD56–120) claimed that, among the Germanic peoples, the priests always dressed as women. He could have seen examples of the practice closer to home: Cybele was one of the most enthusiastically worshipped deities in Rome,

THE DISTRIBUTION OF CREATION MYTHS CONTAINING BISEXUAL BEINGS

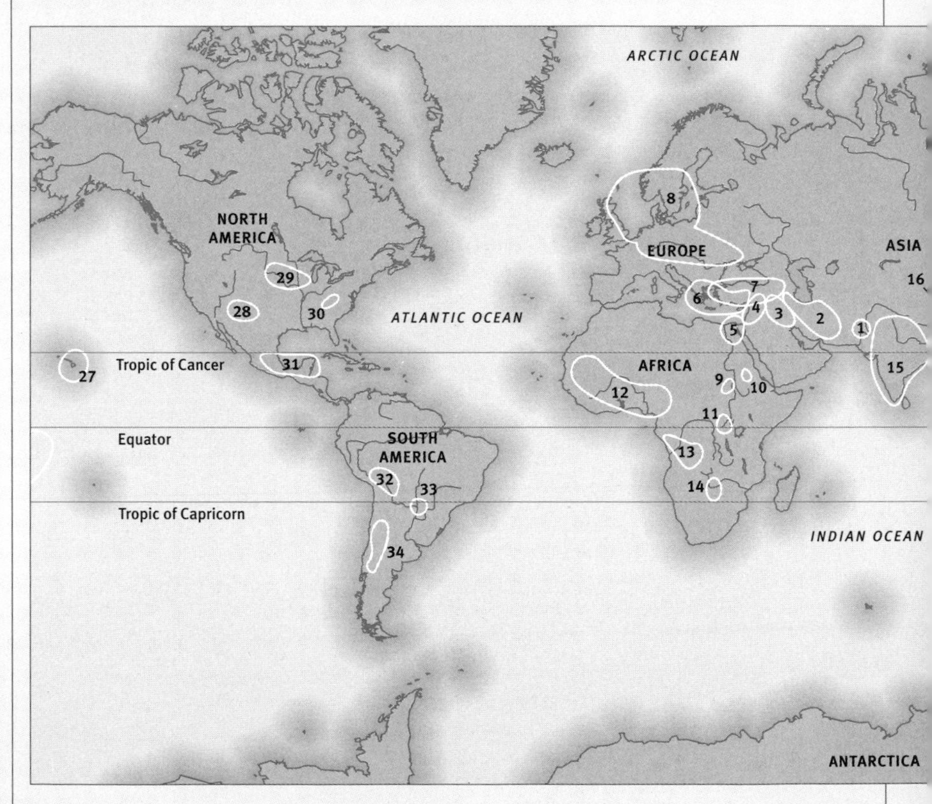

In many of the world's myths, the original creator being is neither male nor female, but both. This bisexual being is able to copulate with itself to generate the world. However, as myths and religions have evolved, the bisexual nature of the creator has often gradually been disguised.

and ritual transvestism was a feature of Roman festivals such as the Lupercalia, which was held every February 15, probably to celebrate the she-wolf who suckled Romulus and Remus. The Church Father, St Augustine (AD354–430), condemned men who clothed themselves as women at the feast of Janus, saying that they could never enter heaven.

Ritual transvestism survives in a number of cultures, often coinciding with areas that retain myths of primordial, bisexual beings that played some part in the creation of the world. For example, among the Navajo, the *nadle* is a man

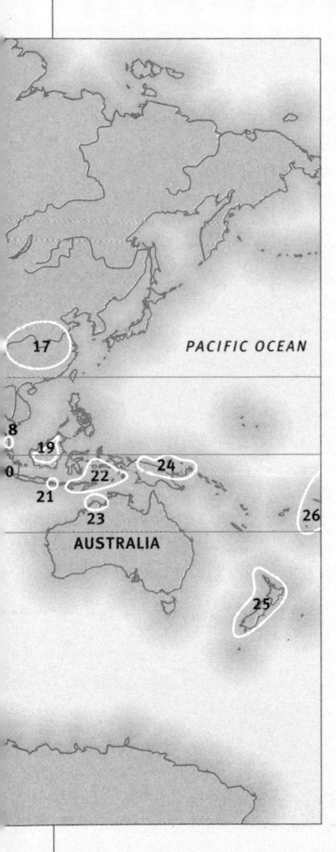

Key

Bisexual creator beings occur or have occurred among the myths of:

1- the ancient Indus Valley civilization
2- ancient Iran
3- ancient Sumer
4- the Phoenicians and other ancient Semitic peoples
5- ancient Egypt
6- Aegean cults, such as Orphism
7- Asia Minor
8- Old Germanic and Baltic peoples, and in various strands of European folklore and mysticism, such as Kabbalism and alchemy
9- ancient Nubia, extending from the Nile to the Libyan desert
10- the Kunama of eastern Sudan
11- the Hunde of Zaire
12- the Dogon-Bambara of Mali
13- the Villi-Kongo, Luba, Lulua and Chokwe of southwestern Angola and Zaire
14- the Tonga Lala of Botswana and Zimbabwe
15- the Vedic, Hindu, Tantric and Shakti-worshipping traditions of India, as well as local groups such as the Musahar
16- the Kochin, Naga, Abor and Khasi of northern Burma and Assam
17- the Taoist and Confucian traditions of China
18- the Se-Plakai of Malaysia
19- groups on Pulaua Nias
20- the Dayak of Borneo
21- Bali
22- groups dispersed through islands from Sumba to Aru
23- the Aboriginals of northern Australia
24- the Widaro, Yatmul and other groups of northern New Guinea, New Ireland, the Admiralties and neighbouring islands
25- the Maori of New Zealand
26- the Tongans, Tahitians and Raiateans of Polynesia
27- Hawaii
28- the Zuni and Navajo
29- the Sauk, Fox, Dakota and Omaha
30- the Cherokee
31- the Aztecs and Maya of Mesoamerica
32- the Aymaras of the central Andes
33- the Araucanians of Chile
34- the Lenguas of Paraguay

who is told to become a woman by the moon, in a dream; and the shamans of the Dayaks of Borneo likewise become transvestites after receiving spirit instructions in their dreams. However, ritual bisexuality does not always coincide with myths of bisexual creators. For example, the Chukchi of Siberia have a type of shaman known as a "soft man", who dresses and behaves as a woman, and sometimes even takes a husband.

There are various explanations for the behaviour of ritual transvestites. It is possible that they are striving, consciously or unconsciously, to attain a state of androgyny in which they unify the complementary aspects of male and female, and thereby attain a superior, divine or near-divine, state. Another suggestion, put forward by some advocates of the supreme Goddess, is that at one time all religious and magical knowledge belonged to women. As a result, when men first began to appropriate religious authority they dressed as women so as to make themselves more acceptable to the spirits and forces of Nature. The proponents of this theory point to the Celebes as an example of a culture that never made the transition from a female- to a male-dominated religion. They claim that, despite the efforts of an incipient male priesthood, ritual power remained in the hands of the women, who nevertheless came to accept assistance from an order of transvestite male priests called *tjalabai*, or "imitation women".

Some ritual transvestites openly claim to be emulating, and in the service of, a goddess. The *hijras* of the Indian sub-continent, in a manner reminiscent of the priests of Cybele, castrate themselves while gazing at a picture of the goddess Bahachura Mata and repeating her name so as to identify with her. The Dayaks usually invoke spirits in the name of a great mother, Ini. The historian of religion, Mircea Eliade, wrote in *Shamanism* (1964) that Dayak religious practice "shows clear traces of a feminine magic and a matriarchal mythology". On the other hand, a Chukchi soft man is not attempting to emulate any goddess. He is instructed to change sex by a male spirit, called a *ke'let*, who becomes his "husband". These male spirits are so powerful and protective that, despite their bashful manner, soft men are the most feared shamans among the Chukchi. Male followers of the Krishna cult in India dress in women's clothes to identify themselves with the *gopis*, or cowherds, who were seduced by the god Krishna. However, this does not imply the existence of a divine female power: on the contrary, this form of ritual transvestism is undertaken because "all souls are feminine to God".

The Romance tradition

A Mon Seul Desir, *a tapestry from a series based on the theme of the lady and the unicorn, made in Brussels at the end of the 15th century. According to legend, the unicorn allowed itself to be captured by a virgin, because of its desire to lay its horn in a maiden's lap. Christian and Romance iconography, inspired by the existence of Mary, the ideal virgin, began to identify Christ as, in the words of one medieval hymn, the "wild unicorn whom the Virgin caught and tamed".*

The songs and poems that comprise the Romance tradition of 12th- and 13th-century France and Germany all share an idealization of women as unattainable, perfect beings, worthy of constant, although hopeless, devotion. The early French troubadours and German *minnesingers* (lyric poets) considered their mistresses to be goddesses, and worshipped them with a devotion that did not seek any physical gratification. Although there is little sign of Mary-worship in the early poems, by the beginning of the 13th century the mistress was regularly being addressed as the Virgin. Another common way in which a troubadour showed his reverence for his mistress was by referring to her as *Midons*, or "My Lord".

Romance literature is preoccupied with chivalry and adventure, detailing deeds of honour and bravery that might make a man deserving of his mistress's attention. One of the most influential works in the chivalric tradition was *Perceval ou li Conte du Graal*, written by Chrétien de Troyes in the latter half of the 12th century. This poem introduced the theme of the Holy Grail into European literature. The idea of the Grail – a vessel promising rejuvenation and eternal life – quickly subsumed the legends of innumerable localized Celtic goddesses, who often possessed life-giving cauldrons. Perceval, or Parsifal, also eventually became Christianized, although originally he was a typical son–lover to a goddess (see pp.80–81). His original titles included the "Green One" and the "Son of the Widow".

Glossary

Aditi ancient Iranian primordial goddess and mother of all other deities and heavenly bodies. Also known as "Cow of Light" and "Freedom"
Amaterasu Japanese goddess of the sun and supreme deity of the Shinto religion
Ana see MORRIGAN
Anahita moon and fertility goddess in the ancient Iranian religion of Zoroastrianism
Anath Canaanite goddess of fertility and war, worshipped alongside her brother–lover, Baal
Andromeda daughter of CASSIOPEIA. She was offered as a sacrifice to appease the sea god, Poseidon, after Cassiopeia boasted that she and Andromeda were more beautiful than the sea nymphs, the Nereides. Andromeda was saved by the hero, Perseus
aniconic symbolizing something without attempting to resemble or portray it
anima the female component of the male personality in Jungian psychology
animus the male component of the female personality in Jungian psychology. Also hostility; and the spirit that moves someone or something to action
Annapurna Himalayan mountain and goddess of plenty
Aphrodite Greek goddess of love
apotropeic protective or tending to ward off evil
apsarases Indian river spirits, and consorts of the Indian pantheon, especially Indra
archetype the original form of some object or phenomenon. In Jungian psychology, primordial images or situations that have somehow become encoded in the genetic fabric of the human mind, and are passed on from generation to generation
Arinna Hittite sun goddess
Artemis Greek moon goddess, most famous as a virgin huntress
Asherah Mother Goddess of Canaan
Ashtoreth derogatory form of ASTARTE
Astarte Canaanite and Phoenician goddess of fertility, love, sexuality and the sea. Often described as being equivalent to ANATH
athame ceremonial witch's knife
Athene Greek warrior maiden and goddess of wisdom and domestic skills
Auchinalgu moon goddess among the Araucanian people of Chile
avatar aspect or manifestation of a Hindu deity, gaining widespread use as the manifestation of any divine being
Badb see MORRIGAN
Barbara Catholic saint often assimilated to OYA
Biman Chan Cambodian moon goddess
Boann Celtic Irish goddess, patron deity of the River Boyne
Branwen Celtic Welsh goddess of love and the moon. Daughter of the sea god, Llyr
Brigit Celtic Irish goddess of healing, smiths and fertility, christianized as St Bridget
Cailleach Bheur ancestral hag-goddess found throughout Celtic Britain, said to have shaped the land and guided the flow of the rivers
Cassiopeia Greek queen, mother of ANDROMEDA, and goddess of night and beauty
Ceres Roman equivalent of DEMETER
Chalchiuhtlicue Aztec water goddess known as "Jade Skirt"
Changing Bear Maiden Navajo Native American figure of evil, also known as Tcikee Cac Nadleehe
Changing Woman Pueblo Native American fertility figure and mother of heroes, existing under many different names
Circe Greek sorceress who lived on the island of Aenea
Coatlicue Aztec goddess of flowers, and mother of the Aztec pantheon
Coyolxauhqui Aztec warrior and moon goddess
Cybele Anatolian Mother Goddess who became the most popular deity of the Roman Empire
Danu Celtic Irish mother of the gods
Demeter Greek goddess of the productivity of the earth. Mother of KORE (or PERSEPHONE)
Devi originally a general Indian term for a goddess. Now usually used to designate the Indian supreme goddess and ultimate power of the universe. Also known as SHAKTI
Devi Sri Indonesian rice goddess
Dharani Indian earth goddess
Diana Roman moon goddess
Dike one of the Greek trinity of goddesses called the Moirae. Her name means "Justice"
Diti Vedic goddess, mother of a race of storm spirits and a race of submarine giants
Durga Indian warrior goddess
Eirene one of the Greek trinity of goddesses

called the Moirae. Her name means "Peace"

Epona Celtic goddess whose precise significance seems to have varied from region to region. Often associated with horses

Ereshkigal Mesopotamian queen of the underworld

Erzulie Voodoo goddess of love

Eshara Mesopotamian goddess of productive fields, patron of the ownership of land

Eunomia one of the Greek trinity of goddesses called the Moirae. Her name means "Good Order"

Europa a family goddess in southern Greece, or one of the Oceanides (sea nymphs). Also one of the names of Demeter at Lebadeia. She was raped by Zeus

Eurynome one of the Greek Oceanides, or water nymphs. Also one of the names of Artemis at Phigalia

Flora Roman goddess of spring and flowers

Fortuna Roman goddess of chance and lotteries

Freya fertility goddess and leader of the Valkyries

Gaia Greek mother earth

Ganesh Hindu elephant-headed god

Ganga personification of the River Ganges in India, sister of PARVATI and wife of all the celestial gods

Gauri Hindu cosmic cow, origin of the world and source of abundance, worshipped with GANESH at wedding ceremonies in central India

Hainuwele food goddess of New Guinea and Melanesia

Hathor Egyptian cosmic cow

Hecate Greek Titan, a powerful witch who forms trinities with ARTEMIS and Lucina, and with DEMETER and KORE

Heket see HEQIT

Heqit Egyptian giver of life, who presides over birth, especially that of kings. Represented as a woman with a frog's head

Hera queen of the Olympian gods

hierodule sacred prostitute

Hi'iaka Hawaiian weather goddess, younger sister of PELE and mistress of the hula

Hine creatrix worshipped in some form throughout Polynesia

Hokhma see SOPHIA

Husbishag Akkadian goddess of the underworld, who knows the hour of every creature's death

Iamanje see YEMONJA

Imberombera Australian ancestor who produced humankind and provided it with food and language

Inanna Sumerian supreme goddess

Indrani Vedic goddess of sensual pleasure, and owner of a celestial tree which rejuvenates all who see it

Ishtar Mesopotamian supreme goddess

Isis Egyptian goddess of the Nile. One of the most popular goddesses of the Roman Empire

ithyphallic possessing an erect phallus

Izanami mother of the Japanese pantheon

Juno queen of the Roman pantheon, corresponds to the Greek goddess HERA

Kali Hindu goddess of eternal time, and bringer of death

Kalwadi northern Australian Ancestor, who is thought to swallow boys during their puberty rituals, and regurgitate them as men

Klu-rgyal-mo Tibetan primordial creatrix

Kore daughter of DEMETER

Kwan yin Chinese goddess of mercy

Lakshmi popular Hindu goddess of wealth and fortune

Lilith Sumerian storm goddess, absorbed into Hebrew tradition as the first wife of Adam

lingam the symbolic, erect penis of the Hindu god, Shiva. Also a general term for penis

Lueji barren form of an African rainbow python which can bring either rain or dry weather, worshipped by the Lunda and Bemba peoples

Macha see MORRIGAN

Machilottu rural Indian goddess, worshipped in the state of Kerala. Patron of wrongly maligned women

Mahadevi Hindu supreme being, also known as DEVI or SHAKTI

Mahakali a personification of KALI as the bringer of cholera

Mahamaya Indian term for the Goddess manifesting herself as Wisdom. Also, the name of the queen who was mother of the Buddha

Mama Ocllo Inca empress and moon goddess, who lived in the 12th century AD

Matronit see SOPHIA

Mawu Lisa creator-being variously worshipped in female, male or androgynous forms

Maya Indian goddess of illusion

Mayi ancient Australian sisters, said to have risen into the sky as the Pleiades
Menesis Baltic moon goddess
Metis Greek Titan, whose name means "Cunning Intelligence". She was the first wife of Zeus, who swallowed her to gain her wisdom
Minerva Roman goddess of intelligence and military skill. Counterpart of the Greek goddess ATHENE
Miru Oceanian goddess of the three lowest underworlds, whose home is called the "door of the night"
Morgan Le Fay evil sorceress in the Arthurian cycle of legends
Morrigan Irish Celtic goddess of war, comprising the trinity of ANA, BADB and MACHA
Nanda Devi Indian goddess of the Himalayas
Nanshe Babylonian goddess of water, judgement, dreams and fishing. The patron deity of Lagash in Sumer
Neith Egyptian creatrix, cow-goddess, and guardian of funerary urns, assimilated to numerous other Egyptian goddesses
Net see NEITH
Nimue Welsh name for the Lady of the Lake, who invested Arthur as king of England
Ninlil patron deity of the Mesopotamian city of Nippur, sometimes conflated with ERESHKIGAL, and later assimilated to ISHTAR
Nuanet see NEITH
Nü-kua "Restorer of Cosmic Equilibrium", an early Chinese creatrix, usually portrayed as a dragon with a human head
Oba Nigerian goddess of the River Oba, wife of the thunder god and protector of prostitutes
Omecithuatl "Woman of Duality", one half of the being that gave birth to the Aztec pantheon
Oshun Nigerian goddess of the River Oshun and wife of the thunder god, also known as Oxun
Oya goddess of the River Niger and wife of the thunder god, to whom she gave power over fire and lightning
Pachamama Peruvian earth goddess, portrayed as a dragon when she causes earthquakes
Parvati the SHAKTI of the Hindu god, Shiva
Pele Hawaiian volcano goddess
Persephone daughter of DEMETER
Radha wife of the Hindu god, Krishna, and a form of LAKSHMI
Ran Scandinavian sea goddess
Saci see INDRANI
Sarama Indian goddess of domesticated animals, especially dogs
Sarasvati Indian goddess of knowledge and the arts, revered by Hindus and Buddhists, and worshipped in libraries with offerings of flowers and incense
Satene Melanesian underworld goddess, through whose arms the dead attempted to pass. Those who succeeded were reincarnated as humans, those who failed as animals
Saule Slavic sun goddess
Sedna Arctic mistress of sea animals
Sekhmet Egyptian lion-headed goddess
Selene Greek moon goddess
Shakti the active, female power of the male Hindu gods, especially Shiva. The ultimate source of the universe
shaman traditional worker-with-spirits
Shekhina see SOPHIA
Sophia personification of Wisdom in Near-Eastern religions and Gnostic and Judaic philosophies. Also known as Shekhina, Hokhma and the Matronit
Spider Woman Native North American creatrix
Styx water nymph inhabiting the river in the Greek underworld that bears her name
Tara Indian and Tibetan goddess of wisdom, the stars and the senses. Occurs in five forms: white, green, blue, yellow and red
Tethys Greek sea goddess, daughter of GAIA
Tiamat Mesopotamian goddess of salt water, described as a mother of dragons
Tonantzin Aztec goddess of earth and corn, who reappeared in Mexican Catholicism as the Virgin of Guadeloupe
Tshimbulu seductive, fruitful aspect of LUEJI
Venus Roman goddess of love
Vesta Roman hearth goddess
Xochiquetzal Aztec goddess of love, beauty and flowers, who is closely associated with child-bearing. Her name means "Flower Feather"
Yemanja see YEMONJA
Yemonja Nigerian goddess of salt and fresh water, also known as Yemanja in parts of Nigeria and Central America, and Iamanje in South America
Zarya Slavic goddess of healing waters

Bibliography

Allen, P.G. *The Sacred Hoop: Recovering the Feminine in American Indian Traditions*, Beacon Press, Boston, 1986

Apuleius, (trans. R. Graves) *The Golden Ass*, Penguin, Harmondsworth, 1950

Arthur, R.H. *The Wisdom Goddess: Feminine Motifs in Eight Nag Hammadi Documents*, University Press of America, Lanham, New York and London, 1984

Asad, T. (ed.) *Anthropology and the Colonial Encounter*, Ithaca Press, London, 1973

Ashe, G. *The Virgin, Mary's Cult and the Re-emergence of the Goddess*, Arkana, London and New York, 1988

Bachofen, J.J. (trans. R. Mannheim) *Myth, Religion and Mother Right*, Princeton University Press, Princeton, 1973

Baring, A. and Cashford, J. *The Myth of the Goddess: Evolution of an Image*, Viking Arkana, Harmondsworth, 1991

Begg, E. *The Cult of the Black Virgin*, Arkana, London, Boston and Henley, 1985

Bennett, G. *Traditions of Belief: Women, Folklore and the Supernatural Today*, Penguin, Harmondsworth, 1987

Berger, P. *The Goddess Obscured: Transformation of the Grain Protectress from Goddess to Saint*, Beacon Press, Boston, 1985

Bishop, C. *Sex and Spirit*, Duncan Baird Publishers, London and New York, 1996

Bolen, J.S. *Goddesses in Everywoman: A New Psychology of Women*, Harper & Row, New York, 1984

Bonnefoy, Y. and Doniger, W. (ed.) *Mythologies* (2 volumes), University of Chicago Press, Chicago and London, 1991

Branston, B. *The Lost Gods of England*, Book Club Associates, London, 1974

Brooks, D.R. *The Secret of the Three Cities: An Introduction to Hindu Sâkta Tantrism*, University of Chicago Press, Chicago and London, 1990

Bryant, P. *Native American Mythology*, Aquarian Press, London and San Francisco, 1991

Budapest, Z. *The Holy Book of Women's Mysteries*, Robert Hale, London, 1990

Caldecott, M. *Women in Celtic Myth: Tales of Extraordinary Women from the Ancient Celtic Tradition*, Destiny Books, Rochester, Vermont, 1992

Caldwell, R.S. (trans.) *Hesiod's Theogony*, Focus Information Group, Cambridge, Massachusetts, 1987

Camp, C.V. *Wisdom and the Feminine in the Book of Proverbs*, Almond Press, Sheffield, 1985

Campbell, J. *Historical Atlas of World Mythology*, Harper & Row, New York, 1988

Campbell, J. *The Masks of God: Creative Mythology*, Penguin, Harmondsworth, 1976

Campbell, J. *The Masks of God: Occidental Mythology*, Penguin, Harmondsworth, 1976

Campbell, J. *The Masks of God: Oriental Mythology*, Penguin, Harmondsworth, 1976

Campbell, J. *The Masks of God: Primitive Mythology*, Penguin, Harmondsworth, 1976

Campbell, J. and Musès, C. (ed.) *In All Her Names: Explorations of the Feminine in Divinity*, Harper, San Francisco, 1991

Caputi, J. *Gossips, Gorgons and Crones: The Fates of the Earth*, Bear & Company, Santa Fe, New Mexico, 1993

Cary, M. et al. (ed.) *The Oxford Classical Dictionary*, Clarendon Press, Oxford, 1949

Clark, E.E. *Indian Legends of the Pacific Northwest*, University of California Press, Berkeley, Los Angeles, London, 1953

Clark, R.T.R. *Myth and Symbol in Ancient Egypt*, Thames & Hudson, London, 1959

Clendinnen, I. *Aztecs: An Interpretation*, Cambridge University Press, Cambridge, 1991

Colum, P. *Legends of Hawaii*, Yale University Press, New Haven and London, 1937

Comay, J. *Who's Who in the Old Testament*, J. M. Dent, London, 1971

Connell, J.T. *Meetings with Mary: Visions of the Blessed Mother*, Virgin Books, London, 1995

Cott, C. *Isis and Osiris: Exploring the Goddess Myth*, Doubleday, New York, 1994

Crawford, O.G.S. *The Eye Goddess*, Phoenix House, London, 1957

Crowley, V. *Wicca: The Old Religion in the New Age*, Aquarian Press, London, 1989

Curtis, V.K. *Persian Myths*, British Museum Press, London, 1993

Davies, O. and Bowie, F. (ed.) *Celtic Christian Spirituality*, SPCK, London, 1995

Deren, M. *The Voodoo Gods*, Paladin, St Albans, 1975

Dowson, J. *A Classical Dictionary of Hindu Mythology and Religion*, Rupa, Calcutta, 1982
Durdin-Robertson, L. *The Year of the Goddess: A Perpetual Calendar of Festivals*, Aquarian Press, Wellingborough, 1990
Eisler, R. *The Chalice and the Blade: Our History, Our Future*, Pandora, London, 1993
Engelsman, J.C. *The Feminine Dimension of the Divine: A Study of Sophia and Feminine Images in Religion*, Chiron Publications, Wilmette, Illinois, 1994
Erndl, K.M. *Victory to the Mother: The Hindu Goddess of Northwest India in Myth, Ritual, and Symbol*, Oxford University Press, New York and Oxford, 1993
Farmer, P. (ed.) *Beginnings: Creation Myths of the World*, Chatto & Windus, London, 1978
Franz, M.-L. von *The Golden Ass of Apuleius: The Liberation of the Feminine in Man*, Shambhala, Boston and London, 1992
Getty, A. *Goddess: Mother of Living Nature*, Thames & Hudson, London, 1990
Gimbutas, M. and Marler J. (ed.) *The Civilization of the Goddess*, Harper, San Francisco, 1991
Gleason, J. *Oya: In Praise of an African Goddess*, Harper, San Francisco, 1992
Grant, M. *Ancient History Atlas 1700 BC to AD 565*, Weidenfeld & Nicolson, London, 1989
Graves, R. *The White Goddess*, Faber & Faber, London, 1961
Graves, R. and Patai, R. *Hebrew Myths: The Book of Genesis*, Arena, London, 1989
Green, M. *Women and Goddesses in the Celtic World*, British Association for the Study of Religions, Leeds, 1991
Green, M. *Celtic Goddesses, Warriors, Virgins and Mothers*, British Museum Press, London, 1995
Green, M.J. *Dictionary of Celtic Myth and Legend*, Thames & Hudson, London, 1992
Grigson, G. *The Goddess of Love: The Birth, Triumph, Death and Return of Aphrodite*, Constable, London, 1976
Grimal, P. and Kershaw, S. (ed.), (trans. A.R. Maxwell-Hyslop), *The Concise Dictionary of Classical Mythology*, Basil Blackwell, Oxford, 1990
Guiley, R.E. *Harper's Encyclopedia of Mystical and Paranormal Experience*, Harper, San Francisco, 1991
Gustafson, F. *The Black Madonna*, Sigo Press, Boston, 1990
Haardt, R. (ed.), (trans. J.F. Hendry), *Gnosis, Character and Testimony*, Brill, Leiden, 1971
Harding, M.E. *The Way of All Women: A Psychological Interpretation*, Rider, London, 1971
Harding, M.E. *Woman's Mysteries, Ancient and Modern: A Psychological Interpretation of the Feminine Principle as Portrayed in Myth, Story and Dreams*, Rider, London, 1989
Harrison, J.E. *Prolegomena to the Study of Greek Religion*, Princeton University Press, Princeton, 1991
Hart, G. *Egyptian Myths*, British Museum Press, London, 1990
Haskins, S. *Mary Magdalen: Myth and Metaphor*, HarperCollins, London, 1994
Heaton, J. Meits, *Divinination, Psychotherapy and Cunning Intelligence*, The Company of Astrologers, London, 1990
Hejaiej, M. *Behind Closed Doors: Women's Oral Narratives in Tunis*, Quartet Books, London, 1996
Hillman, J. (ed.) *Facing the Gods*, Spring Publications, Dallas, 1980
Hollis, S.T., Pershing, L. and Young, M.J. (eds) *Feminist Theory and the Study of Folklore*, University of Illinois Press, Urbana and Chicago, 1993
Houston, J. *The Hero and the Goddess: The Odyssey as Mystery and Initiation*, Aquarian Press, London, 1993
Hurtado, L. (ed.) *Goddesses in Religions and Modern Debate*, Scholars Press, Atlanta, Georgia, 1990
Johnson, A.R. *Sacral Kingship in Ancient Israel*, University of Wales Press, Cardiff, 1967
Johnson, B. *Lady of the Beasts: Ancient Images of the Goddess and Her Sacred Animals*, Harper, San Francisco, 1988
Jones, K. *The Ancient British Goddess: Her Myths, Legends and Sacred Sites*, Ariadne Publications, Glastonbury, 1991
Jung, C. and Kerényi, C. (trans. R.F.C. Hull) *Essays on a Science of Mythology: The Myth of the Divine Child and the Mysteries of Eleusis*, Princeton University Press, Princeton, 1969
Kemp, A. *Witchcraft and Paganism Today*,

Brockhampton Press, London, 1993
Kerényi, C. (trans. M. Stein) *Goddesses of Sun and Moon*, Spring Publications, Dallas, 1979
Kerényi, C. (trans. N. Cameron) *The Gods of the Greeks*, Thames & Hudson, London, 1979
Kerényi, C. (trans. R. Mannheim) *Eleusis: Archetypal Image of Mother and Daughter*, Princeton University Press, Princeton, 1991
King, U. (ed.) *Religion and Gender*, Blackwell, Oxford and Cambridge, Massachusetts, 1995
Kinsley, D. *Hindu Goddesses: Visions of the Divine Feminine in the Hindu Religious Tradition*, Motilal Banarsidass, Delhi, 1987
Knapp, A.B. *The History and Culture of Ancient Western Asia and Egypt*, Wadsworth, Belmont, California, 1988
Koltuv, B.B. *The Book of Lilith*, Nicolas-Hays, York Beach, Maine, 1986
Koltuv, B.B. *Solomon and Sheba: Inner Marriage and Individuation*, Nicolas-Hays, York Beach, Maine, 1993
Kramer, S.N. (ed.) *Mythologies of the Ancient World*, Anchor Books, New York, 1961
Kramer, S.N. *The Sumerians: Their History, Culture, and Character*, University of Chicago Press, Chicago and London, 1963
Larrington, C. (ed.) *The Feminist Companion to Mythology*, Pandora, London, 1992
Lassner, J. *Demonizing the Queen of Sheba: Boundaries of Gender and Culture in Postbiblical Judaism and Medieval Islam*, University of Chicago Press, Chicago and London, 1993
Layard, J. and Bosch, A.S. (ed.) *A Celtic Quest: Sexuality and Soul in Individuation*, Spring Publications, Dallas, 1975
Leeming, D. and Page, J. *Goddess: Myths of the Female Divine*, Oxford University Press, New York and Oxford, 1994
Leland, C.G. *Aradia: The Gospel of the Witches*, Gates of Annwn, London, 1991
LeRoy, J. (ed.) *Kewa Tales*, University of British Columbia Press, Vancouver, 1985
Lévi-Strauss, C. (trans. M. Layton) *Structural Anthropology 2*, Penguin, Harmondsworth, 1994
Long, A.P. *In a Chariot Drawn by Lions: The Search for the Female in Deity*, The Crossing Press, Freedom, California, 1993
MacCormack, C. and Strathern, M. (ed.) *Nature, Culture and Gender*, Cambridge University Press, Cambridge, 1980
Macquitty, W. *Island of Isis: Philae, Temple of the Nile*, Book Club Associates, London, 1976
Mallory, J.P. *In Search of the Indo-Europeans: Language, Archaeology and Myth*, Thames & Hudson, London, 1989
Matthews, C. (ed.) *Voices of the Goddess: A Chorus of Sibyls*, Aquarian Press, Wellingborough, 1990
Matthews, C. *Sophia Goddess of Wisdom: The Divine Feminine from Black Goddess to World Soul*, Mandala, London, 1991
McCall, H. *Mesopotamian Myths*, British Museum Press, London, 1990
McCrickard, J. *Eclipse of the Sun: An Investigation into Sun and Moon Myths*, Gothic Image Publications, Glastonbury, 1990
McLean, A. *The Triple Goddess: An Exploration of the Archetypal Feminine*, Phanes Press, Grand Rapids, 1989
Miles, M.R. *Carnal Knowing: Female Nakedness and Religious Meaning in the Christian West*, Burns & Oates, Tunbridge Wells, 1992
Monaghan, P. *The Book of Goddesses and Heroines*, Llewellyn Publications, St Paul, Minnesota, 1993
Mookerjee, A. *Kali: The Feminine Force*, Thames & Hudson, London, 1988
Moscati, S. (trans. A. Hamilton) *The World of the Phoenicians*, Sphere Books, London, 1968
Neumann, E. (trans. R. Mannheim) *The Great Mother, An Analysis of the Archetype*, Princeton University Press, Princeton, 1972
Nicholson, S. (ed.) *The Goddess Re-awakening: The Feminine Principle Today*, Quest Books, Wheaton, Illinois, 1989
Norman, H. (ed.) *Northern Tales*, Pantheon Books, New York, 1990
O'Flaherty, W.D. (trans.) *Hindu Myths: A Sourcebook Translated from the Sanskrit*, Penguin, Harmondsworth, 1975
O'Flaherty, W.D. *Women, Androgynes, and Other Mythical Beasts*, University of Chicago Press, Chicago and London, 1980
O'Flaherty, W.D. *Dreams, Illusions and Other Realities*, University of Chicago Press, Chicago and London, 1984
O'Hogain, D. *Myth, Legend and Romance, An*

Encyclopædia of the Irish Folk Tradition, Prentice Hall, New York, 1991

Opler, M.E. *Myths and Tales of the Chiricahua Apache Indians*, University of Nebraska Press, Lincoln and London, 1994

Opler, M.E. *Myths and Tales of the Jicarilla Apache Indians*, University of Nebraska Press, Lincoln and London, 1994

Owen, L. *Her Blood is Gold: Reclaiming the Power of Menstruation*, Aquarian Press, London and San Francisco, 1993

Page, R.I. *Norse Myths*, British Museum Press, London, 1990

Pagels, E. *The Gnostic Gospels*, Penguin, Harmondsworth, 1982

Patai, R. *The Hebrew Goddess*, Wayne State University Press, Detroit, 1990

Perera, S.B. *Descent to the Goddess: A Way of Initiation for Women*, Inner City Books, Toronto, 1981

Pintchman, T. *The Rise of the Goddess in the Hindu Tradition*, State University of New York Press, Albany, 1994

Pritchard, J.B. (ed.) *Ancient Near Eastern Texts Relating to the Old Testament*, Princeton University Press, Princeton, 1955

Qualls-Corbett, N. *The Sacred Prostitute: Eternal Aspect of the Feminine*, Inner City Books, Toronto, 1988

Rahner, H. (trans. S. Bullough) *Our Lady and the Church*, Darton, Longman & Todd, London, 1961

Redgrove, P. *The Black Goddess and the Sixth Sense*, Paladin, London, 1989

Rees, A. and Rees, B. *Celtic Heritage: Ancient Tradition in Ireland and Wales*, Thames & Hudson, London, 1961

Robinson, G. *Raven the Trickster: Legends of the North American Indians*, Chatto & Windus, London, 1981

Rodman, S. and Cleaver, C. *Spirits of the Night: The Voudun Gods of Haiti*, Spring Publications, Dallas, 1992

Spretnak, C. *Lost Goddesses of Early Greece: A Collection of Pre-Hellenic Myths*, Beacon Press, Boston, 1984

Sproul, B.C. *Primal Myths: Creating the World*, Harper, San Francisco, 1979

Starhawk, *Spiral Dance: A Rebirth of the Ancient Religion of the Great Goddess*, Harper, San Francisco, 1989

Stone, M. *When God was a Woman*, Barns & Noble, New York, 1976

Tacitus, (trans. H. Mattingly) *Tacitus on Britain and Germany*, Penguin, West Drayton, 1948

Taube, K. *Aztec and Maya Myths*, British Museum Press, London, 1993

Thomas, K. *Religion and the Decline of Magic*, Penguin, Harmondsworth, 1978

Vercoutter, J. (trans. R. Sharman) *The Search for Ancient Egypt*, Thames & Hudson, London, 1992

Voragine, J. de (trans. R. Sharman) *The Golden Legend: Readings on the Saints* (2 volumes), Princeton University Press, Princeton, 1993

Walker, B.G. *The Woman's Dictionary of Symbols and Sacred Objects*, Harper & Row, San Francisco, 1988

Warner, M. *Alone of All Her Sex: The Myth and Cult of the Virgin Mary*, Picador, London, 1990

Wolkstein, D. and Kramer, S.N. *Inanna, Queen of Heaven and Earth: Her Stories and Hymns from Sumer*, Harper & Row, New York, 1983

Index

Page numbers indicate a reference in the main text. There may be references in captions or feature boxes on the same page. Page numbers in *italic* indicate a reference in an illustration caption only. Page numbers in **bold** indicate a reference in a feature box.

A

B

N

O

P

Q

R

S

T

U

V

W

X

Y

Z

Picture credits

The publisher thanks the photographers and organizations for their kind permission to reproduce the following photographs in this book.

Abbreviations:
T top; **C** centre; **B** bottom; **L** left; **R** right

AAA: Ancient Art and Architecture Collection
AKG: AKG, London
BAL: Bridgeman Art Library
ETA: e.t. archive
RHPL: Robert Harding Picture Library
WFA: Werner Forman Archive

1 Tony Stone; **2** ETA; **6T** C.M. Dixon; **6BL** RHPL; **6–7** Michael Holford; **7BL** ETA; **7BR** Trip; **8–9** Panos/Penny Tweedy; **10** AAA; **11** BAL; **12** Fortean Picture Library; **13** C.M. Dixon; **14** C.M. Dixon; **15** Michael Holford; **16** Museum of Modern Art, New York. Gift of Nelson A. Rockefeller; **19L** WFA; **19R** BAL; **20–21** Pepita Seth; **22T** Trustees of the British Museum; **22B** WFA; **23** ETA; **24** BAL; **25** RHPL; **26** WFA; **27** WFA; **28** WFA; **29** Sue Cunningham; **30** Trip; **31** WFA; **32** AKG; **33** ETA; **34** Paul Watts; **35T** C.M. Dixon; **35B** WFA; **36** WFA; **38T** and **C** AAA; **39** AAA; **40** Hutchison Library; **41** Hutchison Library; **42–3** WFA; **44–5** Hutchison Library; **45** WFA; **46T** C.M. Dixon; **46B** Sue Cunningham; **47** BAL; **48T** WFA; **48B** Sue Cunningham; **49** Hutchison Library; **50** ETA; **51** C.M. Dixon; **52** Michael Holford; **53L** C.M. Dixon; **53R** AAA; **54** Fortean Picture Library; **55T** ETA; **55B** WFA; **56–7** RHPL; **58** Wheelwright Museum of the American Indian; **59** WFA; **60** AAA; **61** Michael Holford; **62** Fortean Picture Library; **63** WFA; **64** ETA; **65B** WFA; **67** WFA; **68** WFA; **69** ETA; **70** C.M. Dixon; **71T** Michael Holford; **71B** ETA; **72** ETA; **73** BAL; **74–5** WFA; **76** Michael Holford; **77** Michael Holford; **78T** AAA; **79** Fortean Picture Library; **80** AKG; **81** C.M. Dixon; **82** WFA; **83** AAA; **84** AAA; **86** WFA; **87** ETA; **88** ETA; **89** ETA; **90R** ETA; **91** Bodleian Library, Oxford; **92–3** Trustees of the British Museum; **94** Michael Holford; **95** WFA; **96T** WFA; **96B** Fortean Picture Library; **97** WFA; **98** AAA; **99T** ETA; **99B** Images of India; **100** ETA; **101L** Michael Holford; **101R** ETA; **102** ETA; **103** C.M. Dixon; **104** WFA; **105** AKG; **106** BAL; **107** BAL; **108–9** Stephen Trimble; **110** RHPL; **111** ETA; **112–3** Stephen Trimble; **114B** AAA; **115** WFA; **116T** ETA; **117** BAL; **118** AKG; **119** AAA; **120** AAA; **121** Michael Holford; **122** AKG; **123** ETA; **124** BAL; **125** Fortean Picture Library; **126** BAL; **127T** ETA; **127B** WFA; **128–9** Fine Arts Museum of San Francisco. Gift of Peter F. Young; **130** BAL; **131** BAL; **132** AKG; **133** Pepita Seth; **134T** BAL; **134B** WFA; **135** BAL; **136–7** RHPL; **138** Michael Holford; **139T** AAA; **139B** Trustees of the British Museum; **140** WFA; **141** AKG; **142** BAL; **144** Wheelwright Museum of the American Indian; **145** Michael Holford; **147** Ann and Bury Peerless; **148–9** Sue Cunningham; **150** Mary Beth Edelson; **151** Stuart Littlejohn; **153** Stephen Trimble; **154** BAL; **155** Harper Collins, San Francisco; **157** Arks Gallery/Gogisaroj Pal; **158T** ETA; **159** Network; **160** BAL; **163** ETA; **167** C.M. Dixon

Commissioned illustrations:
66, 78B, 114T Hannah Fermin
37, 162, 164–5 Russell Bell

Every effort has been made to trace copyright holders. However, if there are any omissions we will be happy to rectify them in future editions.

FRONTISPIECE Ceres, *by Baldassare Peruzzi (1481–1536).*

For Jessica Burnstone, my god-daughter, on the threshold of her Classics career.